Learning to Compose

Learning to Compose

Modes, Materials and Models of Musical Invention

Larry Austin / Thomas Clark
University of North Texas

wcb
Wm. C. Brown Publishers
Dubuque, Iowa

Cover Design: Ben Neff

Frederick Westphal/Consulting Editor

Library of Congress Catalog Card Number: 88–070484

ISBN 0–697–03495–X

Printed in the United States of America by Wm. C. Brown Publishers
2460 Kerper Boulevard, Dubuque, IA 52001

10 9 8 7 6 5 4 3 2 1

To Edna and Beth

with love and thanks
for their patience and support

CONTENTS

CODA

PREFACE

Our musical culture has always been fascinated with the central role its composers play in making music. Composing is an exciting and challenging pursuit. Its practice has always held a certain mystique as a secret art drawn from unseen and even indescribable inspiration. Of course, much has been written exploring the craft of composition, with particular ideas and methods for constructing various aspects of musical structure. Such writings invariably have restricted the scope and depth of their thoughts, explaining one compositional approach mainly by describing its outcome. There remains a deeper challenge of writing about writing music: to explore how we begin learning to compose, how compositions are conceived as inner images growing out of infinite possibilities through imagination, and how they can be planned as designs for building complex experiences in time and sound. These processes are the essence of composing, the important objects of compositional study, and the subjects of this book.

We hope that an exploration of these processes, rich in potential to focus and refine musical thought, will offer a valuable new tool to the composition student and teacher—a rigorous yet wide-ranging guide to their creative endeavors. Other studies of music—music theory, arranging, and comprehensive musicianship education—may also be informed and edified by the insights gained from examining the creative process itself in music.

Composing is a very personal activity, as is most artistic creating. This is why most of us composers are reluctant to discuss how we work. When we do, usually we try to avoid deeply personal disclosures by being technical and superficial, describing the most prosaic aspects of our work. It is difficult to explain composing's private dimensions, difficult also for teachers and students of composing to accept as universal any one person's account of its inner processes. Our confidence and, perhaps, foolhardy enthusiasm to accept this challenge came only in the consolation of sharing a task we individually thought impossible. As colleagues, fellow composers, and teachers, we have often collaborated closely on large projects, learning to trust shared experiences and insights to transcend our individual limits.

An important trend in compositional activity in the last three decades has been a growing awareness and utilization of a vast range of sources for musical ideas, models for provocative approaches to the processes of compositional thinking. Many important and recent concepts from the fields of mathematics, perceptual psychology, philosophy, computer science, and music theory are incorporated in this book, but with a fresh point of view—that of the composer. The examination of topics is wide-ranging—from the ancient origins of composing to the impact of technology; from sketching a narrative curve to drawing a manuscript note/symbol; from the mystery of experiencing time to the almost tangible experience of pitch; from the magic of sound color to practicalities of performance. The emphasis with each is not on categorizing specimens or prescribing models but on processes of connection and variation which give music coherence.

To equip the reader with a broad set of concepts, a language of terms is developed to crystallize these concepts. Extensive examples from a collection of exemplary contemporary compositions illustrate the concepts in detail. Many chapters include lists of suggested listening and readings, thought-provoking essays and books by other composers and writers.

Finally, guidelines for creative projects suggest avenues for gaining actual experience using processes to compose. Writing assignments with a totally prescribed result, however, accomplish only the most limited rehearsal of basic techniques. Instead, we offer what we call "inventions" designed to suggest many outcomes, allowing a student to exercise real creative choice and evaluation. They are road maps for individual exploration of the possibilities illuminated in each chapter. Thus, techniques of craft are exercised in the service of living ideas, with results that may stimulate further exploration.

In developing this text, we relied on our shared teaching and learning experiences as composers. Always important were remembrances of how we ourselves, learned to compose, how our teachers guided us, and how our work progressed and matured. As teachers of composition, we have come to appreciate deeply the fact that composers never cease being students of their art. With insatiable appetites for inventing new music, the finest composers are always probing, listening, studying their own and others' music—assimilating their musical environment. We have endeavored to create a book which models such a process of assimilating the world of new music.

Ideally, *LEARNING TO COMPOSE* is a composer's companion—a handbook—in the ongoing process of creating new music. The composer's teacher (who might even be the composer!) uses the book as a catalyst for the dynamic process of learning to compose, guiding the student through or selectively exploring the substance of the book. In private composition lessons, this process is personal and interactive. Knowing a student's past work and future potential, the teacher can readily chart a course, using progressively the Inventions and model score excerpts from the **PORTFOLIO** to stimulate the student's musical imagination and compositional fluency.

In the context of a class, the book can be valuable in discussions of compositional approaches and a stimulus for peer interaction. The nonprescriptive nature of the Inventions suggests diverse outcomes, ideal and even fun for students to compare their "solutions" with each other's in class. The teacher, too, may well want to participate by composing an Invention or two. Both students and teacher could and should also invent their own Inventions!

Such direct use of *LEARNING TO COMPOSE* is not meant to be exclusively limited to compositional study; a survey of contemporary music, form and analysis courses, and comprehensive musicianship sequences are highly appropriate contexts for studying the modes and materials of contemporary musical expression from the composer's point of view. The **PORTFOLIO** offers selected models for further explorations in new music since 1950.

Thus, *LEARNING TO COMPOSE* is meant to be used in a variety of ways. It serves as an undergraduate composition textbook, progressing with students who might spend about a month per chapter. With two-year course sequences, the second year can concentrate on the more challenging Inventions, using them as models for full-blown composition projects. At the senior or beginning graduate level, the reading lists of books and articles and many references to composers and their works can be examined and absorbed for a broader and deeper understanding of the great diversity in compositional thought today.

In short, we intend this book to be a companion, a resource for creative thinking and music making: a progressive textbook for learning to compose or an open, dynamic reference for the more experienced student of the art and its new music.

For teachers and students of music, we hope *LEARNING TO COMPOSE* will be a valuable stimulus, an inspiration to understand and create fine music. In turn, we acknowledge the great debt we owe to our students, who have stimulated our thoughts with their interests, refined our ideas with their questions, inspired us with their struggles to learn, and prompted us to write this book for them.

A special note of appreciation is extended to Professors Eric Ziolek (University of Iowa), Susan Cohn Lackman (Rollins College), David Mathew (Georgia State University), David Ernest (St. Cloud State University), Gary White (Iowa State University), Charles Dodge (Brooklyn College Conservatory) and John Fonville (University of California–San Diego) for their very helpful reviews of the manuscript.

CHAPTER 1
CONTEXTS FOR LEARNING

As composers, we learn our art through its practice. We work to find our music's profile, modeling our pieces on master composers' works we admire. Coached and inspired by composer-teachers, we build our portfolio of successfully completed works. Our teachers are important to us, the best providing technical expertise, sympathetic ears, stern critical analyses, and, most important, their own "secrets of composing." They follow the progress of our piece, appraising its effect according to our stated intent, in the process teaching us principles of composition through our own work.

Generation after generation of composers have followed this time-honored practice of studying composition, acknowledging its importance by declarations that they have studied with this or that distinguished composer. Yet, the frequently heard assertion by composers (and often teachers themselves!) that, "Composing can't be taught," goes effectively unchallenged. Accepted, doesn't it follow that, "Composing can't be learned?"

We composers have, indeed, developed ways to learn our art. The products of the art, the compositions, prove that. Can the composer's art be learned completely from a book? No, no more than a book in any other field of endeavor can claim to offer comprehensive treatment, there to be fully assimilated by the student alone. But we can describe and elucidate, even enlighten ourselves about those elusive aspects of the composer's art—imagery, invention, and form. These essences of composition and process draw us to undertake this challenging task: to explore the fascination with thoughts that coalesce in a piece, how we come to have them, and how we translate them into music. Projecting possible outcomes for a piece, deciding obvious things like overall duration and subtle things like nuances of color from moment to moment, all these things go to make up the composing of a work of art. Can we find words to describe the modeling of the compositional act? If we do so well, it will be stimulating and provocative and, most of all, helpful both to students who are at the beginning of their work as composers and those who are already in the midst of a composing career with tens of pieces composed.

ATTITUDE AND ASSUMPTIONS

Composers, in creating their music, work first in the world of the mind. Asked to explain our thoughts, we rarely speak of a particular compositional method. Instead, we usually describe the landscape of the composition, its surface characteristics. We find it much more difficult to talk about the imaginings of a piece of music, its inner workings. Or, when explaining a piece, we will describe its specifications, logistics, or where and when it was written—not its imagery, its effect, its content, or its substance. In this book we will explore and explicate, detailing ways that composers can proceed from the first blurred images of a new piece of music to its full, sonic realization. We will strive for clarity and precision, especially in the terminology of composing. To do this we will not hesitate to go outside the field of music into the fields of phenomenology, psychology, psychoacoustics, and physics to find terms to fit what it is we need to explicate.

Certainly, the craft of composition that we study early on and continue to refine through the rest of our lives helps greatly to bring out beautiful imagery in a piece. But the most skillful, most expert, most craftsmanlike piece of music will disappoint if its initial stages of conception are ill-formed. Then, how do composers work to form the image of a piece? Once that image is formed, how do we invent material that fulfills that image? How do we judge what material goes where? What processes do we use to form the material into a compelling piece of music? What makes it art? What makes it special? What gives a piece its character? Why does one piece seem to have all the right things interacting with each other and another piece seem flat and uninspired?

Composition is an art, not just a craft. Craft is an essential discipline of execution and absolutely necessary for the composer to become a masterful artist. That said, it remains that *art* is the ultimate end, striving to create works that are elegant in conception and thorough in realization, original to the best of the composer's ability. The artwork, then, aspires beyond the common practice. Ideally, truly fine art is an uncommon practice, separate from the common, unique in experience and valuable to our culture. Thus, art is the end—consummate craft, control, the means.

This surely must have been what Hindemith in 1948 really intended when he wrote his pedagogical treatise, *The Craft of Musical Composition.* As younger composers, we eagerly purchased a copy of the book, avidly studying its contents. We soon realized that *The* Craft was *a* craft, very much a statement of Hindemith's own specialized theories of how musical materials—mainly in the pitch domain—should be understood and controlled. Nevertheless, the book was important to study for its many useful concepts and approaches, ways of thinking about the selection of musical materials, a style of proceeding, a method of composing.

It is important to learn from composers of the past, to study their work, accepting the challenge of their best works to be masterful, original, and to strive for beauty in our own new works. New, artful compositions grow out of the past but are not obeisant to it. In this healthy relationship to the past, composers have traditionally been students of their art, not just during their novice period as intern composers but throughout their composing careers—always probing, always learning, always listening, intimidated only by the fear that they may not yet know enough.

This book puts itself into that same ongoing process of creative learning by all composers. Consequently, there are no precise criteria about the preparation of the composer coming to this book, nor are there precise criteria about how this book will be used by the composer, nor when it will be set aside as the composer moves on to another stage of creative learning.

It is assumed that composers are curious, adventurous, skeptical and speculative. At the same time it is important to be thoughtful and disciplined in creating music. Such serious intent about composing is happily leavened with the joy of making a good piece of music, sometimes tempered with irony and wit, even puns and paradox.

It is assumed that a student reading this book has already begun to compose independently or with a teacher, possibly in a class, and has at least tried their hand at free-form composition, free of restrictions, defined only by constraints the composer invokes. Along with this concept is the fact that to create such works the artist must feel free—free from intimidation by tradition; free from the motive of making a piece solely for some nonmusical gain; and, most difficult of all, free from undue consciousness of hoped-for personal success. To explain this last assumption, a freely composed piece is not really free art if it is a contrivance of the composer personally to succeed economically or socially. To sustain oneself economically is, of course, gratifying and quite necessary. It is hoped the music the composer creates will help with that, and we will speak to those issues in the final chapter, **CONTEXTS FOR COMPOSING.** But Grand Personal Success as an end in itself is not—in this book—a factor in composing. Instead, making a successful work of art is the end and achieving personal success only a by-product of the freely creative process. This is to say that a composer should strive for the success of the piece as the primary pursuit, reflecting the thought, care, and profundity of its concept and realization.

Freely composed music is, by nature, speculative, even experimental. To what degree is up to the artist. It is assumed that composers want their works not to be overtly derivative either of another composer's works or even of their own. Of course, new pieces do not simply spring forth, uninfluenced by previous work and experience. There are often series of pieces in a composer's output that share a particular compositional approach. But each piece or series of pieces should be a new adventure for the composer, new imagery, a new land of free composing to explore.

We strongly believe that it is at the forming stage, the imagery stage, that the essential elements for a successful piece come together. Is forming the image of a piece just "getting an idea?" Often younger composers declare: "I've got an idea for a piece," or "This is only an idea," or "I think I've got an idea." In terms of the steps that go into making a piece, such statements are innocent, of course. No human has trouble having an idea. But master composers go beyond that and focus on achieving a coalescence of ideas around a particular musical **image,** a focus likely to result in a compelling piece of music.

Ideas, then, are the fuel for the engine driving a piece; ideas are nothing without the engine. The engine is a process for generating cogent material and strong coherence for the piece. "Idea" has more to do with the spontaneous, innocent, improvisatory thinking on the periphery of serious conception in the act of composition. However innocent the statement, "I've got an idea for a piece," it can typify an attitude of creating a piece in a facile way, of inventing something on the spur of the moment, not giving too much thought to it. Great credence is given to a particular thought because it was spontaneous, attributing worth to it because it was created quickly and without apparent effort. The important judgment to be made by the composer is where the line is between glib, improvised ideas and profound, controlled thinking. This is at the core of what we mean to study; as artists of composition, we should be concerned with all aspects of the artwork, not just the superficial—not only concerned but responsible for them. Fine artwork comes about that way. Conveniently, we could allow ourselves to accept the quick fix of a "good idea" for a piece without serious examination of it as a really beautiful concept, one that can become profound.

Technique for its own sake at times can result in a viable piece. More often such facile results are a warmed-over, workaday version of something that particular composer or some other composers have done before with more originality. This book is about giving deep thought to composing, every aspect of it, not only its craft but its artistic content.

COMPOSITIONAL THINKING

How do composers compose? Are composers blessed with some mysterious power they can invoke to create a fine piece of music? We hear, "They do it intuitively, a God-given talent." Is it really that mysterious? Don't such notions arise from ignorance rather than from knowledge of the compositional act? Literally, intuition is the direct knowing or learning of something without conscious use of reason, immediate apprehension or understanding. If intuition is, then, something known or learned in this subconscious way, and if intuition is the ability to know or perceive things without conscious reasoning, it certainly doesn't seem to fit the profile of the master composer—they consciously reason; they plan their pieces; they know what they're doing. In spite of this, many composers themselves claim that composition can't really be explained, that it's a mysterious process and that you can only learn about it by doing it, aping other composers and their pieces. Carried to the extreme, a composer may state, "I can't explain how I compose. It just comes to me."

The prolific French composer Darius Milhaud, it is said, was asked by a concertgoer after a concert of his music, "How did you compose that wonderful piece?" He answered, pulling out his pen from inside his coat, "My dear, with this." It's true, in fact, that Milhaud was known often to start orchestral works with pen and ink on a full-sized manuscript page, inking the piccolo part on the first staff of the first page, straight across, followed by all the other instruments in order. Without sketches of any kind lying about, apparently all "inside his head," the music seemed to emerge magically from inner ear to finished score. Or there was Stravinsky's declaration that he was only a vessel from which the music came—filled by God and poured by Stravinsky. And the legendary Mozart, of course—his intuitive powers were deemed godlike, so effortlessly did he create music. It is often thought, based mainly on his letter to his sister (April 20, 1782), that Mozart worked out his compositions intuitively before setting pen to paper. But sketches in his hand (the *Piano Concerto in A major,* K.488) detail planned textures, themes, and harmonic movement, showing that he did, indeed, work from the inception of a piece with a thought-out plan. "Composing at the keyboard" was actually a transfer of that plan to his fingers, a realization, a test of the plan's workability. Milhaud's music is certainly "reasoned," not at all "unconscious," doubly so Stravinsky's! Certainly, Mozart's super-fluency gave him more, not less, control over the profoundly thoughtful, deep structure of his works.

Still, we composers, experienced and beginning alike, are rarely openly disputed when saying, "I can't explain how I composed it. It just came to me." We composers seem encouraged, in fact, to invoke such mystical innocence, even dogmatically declaring that music not created intuitively is not truly formed art, a doctrine that all things are apprehended in their real nature through intuition. At its most radical, this doctrine of intuitionism can even become an ethical principle, where the rightness of acts are apprehended only by intuition. Some conclude that if a composer doesn't write a piece exclusively with intuition, it can't be called a true artwork, that conscious planning, process, and method are anti-intuitive and anti-art.

Such a radical stance would seem to deny the existence of cognition, the result of the process of knowing in the broadest sense, including consciousness, memory, perception, conception, and judgment. If a composer believed only in the intuitive compositional approach, it would mean that the composer never consciously thought about how the piece would be perceived, judged and understood, since that composer would deny that those factors entered into the creation of the work. That's illogical, of course. Every composer thinks about his/her work, even if it's real-time composition, such as improvisation. A fine improviser thinks about the outcome of the piece at all levels at once, creating the final form of the work as it is being performed. The moment the composer sits down at the piano or picks up an instrument or sings, a conscious choice of medium has already been made, if nothing else. In fact, conscious compositional decisions are constantly having to be made by such real-time composers as well as their sit-down, studio counterparts composing "out of real-time." This kind of cognitive process at work is both deductive and inductive—deductive, where the composer proceeds from a known assumption to an unknown, from the general to the specific, from a premise to a logical conclusion; and inductive, where the composer proceeds by method, logically reasoning from particular facts to general conclusions. Composer Arnold Schoenberg, in his essay, "Heart and Brain in Music" (1946), explained the thought processes of composing:

> It is not the heart alone which creates all that is beautiful, emotional, pathetic, affectionate, and charming; nor is it the brain alone which is able to produce the well-constructed, the soundly organized, the logical, and the complicated. First, everything of supreme value in art must show heart as well as brain. Second, the real creative genius has no difficulty in controlling his feelings mentally; nor must the brain produce only the dry and unappealing while concentrating on correctness and logic.
>
> But one might become suspicious of the sincerity of works which incessantly exhibit their heart; which demand our pity; which invite us to dream with them in a vague and undefined beauty and of unfounded, baseless emotions; which exaggerate because of the absence of reliable yardsticks; whose simplicity is want, meagerness, and dryness; whose sweetness is artificial and whose appeal attains only to the surface of the superficial. Such works only demonstrate the complete absence of a brain and show that this sentimentality has its origin in a very poor heart. (*Style and Idea,* 1975, 53–54)

Compositional thinking is, then, a dynamic interplay of intuitive and cognitive reasoning, of heart and brain, of *yin* and *yang,* of fluency and control. The process of composing a new piece is, in fact, an ongoing critical analysis by the composer of the value of materials the composer invents and the concepts for their use. The composer asks: What is involved in making this piece? Is there a valid concept? Are the materials original and beautiful? Is the substance of the work imbued in its image meaningful and telling? Does the shape given the piece have integrity? Does the intent for the work—the image-form of the piece—manifest itself in an elegant process or in an obscure or, worse, an obvious way? Does my understanding of the materials generated lead to consummate control, in turn making the most appropriate decisions for the piece? Am I communicating meaning through articulate, fluent use of distinctive music idioms, thoughtfully controlled as a result of mastering materials and language and their implications in the composition? Finally, am I careful to see that the piece is well performed and presented in a conducive context?

Today, the field of composing as an art is diverse and multifaceted. It hasn't always been that way. The role of the composer in society as an artist is a recent phenomenon in the history of music, mainly growing out of what composers began to become in relatively recent history.

ORIGINS OF MUSICAL COMPOSITION

As we come of age as musicians, and later as composers, our notions of what constitutes a piece of music are clear. A piece has a beginning, middle and end, is usually, but not always, notated on music paper, composed, and meant to be performed and appreciated. Simple . . . no, not so simple. The earliest known, recorded pieces of Western music that have survived from Greek antiquity weren't compositions as we know them today. They were poems, intoned and chanted in rhythms as speech-songs.

For us, today, it is difficult not to think of a piece of music from any period as an object of sounding art, a thing created for itself, for the artist's conscious expression of beauty. But this perception is, it turns out, very special, developing only since the sixteenth century, coming into its own in the eighteenth and, of course, flourishing through the nineteenth, twentieth, and now into the twenty-first century. We have learned to define the musical art object by distancing ourselves from it, by placing it in an aesthetic realm. The ways in which we set the piece apart in its own kind of artistic space affect our appreciation of its beauty. The musical art object is beautiful, complete, having no corporeal model but itself, transcendent from the "real" world.

The entire tradition of music in the West has been devoted to defining further the beauty of the musical object, to refining our understanding of musical processes so that the processes can yield desired results. This further and further distances us from the object, making it exist for its own sake, an object of thought, of contemplation. Such objectivity in the art of music is heightened by distinguishing between the action—the doing—of making the piece and the contemplation—the knowing—of the art.

Music in this sense was the last of the arts to develop. Music became a conscious artform only in the second millennium of its existence. Of course, there had been an awareness of the sounds that can make music since humans first heard. But what we call music was not understood in the same way by ancient people. Three thousand years ago they intoned speech in verse and they danced their rituals to rhythmic beating sounds, but they were not conscious of any artful essence. The ancient music-maker was not yet capable of understanding these activities as an art.

Why this slow development of music as an art? Weren't there always composers, even though they may not have written their music? Poets, yes, composers, no. Distinct from the other arts developing in antiquity, music had elusive and ephemeral models to imitate. The sound world provided nothing as vivid and corporeal as the painter's representations of visual objects and scenes or the poet's stories of human drama or the dancer's ritualized bodily movements. True, birdsongs, the howling wind, animal cries must certainly have mesmerized ancient ears, but short, repetitive birdsongs or the wavering pitch and drone of wind and animals hardly provided a clear idea for the creation of music as a unique artform. Music's models did not offer as direct a relationship as did pictures to the visual, drama to action, poetry to story, all Platonic copies or Aristotelian imitations of nature.

Music, instead, was gradually abstracted from the elemental rhythms of life and the environment, at the same time synthesized with the voiced intoning of speech in poems. Rhythm and words, thus abstracted and fused, became the first music. Still, in antiquity the fusion was mysterious, not a consciously creative act. Music had the most difficult model of all—itself.

When did these sounded poems of Greek antiquity become choral verse leading to music, and when did composition become a manifestation of that artform? The distinguished psychologist and anthropologist, Julian Jaynes (1976), traces the development of poetry and music in ancient Greece as part of his view of human behavior in his book, *The Origin of Consciousness in the Breakdown of the Bicameral Mind.* Jaynes presents compelling evidence that human consciousness as we perceive it today was a learned process, presenting the argument that the human being of three thousand years ago had a hallucinatory mentality, "a human nature split in two, an executive part called a god," in the right hemisphere of the brain, "and a follower part," in the left. Neither part of this bicameral mind was conscious, a fact almost incomprehensible to us today. Bicameral man reacted to all of life's situations by experiencing auditory hallucinations, hearing his own "bicameral voice . . . which with the stored-up admonitory wisdom of his life would tell him nonconsciously what to do." (p. 85) Important evidence for Jaynes' theory derives from his study of poetry and music of ancient Greece:

> I shall state my thesis plain. The first poets were gods. Poetry began with the bicameral mind. The god-side of our ancient mentality, at least in a certain period of history, usually or perhaps always spoke in verse. This means that most men at one time, throughout the day, were hearing poetry (of a sort) composed and spoken within their own minds. (p. 85)

As the bicameral mind began its evolution to consciousness three millennia ago, man came more and more to rely on poetic utterances to invoke the "voices", so important to his survival. Poetry, as divine knowledge, sustained the sound and the godly authority of those voices well into the "conscious period," slowly manifesting itself after 1000 B.C. Early poetry, as the language of the gods, was sung, and, as Jaynes points out, scientific studies conclude that singing is primarily a function of the right cerebral hemisphere, "more specifically . . . the posterior part of the right temporal lobe . . . responsible for organizing divine hallucinations together with adjacent areas which even today are involved in music."

Jaynes expands his argument to point out the close relationship between ancient Greek poetry and instrumental music, "suggesting . . . that the invention of music may have been as a neural excitant to the hallucination of gods for decision-making in the absence of consciousness. . . . It is thus no idle happenstance of history that the very name of music comes from the sacred goddesses called Muses. . . . For music too begins in the bicameral mind." He theorizes, then, that the use of the lyre by early poets was meant to stimulate "divine speech."

Up to the seventh century B.C., the poet's creativity was bicameral. By the sixth century poets were "learning the gift of the Muses" (Solon, Fragment, 13:51). By the fifth century B.C. writings describe poets' ecstatic trance to induce the Muses; Democritus insisted that no one could be a great poet unless entering an ecstatic state of fury. In the fourth century B.C., Plato describes the poets' possession by the Muses, thus:

> . . . all good poets, epic as well as lyric, composed their beautiful poems not by art, but because they are inspired and possessed . . . there is no invention in him until he has been inspired and is out of his senses and the mind is no longer in him. (p. 370)

Poetry, then, began as the gods' language of the bicameral mind. Even as the bicameral mind broke down, poets continued to invoke the gods with sung, accompanied poetry. As consciousness dawned, though, the poets had more and more difficulty achieving the necessary ecstatic state and found they had to teach themselves to learn the ritual process. They now had to record their poetry/music to retain it and pass it on. The first fragments of recorded ancient Greek music we have today come from the third and second centuries B.C. Jaynes explains:

> And then indeed toward the end of the first millennium B.C., just as the oracles began to become prosaic and their statements versified consciously, so poetry also. Its givenness by the unison Muses had vanished. And conscious men now wrote and crossed out and created and rewrote their compositions in laborious mimesis of the older divine utterances. . . . The continuance of poetry, its change to a human craft is part of that nostalgia for the absolute. The search for the relationship with the lost otherness of divine directives would not allow it to lapse. And hence the frequency even today with which poems are apostrophes to often unbelieved-in entities, prayers to unknown imaginings. . . . The poet's task now is an imitation or mimesis of the former type of poetic utterance and the reality which it expressed. Mimesis in the bicameral sense of mimicking what was heard in hallucination has moved through the mimesis of Plato as representation of reality to mimesis as imitation with invention in its sullen service. (pp. 374–375)

Only twenty notated pieces or fragments of pieces survive today from ancient Greece. The earliest is dated from the third century B.C., and the last from third century A.D., a span of about seven centuries. The texts for the speech-songs were religious paeans to the gods (for example, the *First Delphic Hymn to Apollo*), satyr plays, tragedies, and hymns, the last, the Oxyrhynchus papyrus, one of the early Christian church.

Music of the early Christian church was no better preserved than ancient Greek music. It is known, though, that music was very important in the liturgy, with texts sung in the manner of the Greeks. Unlike the Greeks, however, the early Christians discouraged instrumental music, probably because of the association it had with what the Christians considered pagan, those invocations to the ecstatic state referred to by Jaynes. The Fathers of the Church encouraged communal vocal music, the sounded repetition of holy words, so that the worshippers could learn the holy texts, which only the Fathers could read. Thus the Church sustained music as a function of the liturgy, not an art, well into the Middle Ages.

Through the Middle Ages, music theorists were held in high esteem, higher actually than the practitioners of music. The music theorists, who often were also religious clerics, were fanatic codifiers of accepted musical practices—those practices which seemed not to offend or contradict the views of the Church. Innovation was held to be a deviation and considered almost heretical. Consequently, because of such intimidation, music was much slower than the other arts to reach its renaissance when, finally, color and dynamism in music began to flourish.

In the humanistic period of the Renaissance in the sixteenth century the idea of creating a musical composition became more than the fabrication of a product by a practicing artisan of music. In tune with the changing attitudes then about music, not only in its liturgical function in the church but in its humanist function as true art, composition became *musica poetica,* and was thought of as *opus perfectum et absolutum* (Nikolaus Listenius, *Musica,* 1530). The concept of a musical composition was to make it perfect, absolute, complete art in itself, with the artful spirit of poetry, now ineffably expressed in the world of music.

This perception of the composition as a work of art gave new importance to notated, published compositions. It is no accident that the concept of *musica poetica* perceived as autonomous work and the new appreciation of abstracted musical objects should appear in the "Gutenberg galaxy," as Marshall McLuhan observed, just after the advent of printing. Then, in fact, the piece could actually be appreciated and performed by others, independent of the original composer/performer and his craft. The composer had become not only a practitioner of music but a creator and an artist. With this realization came new and more focused expressiveness in the music itself and a new significance given to the act of composing. To that time, the words "composer" and "composition" had been used only incidentally in connection with music. Now the words began to appear more and more in published musical treatises.

Etymologically, the term *composition* is rooted in the concept of "a putting together." Today, it connotes putting music together, integrating the materials with skill, planning, and artful originality to satisfy the requirements of a particular musical genre. This modern usage of the term refers especially to music composed since the rise of the orchestral score in the eighteenth century. Tracing the term's earliest usage in Latin, *compositio* or *compositus* referred first to writing a poem or tale before setting it to music (if at all). The Latin gerund form *componenda* for "composing" was used in the first known direct reference to music composition by eleventh century music theorist Guido of Arezzo in his great treatise on music practice, *Micrologus* (c. 1026). He used the term to describe the process for "putting together" the neumes of plainchant notation. Guido's treatise was widely copied and circulated through the Middle Ages (eleventh to fifteenth centuries) in both monasteries and, later, in universities. In it, Guido not only helped spread the use of the term but was responsible for creating a systematic method of music notation, so important for the development of the score. Still, around 1335, when Dante referred to the *composizione* of a canzone, he meant a poem, not a piece of music.

In the Renaissance, beginning in the sixteenth century, the term "composition" came to be used in the plastic arts as well as in descriptions of architecture and sculpture, and in philosophy and alchemical writings when referring to diverse constituent elements. Thus, in 1597, when composer Thomas Morley declared his aim to instruct music students to be "quicke in your compositions," he was still really using the term in its generic sense. In fact, "composition" still implied "a putting together," a gathering of diverse parts, well into the nineteenth century. It remained for the emergence of the orchestral score in the eighteenth century to narrow and focus the meaning of the term more and more toward our modern usage.

Today, "composition" connotes synthesis and integration, as well as a putting together. This change can be traced from the eighteenth century, when dance suites with many diverse movements were "put together," to the nineteenth century symphonic form "composed" in a closely related four-movement sequence, to Wagner's unifying integration of his *Gesamtkunstwerk* ("whole art work"), to our diverse and multifaceted syntheses of all forms and mediums of music today.

The history of music as art and of musical composition, then, is a history of the development of growing consciousness—the consciousness of change, consciousness of the beauty of change, and the resulting consciousness of creating processes of change as beauty. Though music had a much longer gestation period than the other arts, its development, finally, led to a new understanding of the creative idea, not bound by or dependent on any model but itself. Music became art when it was created for itself, not model-bound like the other arts. Philosopher Susanne Langer (1942), in her definitive *Philosophy in a New Key,* concludes:

> It is easier to grasp the artistic import of music than of the older and more model-bound arts. This artistic import is what painters, sculptors, and poets express through their depiction of objects and events. Its semantic is the play of lines, masses, colors, textures in plastic arts, or the play of images, the tension and release of ideas, the speed and arrest, ring and rhyme of words in poetry. Artistic expression is what these media will convey. The import of artistic expression is broadly the same in all arts as it is in music—the verbally ineffable, yet not inexpressible law of vital experience, the pattern of affective and sentient being. This is the "content" of what we perceive as "beautiful form"; and this formal element is the artist's "idea" which is conveyed by every great work. It is this which so-called "abstract art" seeks to abstract by defying the model or dispensing with it altogether; and which music above all arts can reveal, unobscured by adventitious literal meanings. (p. 257)

Today, the art of composing a piece of music, rather than a simple process of musical realization, is really a highly developed abstracting of sounding images in the composer's mind—music as a sounding object, music as metaphor, music as dramatic expression, music as abstract expression, music as nonexpression, music as sounding sculpture, music as environmental art, music as the beauty of change.

COMPOSING TODAY

Today, composers are free to exert a degree of control over every aspect of a composition: creating its form, its process, even inventing the medium for its performance, building instruments for its own "orchestra" or composing computer algorithms to automatically create compositional material! Or the composer may choose, at the other end of the spectrum, the complete relaxation of accepted compositional prerogatives, composing only the essential, conceptual framework within which choices are to be made by the performers of the piece!

Examples abound, for instance, concerning the importance the composer today attaches to getting the right timbres—instruments—for the proper realization of the concept of the piece. In an interview with percussionist Michael Udow, composer Karlheinz Stockhausen revealed,

> For every work with percussion instruments I have composed since 1951, I have purchased the unusual instruments myself. When percussion players have worked with me on these works, I have shown them the instruments, and they have gone to the same factories, to the same dealers in order to get the right instruments.
> (*Percussive Notes*. Research Edition 23, Sept. 1985, 6:4)

Similarly, John Cage provided precise instructions about how to "prepare" a conventional piano with tacks, screws and bolts for his *Sonatas and Interludes* (1946–48) for prepared piano. Modifying the conventional piano in this way, it became a multitimbral percussion instrument for the freely composed conception Cage wanted to achieve. He made the piano a new instrument of his own "composing." As audacious as this may have seemed in 1938 when Cage first experimented with such modifications of the piano, this open attitude about altering the sound of instruments is accepted today as part of the composer's field of exploration. The composer is in charge of every aspect of the composition, free to compose every aspect of the piece.

At the same time, composers can choose to relax control of certain aspects of a piece. Not long after composing the *Sonatas and Interludes,* Cage came more and more to rely on chance operations in his compositions. First represented in his *Music of Changes* (1951) for solo piano, pitch, rhythmic, registral, and loudness parameters are composed as the result of chance operations taken from the *I Ching* and exactly notated in the score. Between 1958 and 1966, Cage went further, now with almost complete abrogation of composerly prerogatives, composing six context-controlling pieces, the *Variations I–VI.* Instead of specific instrumentation and notated music, parts are to be prepared by the performers, "with or without materials provided," with "any number of players, any sound-producing means" (*Var. I, II*), or "any sounds or combinations of sounds produced by any means, with or without other activities" (*Var. IV*), or "for a plurality of sound systems," (*Var. VI*) or, the most free of all, "for one or any number of people performing any actions" (*Var. III*). In such a seemingly wide-open context as *Variations III,* Cage goes on to invoke conditions for the performers to ponder, as follows:

> Two transparent sheets of plastic, one having forty-two undifferentiated circles, the other blank. Cut the sheet having circles in such a way that there are forty-two small sheets, each having a complete circle. Let these fall on a sheet of paper, 8½ × 11. If a circle does not overlap at least one other circle, remove it. Remove also any smaller groups of circles that are separated from the largest group so that a single maze of circles remains, no one of them isolated from at least one other. Place the blank transparent plastic sheet over this complex.
>
> Starting with any circle, observe the number of circles which overlap it. Make an action or actions having the corresponding number of interpenetrating variables (1 + n). This done, move on to any one of the overlapping circles, again observing the number of interpenetrations, performing a suitable action or actions, and so on. Some or all of one's obligation may be performed through ambient circumstances (environmental changes) by simply noticing or responding to them.
>
> Though no means are given for the measurement of time or space (beginning, ending or questions of continuity) or the specific interpretation of circles, such measurement and determination means are not necessarily excluded from the 'interpenetrating variables.' Some factors though not all of a given interpenetration or succession of several may be planned in advance. But leave room for the use of unforeseen eventualities. Any other activities are going on at the same time. (Copyright 1963 New York: Henmar Press, used by permission)

Here, the two extremes of complete exertion and almost complete abrogation of compositional prerogatives over the outcome of his piece are at work, creating the ultimate variation of constant flux Cage wanted to achieve. Thus, in the *Variations,* Cage was composing contexts for the form the pieces would take in performance, consistent with his definition of form in 1961 as "the morphology of a continuity." (*Silence,* 1961) Rather than accepting models from the past into which the composer's music is "poured," the form is composed to fit the musical conception, to have a better musical effect. *Variations III* exhibits, as well, the integration of form and process. The composer composes a process in which, even as the piece is being performed, the piece's material is being invented, also creating the form the piece is taking.

Experimentation with and exploration of tuning systems other than the equal-tempered twelve-note scale provides abundant examples of the composer's emergence as an instrument builder and microtonalist in our century. Unequal microtonal divisions of the scale have been developed, such as the forty-three tone scale developed by composer Harry Partch. He built a complete family of instruments for the performance of his microtonal music, which he labeled "corporeal." He went further to develop a form of music theater, modeled after ancient Greek theater. Partch's book, *Genesis of a Music* (1949, rev. and enlarged, 1974), is testament to his singleminded goal of disavowing the whole tradition of Western music in favor of his unique theories about tuning. He created a complete world of music of his own devising.

Since World War II, the rise and the now ubiquitous development of electroacoustic music systems has offered composers the potential of creating not just one musical microcosm in a particular system but a whole new world every time a new piece is conceived. Here the composer has had the opportunity and the challenge to invent new harmonic languages, organizing principles, new instruments and timbral collections, as well as new forms and processes. No longer was the composer limited by the breath capacity of the lungs or the length of time a sound could be sustained on a string instrument before changing bow direction or the decay factor of a piano string struck by its hammer. Electroacoustic music didn't have to breath or be bowed or concerned with how long a note could be sustained at all. Nor did the composer, for that matter, have to be so concerned with how loud or soft the music could be. The limits were simply those of human hearing. It could be that it was the electroacoustic media that gave rise in the last half of the twentieth century to this new attitude about composition: that the composer was now free of all the restraints of music performed on acoustic instruments, free to experiment.

A finished tape music composition is, in itself, an authentic performance of that piece, and the composer is a kind of audience for it—a small but whole, self-sufficient microcosm of music. Along with this development, music has become more personalized, again making freely composed personal art music its logical extension. No longer are the venues for compositions only the concert halls, opera halls and salons of the nineteenth century. The new venues are the living rooms, the studios, the lofts, the streets, radio, television, film, recordings, or any place human beings can gather to listen.

The degree of control the composer exerts over the materials of a composition is, in our time, a central issue. How much will the composer leave to the performer? Does the composer wish for the piece to be the same each time it is performed? Or how important that it be different each time? How precisely will the composer indicate his image of the piece?

> Thoreau's advice to all of us in *Walden* is to simplify, simplify. If you look at his journal, you can see a beautiful thing that happens. At the beginning, there are many adjectives, and the style is very wordy. By the end, he has moved from that floridness to a great simplicity.

The theme of Joyce's *Finnegan's Wake* is just the opposite of simplify, simplify. Its goal is to move as close as possible to confusion, a rich confusion, reaching for an enormous abundance of information. Mozart I love. Before that, I loved Bach. Bach reassures about the presence of order, while Mozart moves, as does James Joyce, toward a greater and greater complexity. (John Cage in the *Dallas Observer,* Feb. 20, 1986)

OTHER READINGS

Books:

Childs, B., and E. Schwartz. *Contemporary Composers on Contemporary Music.* New York: Holt, Reinhart and Winston, 1967.

Clifton, Thomas. *Music as Heard.* New Haven, Conn.: Yale University Press, 1983.

Copland, Aaron. *Music and Imagination.* Cambridge, Mass.: Harvard University Press, 1952.

Edwards, Allen. *Flawed Words and Stubborn Sounds: A Conversation with Elliott Carter.* New York: W. W. Norton, 1972.

Hindemith, Paul. *A Composer's World.* New York: Doubleday, 1961.

Ives, Charles. *Essays Before a Sonata.* New York: W. W. Norton, 1962.

Lutoslawski, Witold. *Lutoslawski Profile: W. L. in Conversation with B. Varga.* London: Chester Music, 1976.

Meyer, Leonard. *Emotion and Meaning in Music.* Chicago: University of Chicago Press, 1956.

Partch, Harry. *Genesis of a Music.* New York: Da Capo Press, 1949.

Samuel, Claude. *Conversations with Olivier Messiaen.* London: Stainer and Bell, 1976.

Schoenberg, Arnold. *Style and Idea.* Leonard Stein, ed., Leo Black, trans. Berkeley, Calif.: University of California Press, 1984.

Stravinsky, Igor. *The Poetics of Music in the Form of Six Lessons.* A. Knodell, I. Dahl, trans. Cambridge, Mass.: Harvard University Press, 1970.

MODES OF INVENTION

CHAPTER 2
FORM MODELING

Unlike the other arts, music is self-modeled. The plastic, literary, dramatic and choreographic arts with their concrete and "real-life" models are, of course, integrated with music in operatic and intermedia genres. But even when combined with these other artforms, music's sounds can't be seen or touched, can't really be understood as symbols representing anything.

Yet, we perceive music as tangible, its models clear, part of our cultural heritage, existing in our mind's ear as real and valued. Music's models are its own vast array of musical compositions. Other art forms often emulate this abstract and highly desirable quality of self-modeled design:

> Drawings which attempt to *be* life always melt away under the wearing drip of time. Drawings are *not* life but simply a translation of its elements into visual terms of line, dark/light and color which are used in [an] abstract way. In other words, a drawing is a design and a thing unto itself. (Texas artist Alexandre Hogue)

Do we conclude, then, that the form of a musical composition is fashioned in its own image? Yes, both when the composer works to model a piece whose form is meant to be original and also when it is a variation or emulation of preexistent forms.

Intuitively, we understand how we model the form of a new piece after our own or other composers' pieces. It is more difficult to understand how we model wholly original compositional forms. Understanding this modeling process requires a grasp of fundamental concepts of musical form, how they have developed and are still evolving.

FORM IN MUSIC

In music, form is the shaping of musical time through change. Form is the wholeness in time of a piece. Form subsumes structure, which we know as the relatedness, "out of time," of the piece's largest to smallest elements, its surface to deepest levels. Thus, everything in a piece of music, including all its structures, makes its form. Form is all the attributes the composer gives a piece, its whole sonic and temporal effect, its essence.

> Used in the aesthetic sense, form means that a piece is organized, i.e., that it consists of elements functioning like those of a living organism. (Arnold Schoenberg 1967, 1)

Let us take, from our training as musicians, a typical example of what is often given to describe a "standard" form: the first movement in a classic sonata from the late eighteenth century. *The form is sonata form, having three successive sections: an exposition with two contrasting themes, the first in the tonic, the second in the dominant or relative major; a development of this thematic material; and a recapitulation of material from the exposition, both themes returning in the tonic.* Such a bare description of thematic and tonal schemes in parts of a piece is not an explanation of its form. The sonata form, as Charles Rosen (1972) explains in his book, *The Classical Style,* is "a way of writing, a feeling for proportion, direction, and texture rather than a pattern." In fact, since the term "sonata" (meaning sounding piece) was first used, sonata form has had a multiplicity of formats, some like, some quite unlike our classic, academically "correct" format described above. Sonata forms actually were understood by composers in the late eighteenth and into the nineteenth century to be beautifully ambiguous in form. Eighteenth century musician J. A. P. Schulz, in describing the merits of the classical sonata of the day, wrote:

> Clearly in no form of instrumental music is there a better opportunity to depict feelings without words . . . there remains only the form of the sonata, which assumes all characters and every expression. (Charles Rosen 1980, 14)

Composers then, as now, seek diversity and originality, not conformity in musical terms. The meaning of form today remains in flux, remains beautifully mysterious. In the composer's search for the truth of a piece, form is thus redefined as each new work is conceived and modeled. Were form officially defined, a creative modeling process would not be part of composing. Composers would no longer make art in their compositions, but—provided with the correct form—would simply "follow the recipe," mixing the requisite materials in the right amounts, pouring them into the proper mold and—*Voila!*—produce the perfect piece of non-art. Such lock-step manufacture with no creative modeling is antithetical to artistic values.

> . . . the pleasure of discovering musical processes and composing the musical material to run through them. . . . Material may suggest what sort of process it should be run through (content suggests form), and processes may suggest what sort of material should be run through them (form suggests content). The distinctive thing about musical processes is that they determine all the note-to-note details and the overall form simultaneously. (Reich 1974, 9, 11)

Understandably, as we first study in depth the art of music and learn through analysis about the workings of music's great, inspiring pieces, we quite naturally but mistakenly ascribe aesthetic value to a piece because it is found to be an ideal realization of some traditional form. What we often fail to understand is that the modeling process is aesthetically creative, not analytically derivative. The modeling process is not analytical method turned around to generate the form a piece will take. It is, instead, a staging process for the form of a piece, evolving from its first blurred image, in turn becoming a series of trial realizations, exploring ways its materials can be made and combined. Each trial realization, a sketch, is a test informing the next, until complete synthesis of the piece's form—its shape in time—is achieved.

As the composer works with the materials of a piece, they begin to coalesce, conveying their own essence. Composers are students of their own work. It teaches them how it should be formed. As the composer works through the modeling process, more and more is learned about the piece's nature, looking at it again and again. Other composers' works are studied that either share characteristics or are even totally disparate in form. The composer imagines having composed such pieces and what modeling processes these composers might have used. What we learn, for instance, from studying works created using sonata-like models of form is a modeling process that invokes the power of dramatic polarity and duality of materials, expressed through contrasting lines, textures, tonalities—transformed and juxtaposed. Studying the modeling processes of a composer's past works, essences of form not realized before may be discovered, gaining a new understanding of one's own creative behavior. But the composer always returns to the creative modeling process, refining and developing its form.

PROCESSES OF CONCEPTION

For a piece of music to come into being, it first must be imagined. Imagining its creation and design involves a working strategy, a modeling process. Modeling a piece calls for the composer to imagine, then assimilate the image of the form it will take. At every stage of the modeling process, the composer is imagining the piece's existence in time and space. Such modeling in the mind's conception of time and space can, at will, move very quickly or very slowly over the large and small detail: large details of scope and instrumentation, small details of the relationship in time, distance, and color of individual notes to one another. The composer hears, sees, and makes the piece materialize in what psychologist Julian Jaynes terms "mind-space" and "mind-time."

Three interacting spheres of creative modeling are involved in this process of conception: **temporal modeling, spatial modeling** and **narrative modeling.** Each sphere is a realm of metaphors for a piece's actuality, from its earliest stages to its completion as a work of art. A piece of music, out of time, is imagined as an object with qualities and measurable quantities—a **spatial metaphor**—or as chains of events happening in consequence to one another—a **narrative metaphor**—or as a piece of music as an elaborately articulated piece of time's flow—a **temporal metaphor.**

The most readily understood of these processes is **temporal modeling,** where the sonic materials of the piece are invented and shaped in real or imagined performance time. This modeling typically might take place at a keyboard instrument, usually a piano; or simply singing the music aloud; or silently "playing through" and "hearing the piece in your head" in "mind-time." Here, the composer invents, combines and tests material, working to refine and perfect its form in time. This classic modeling process is integral to composing and is most important to the synthesis of form.

Spatial modeling is the conscious visualization in "mind-space" of the piece of music as an object with measurable dimensions in a network of spatial characteristics: how long, how many, how few, how high, how low, how thick or thin, what color, what texture, where placed, where heard, what structure—all metaphors for spatial images, thinking of the piece as an object. The choice of musical medium, for example, involves spatial modeling in a direct way. In composing a work, say, for trombone alone, the composer imagines the presence of the trombone, certainly an intriguing object in itself. It also has impressive dimensions of range and color. Modeling the trombone piece's dimension of length, say, is concerned first with the practical, outward limits of sheer endurance an ideal trombonist can abide. Since vibrating lips can, after a lot of continuous playing, cause the player to tire and lose the high degree of control of range and color, the length of a relatively continuous piece should be under about ten minutes. With this single decision, we have caused the piece to form—as a spatial object—in our mind. We have begun the synthesis of the piece through spatial modeling.

Narrative modeling involves the plot or the eventfulness of a piece. We can understand this modeling process through our characterization of our piece of music as it begins, develops, continues, reaches its denouement, if one is desired, and finally, its conclusion—all metaphors for a story. As with spatial modeling, we can imagine the story, the plot "out-of-time" as a collection of characters. Like temporal modeling, we can think or hear the story of our piece "in-time" as a complex of interacting events.

In composing his masterful *Sequenza V* for solo trombone, Luciano Berio not only modeled the piece on a storied performance of the legendary Italian clown Grock, but went further to characterize the trombone itself as a noble clown, creating a beautiful melding of medium and metaphor.

> On the stage, a very low stand and chair. Walking on the stage and during the performance of section A the performer (white tie, spot from above etc.) strikes the poses of a variety showman about to sing an old favorite. Inspired, he extends his arms, he raises or lowers his instrument with movements which should appear spontaneous, he hesitates. Just before section B he utters a bewildered "why?" and sits down without pausing. He must perform section B as though rehearsing in an empty hall. (Berio's performance notes in the Universal Edition)

Trombonist Stuart Dempster, who commissioned Berio to compose *Sequenza V,* adds this scenario for its performance:

> A medium height stool in center stage will create a more dramatic effect and should be the only item on stage. It should, along with the lighting, convey a sense of distance and loneliness. Enter and proceed to stool without acknowledging audience. Stand facing front, pause, and look upward for imaginary prey while at the same time slowly "taking aim" with trombone. Begin playing as though shooting, the sound being like gunshots. . . . Section B is best performed with closed eyes and the final bows should be somewhat stiff and aloof as though hall were empty.

Here, the medium of the piece suggests to Berio the nature of its form. But we do not model the same way for the voice as for, say, percussion. Nor do we compose music for orchestra without regard to its large, instrumental ensemble potential. In fact, we quite logically associate the term form with medium: the "song form" and the "symphonic form" most often thought of. The medium has profound effect on musical form, and we refer the reader to chapter 3, **MEDIUMS AND IDIOMS,** for elucidation of that importance.

The purpose and **context** for writing a piece can be an extension of medium, but not always. For instance, the composer may have a particular auditory/visual space in mind for the piece, such as a concert hall. Or a particular set of circumstances will surround its performance, say, a piece primarily for very young audiences. Or the piece may be for a particular performer as soloist. Or the piece is an opportunity for important experimentation with certain materials. These contextual considerations can profoundly affect the composer's thinking by providing the seed of a story with which to initiate the modeling process.

A good modeling process involves just such a dynamic interaction of these metaphorical spheres—spatial, temporal, and narrative imagery. As refinement of the process advances, so does the form of the piece; its time shape, sound space, and eventfulness gradually emerge.

Before going further, we should make certain we understand the use of the term *model* as a metaphor and not as a theory. In learning scientific principles, we often encounter explanations of natural phenomena presented according to some familiar theoretical model. In fact, in science, though the terms *theory* and *model* are sometimes used interchangeably, they have distinctly different meanings. A model represents some real thing. A theory is the relationship or similarity the model has to that thing. A model can be inappropriate, perhaps, but it can't be wrong or right. It simply exists. A theory, however, can be wrong or right in the way it explains the relationship or similarity of the model to what it represents. As Julian Jaynes explains, "A theory is a metaphor between a model and data. And understanding in science is the feeling of similarity between complicated data and a familiar model." (1976, 53)

Another term sometimes used interchangeably with model is the term **analog.** An analog is a special kind of model, not like the theoretical model explained above. Instead, an analog is, at every point in time and space, generated directly by the thing it is tracking. A map, for instance, is an analog of the features of the land area it represents, and this relationship between the land and the analog map is itself a metaphor.

CHOICE OF ENTRY

We have used the terms *metaphor* and *metaphorical* to explain the spheres of our compositional design strategy in the modeling process. It is important to understand the power of these terms in relation to the way composers invoke intuitive thinking in subjective, conscious thought.

In which metaphorical sphere of modeling does the composer begin? We are always, of course, in all three at once. But, in a more deliberate sense, we are, at any one moment, concentrating more intensely in one sphere than the others. And so the subjective decision making begins. At the very beginning of a piece's modeling, though, we normally choose a particular, usually familiar strategy as an entry point into one sphere. Entering, we explore and examine (again, the spatial metaphors to describe the process). For instance, we tell ourselves a story from our experience as a person. Or, we imagine sounds "colliding in space." Or, we simply "hear a tune in our head." The entry point may be suggested by some feature of a model piece—our own or another composer's.

Let's say that we have entered the sphere of spatial modeling and, just as we described before in our trombone piece example, we have already attributed a spatial quality to the instrument in our mind. When we decided to limit the length of the piece to ten minutes, we modeled time spatially, in a metaphorical left to right, from the start (left) to the finish (right). There is, of course, no left or right time, but we do it, nevertheless, by analog, a kind of "time-map." In fact, it is impossible to think of a span of time without spatializing it.

Or, let's say the entry point used is the sphere of narrative modeling. We can understand, for instance, that Berio might have done so by imagining himself as the trombonist, who, in turn, imagines that the trombone is performing the clown's act, declaring, "Why?"

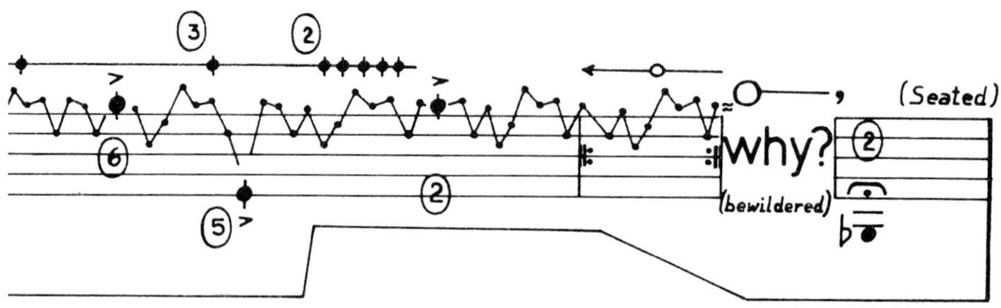

Figure 2.1 Excerpt from Berio's *Sequenza V* for trombone

The clown is a metaphor for the ironic, absurd and paradoxical in our lives. "In consciousness, we are always seeing our vicarial selves as the main figures in the stories of our lives." (Jaynes 1976, 63)

Only if our entry point is the temporal sphere must we create an immediate, assimilated image in time of spatial and narrative metaphors in our modeling process. In this sphere, as we work directly with the sounding successions of the piece, what we hear is immediately projected in both spatial and narrative senses. We hear the music we just invented and imagine the music that will come after the present sounding moment, a story taking place in some space. Incidentally, one of the most powerful modeling tools for the composer today is the practical temporalization of the materials for a piece with a computer system. At any stage of the modeling process, the composer can hear the music, creating an updated prototype of the piece in actual performance.

ASSIMILATION

It is, indeed, the **assimilation** of the emerging materials of a piece that gradually reveals the kind of engine our piece will have and where it will take us. Assimilation, the intuitive phenomenon in the modeling process, is the combustion of the fuel in the engine, the all-important melding force. It is learning about our composition in progress. Often, in the early stages of a piece, objects and events existing "separately" in the spatial and narrative spheres can seem in conflict when tested together in the temporal sphere. When this occurs, the composer, recognizing their incompatibility, may reject both the object and event but more often will work to reconcile them. Assimilation is the automatic reconciliation process. Jaynes explains:

> We assimilate a new stimulus into our conception or schema about it, even though it is slightly different. Since we never from moment to moment see or hear or touch things in exactly the same way, this process of assimilation is going on all the time as we perceive our world. We are putting things together into recognizable objects on the basis of the previously learned schemes we have of them. Now assimilation consciousized is *conciliation* . . . doing in mind-space what *narratization* does in mind-time or spatialized time. It brings things together as conscious objects just as narratization brings things together as a story. And this fitting together into a consistency or probability is done according to rules built up in experience. (p. 64)

Assimilation smooths rough edges, corrects imbalances, puts things in order and relation. The composer's intuitive powers are at work. Temporal assimilation of the spatial dimensions and narrative continuity invented for a piece consummate the process.

CONDITIONS

> The chief requirements for the creation of a comprehensible form are logic and coherence. The presentation, development and interconnexion of ideas must be based on relationship. Ideas must be differentiated according to their importance and function. (Schoenberg 1967,1)

As a piece is formed, the composer is at the same time modeling the piece on its own "rules." As temporal modeling tests new materials for the piece, applying earlier rules may not work. Then the composer either invents new material, invents a new rule, or alters the now unapplicable rule. There is a conciliation of rule and material or object and event. This part of the modeling process is the **synthesis of form.** Jaynes provides a vivid nonmusical example of this phenomenon:

> If I ask you to think of a mountain meadow and a tower at the same time, you automatically conciliate them by having the tower rising from the meadow. But if I ask you to think of the mountain meadow and an ocean at the same time, conciliation tends not to occur and you are likely to think of one and then the other. You can only bring them together by a narratization. Thus there are principles of compatibility that govern this process. . . . (1976, 65)

What Jaynes terms "rules" we will term **constant conditions.** What he terms "principles of compatibility," we will term **variable conditions.** A constant condition is an unchanging constraint or limit the composer invokes uniformly in the modeling process. An example is the adoption of a fixed set of pitches, a scale, used to invent melodic patterns. A variable condition is a changeable constraint or limit invoked when deemed appropriate. An example is the chromatic altering of pitches in that same fixed set when the composer wishes to inflect or replace a tonality.

Constant and variable conditions are integral to the modeling process, not only in temporal modeling but, of course, in the spatial and narrative spheres. The two example conditions above certainly would be decided early on. However, the composer, in working through the modeling process, does assimilate and invoke new constant and variable conditions as the piece forms. Each of these constant and variable conditions is a metaphor in the combined temporal, spatial and narrative spheres. Each such metaphor becomes more and more apt as the modeling process continues, culminating in the finished piece, itself a metaphor for the synthesis of its own form.

Good pieces come from good modeling processes, though that's never guaranteed! In fact, the modeling process the composer creates and uses is itself changing as each new piece provides valuable experience, learning what works well and less well. Though a composer may compose a series of similar works—in genre or medium—that have been created with similar modeling processes, composers should always be intent on refining the effectiveness of this mode: composing as process.

A MOLECULAR MODELING PROCESS

How, then, does a complete modeling process work? It depends on the piece, its context, and the composer's intent. Composer Iannis Xenakis, in his book, *Formalized Music: Thought and Mathematics in Composition* (1971), presents his modeling process as a list of "Fundamental Phases of a Musical Work." Simply paraphrased, they are

1. Initial conceptions, intuitions, provisional data
2. Definition of sonic entities, elements, and their symbolism

3. Definition of transformations, setting up relations between entities and arrangement of operations in time by succession and simultaneity
4. Microcompositional choice, detailed fixing of elements outside-time
5. Sequential programming of the work's pattern in its entirety
6. Modifications of the sequential program
7. Final symbolic result, setting out the music on paper
8. Sonic realization, e.g., performance or electromagnetic construction

Clearly, the modeling process is central to Xenakis' work. In fact, its seemingly all-too-scientific rigor is, at first, intimidating until you read further. "The order of this list is not really rigid. Permutations are possible in the course of the working out of a composition." Intuition gently qualifies the hard-edged mathematical terminology. What he terms "provisional or definitive data" are metaphorically our constant and variable conditions. He invokes spatial metaphors "outside-time," as well as temporal, "in-time." Objects—entities—and narrative metaphors—symbolism—combine with images of temporal reality. In fact, his "Fundamental Phases . . ." are metaphorical all through.

Then, in what at first may seem a quantum leap, we see that Xenakis and Mozart, of all people, turn out to be soul-mates! Mozart's letter to his father, describes his frustration with a student's slowness in understanding his modeling process:

> She plays the harp magnificently; she has a great deal of talent and genius, and, above all, a wonderful memory. She, however, doubts much whether she has any genius for composition, especially as regards ideas or invention. . . . I gave her today her fourth lesson on the rules of composition and harmony and am pretty well satisfied. But, alas! all must be done by rule; she has no ideas, and none seem likely to come, for I have tried her in every possible way. Among other things it occurred to me to write out a very simple minuet, and to see if she could not make a variation on it. Well, that utterly failed. Now, thought I, she has not a notion how or what to do first. So I began to vary the first bar, and told her to continue in the same manner, and to keep to the idea. When it was finished, I told her she must try to originate something herself—only the treble of a melody. So she thought it over and nothing came. Then I wrote four bars of a minuet. . . . I told her then to complete the minuet—that is, the treble only. The task I set her for the next lesson was to change my four bars, and replace them by something of her own, and to find out another beginning, even if it were the same harmony, only changing the melody. I shall see tomorrow what she has done. . . .
> (Paris, May 14, 1778)

Of course, Mozart, at 22 years of age an impetuous young genius and not a patient teacher, was "overkill" for such an innocent as the harp-playing child of a rich eighteenth century duke. But the modeling process Mozart used is there in his description of the lesson. Here, all at once, in the temporal sphere, all the "rules of composition and harmony"—again, our constant and variable conditions—are invoked. The rules were learned but ideas didn't follow because the rules were not yet part of an active modeling process.

Both Xenakis and Mozart stress the importance of imagining a piece's existence, the image of its form—Xenakis in his scientific thoroughness, Mozart in his consummate instinct for musical style. Through modeling, both envision the piece they will compose, both "hear" the likely outcome.

As aesthetician Susanne Langer believes:

> . . . however the total Gestalt presents itself to him, (the composer) recognizes it as the fundamental form of the piece. . . . This form is the 'composition' which he feels called upon to develop. . . . Once the essential musical form is found, a piece of music exists in embryo. . . . One might call that original conception the 'commanding form' of the work (1953, 122–123)

. . . what Arnold Schoenberg termed a *Grundgestalt.*

Inevitably, one expresses the modeling process as steps, stages or items in a list, and the list becomes a nominal order, despite disclaimers such as Xenakis' about ordering. But in our own mapping of the modeling process, we will represent it graphically as a three-dimensional world, a network of spheres swirling with coexistent potentials for routes and interconnections to reach its center.

RELATING FORCES

Now we can visually conceive of how the three types of modeling, temporal, spatial, and narrative, come together in a synthesis of form. Three important **relating forces** assimilate and fuse the distinctly modeled but incomplete images, synthesizing the ultimate form of a composition. These relating forces are fluid, channels of flow where images of time, space, and plot intermingle simultaneously and gravitate toward a common pool. The order and direction of flow is not specified—those are priorities for the individual composer to make. Any course through the connected channels, even a circuitous one, will lead to the creation of a unique form, a full and organic conception of a new artwork (see fig. 2.2).

Now that we have identified these forces as coexistent and co-equal, we can discuss their significance in the modeling process without risking unintended implications of priority.

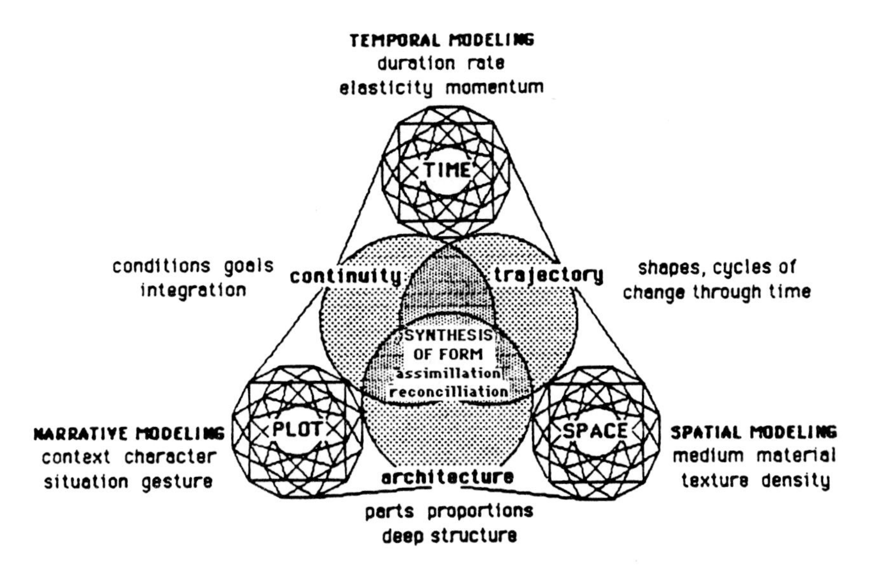

Figure 2.2 Spheres of image and relating forces in the modeling and synthesis of form: a molecular diagram

One of the relating forces in modeling is **architecture.** Qualifying the term structure, it was defined earlier as the relatedness, out of time, of the piece's largest to smallest, deepest to surface elements. Architecture connotes the deep structure, the large organizing elements of entire sections of a piece, their proportions, relations, functions in the overall coherence of structure. Architecture merges conceptions of character and space, involving the composer's strategies for qualities of material and its physical arrangement—where it comes from, where it is to be "placed," what is largely similar and what contrasting, and what types of sounding forces will carry out the plan. These strategies are studied in detail later in chapter 8, **MUSICAL ARCHITECTURE.**

As will be discussed in chapter 5, **TIME STREAMS, trajectory** is an important quality of the unfolding of events, the shape of change through time. A classic shape, for example, is the arch: its opening expressed as an ascending growth and development curve, reaching its peak usually past midway; then descending to its resolution and closure. Another example would be a piece whose surface is what James Tenney describes (in his definitive treatise on form, *Meta (+) Hodos* [1985]) as "ergodic," a process of moment-to-moment change in trajectory, a complex curve "whose statistical properties as a whole are the same as the statistical properties of each part at the next lower hierarchical level." The arch, then, would not be an ergodic shape.

Continuity, with its metaphorical aspects, is an all-important cohesive force in musical change through time. The morphology of a piece means tracing its course, what events occur, when, and how they relate. Composer John Cage has described form in music as "the morphology of a continuity," an apt mixing of all these forces and metaphorical models (and an apt description of the ergodic surface of many of his compositions). Previously in this chapter, we have explained how constant and variable conditions affect a piece and its "glue." Materials of similar and contrasting characters interact in time according to such conditions, interrupting or succeeding one another in their lifelike, individual progressions from inception to completion. Models for the continuity of a piece give essential qualities of tension and relief to its trajectory. Weakly modeled continuity—as, for instance, in a piece that too quickly and too often brings its ideas to neat closure without any conflict seeking eventual resolution—is a subtle but serious flaw common to many novice compositions.

It is, in fact, useful to understand through the relating forces how breakdowns or imbalances can flaw a modeling process. For example: a narrative model that identifies too many individual, distinct characters can disturb continuity; too little distinction of characters can weaken the architecture. Too little density of materials or a very thin texture prescribed by the spatial model can also weaken the architecture; too great a density in space can stifle the trajectory. Rigidity or a lack of elasticity in the temporal model will likewise inhibit trajectory; or an extremely elastic sense of time can confound continuity. In other words, an effective modeling process must balance all three spheres of image, bringing from each its unique contribution to architecture, trajectory, and continuity.

Balance need not mean simple equality, however. Like a trained dancer or acrobat poised in an extended position on the verge of falling but always in control, the modeling of a musical work can emphasize, even exaggerate characteristics on the exciting brink of imbalance. In fact, most great pieces do just that, stretching the boundaries of what can be controlled and kept in a dynamic balance.

Finally, there is the composer's process of assimilating all these images and forces. Through fluency and control of creative thought, through testing and revising, by seeking balanced but vivid images of time, shape, and plot, **synthesis of form** becomes fully realized.

Returning once more to *Sequenza V,* we can see that an elegant and effective model of form emerges from a balancing of vivid and coexistent images. The physical presence of the trombone and the character of the solitary clown performer suggest an architecture of sounds and gestures, changes which through time give perceptible shape to a trajectory. Thus, a continuity of dramatic events in time is achieved.

INVENTION 1 Begin to imagine a piece of music. Think about the molecular diagram of spheres of image and relating forces. Choose an entry point, a kind of image to start modeling. Say, "This piece will be about ______________." Keep a log, describing in detail the evolution of your compositional thoughts and actions as they work to form the piece. Let the log be a free-flowing journal including everything you think about related to the piece. If you are unsure of an idea, whether it will be right for the eventually composed piece, log it anyway. Continue composing in more detail, extending your log into a sketch book using suggestions from chapter 4, **DRAWING MUSIC.**

When the piece is complete, compare its final realization to its initial conception in the modeling process you created and logged.

INVENTION 1 VARIATION Use the same modeling process, but compose an entirely different piece. Choose a stage in the log at which to depart in a different direction of thought and design. This may involve designating new variable conditions which will lead to new kinds of variation in the basic materials suggested by the initial image.

If the point of departure from the original plan is before the selection of sound sources, then this new piece could be for a dramatically different medium. Could the same generating image lead naturally to both an instrumental piece and a vocal piece? Try an entirely new choice of medium and find out.

INVENTION 1 REPRISE Try another sphere of image as the entry point into a modeling process. The sphere of image you originally chose to start with may be the easiest for you—the most vivid imagery in your experience. Perhaps it is narrative modeling, thinking of a dramatic plot for emotional development. Trying to start with an entirely different kind of image will strengthen your imagination and broaden your modeling experience. Keep a log again, and when done, compare it with the logs of the other experiments to see how the process was affected by a different kind of starting image.

INVENTION 2 Study a score of Berio's *Sequenza V.* Listen to a recorded performance or, better yet, if possible, hear and see a live performance of it. Then design a variation of Berio's modeling process as you understand it. As his resulted in a kind of soliloquy, make yours into a composition which is a *dialogue* between two instruments. Use your own idea of their inherent characters or their physical natures as a generating image with which to begin modeling the dialogue.

Other pieces you know or have heard may strike you as vivid and exciting in their conception. Choose one and study it as *Sequenza V* was explored, getting to know its basic images and how they spin out into a fully modeled piece. Don't be reluctant to imitate and adapt a successful modeling process; in doing so, the opportunities for learning are potent, and the final result still cannot help being uniquely *your* piece.

OTHER READINGS

Books:

Arnheim, Rudolf. *Visual Thinking.* Berkeley, Calif.: University of California Press, 1969.

Berry, Wallace. *Form in Music.* 2nd ed. chapter 12 "Free Approaches to Musical Form" Englewood Cliffs, N.J.: Prentice-Hall, 1986.

Cage, John. *Silence.* Middletown, Conn.: Wesleyan University Press, 1961.

Clifton, Thomas. *Music as Heard.* New Haven, Conn.: Yale University Press, 1983.

Langer, Susanne. *Feeling and Form: A Theory of Art.* New York: Scribner & Sons, 1953.

———. *Philosophy in a New Key.* Cambridge, Mass.: Harvard University Press, 1942.

Meyer, Leonard. *Music, the Arts and Ideas.* Chicago: University of Chicago Press, 1967.

Rosen, Charles. *The Classical Style.* New York: W. W. Norton, 1972.

———. *Sonata Forms.* New York: W. W. Norton & Co., 1980.

Schoenberg, Arnold. *Fundamentals of Musical Composition.* Gerald Strang, ed., New York: St. Martins Press, 1967.

———. *Style and Idea.* Leonard Stein, ed., Leo Black, trans. Berkeley, Calif.: University of California Press, 1985.

Tenney, James. *Meta (+) Hodos.* Sante Fe: Soundings, 1985.

Xenakis, Iannis. *Formalized Music: Thought and Mathematics in Composition.* Bloomington: Indiana University Press, 1971.

Articles:

Brown, Earle. "Form in New Music." *SOURCE, Music of the Avant-Garde* 1(1967)1:46–51.

Clark, Thomas. "Duality of Process and Drama in Larry Austin's *Sonata Concertante.*" *Perspectives of New Music* 23(1984)1:112–25.

Dahlhaus, Carl. "Some Models of Unity in Musical Form." *Journal of Music Theory* 19(1975)1:2–30.

Tenney, James. "Form." *Dictionary of 20th Century Music.* John Vinton, ed. New York: E. P. Dutton, 1974.

CHAPTER 3
MEDIUMS AND IDIOMS

"Oh, you're a composer? How interesting. What kind of music do you write?"

Such a simple, friendly question—often asked of composers in getting acquainted with some person—is never simple to answer and sometimes causes the composer to pause a moment or two to reflect on what the question really means. The "kind of music" a composer creates, though hard to describe, is certainly understood and appreciated in a very personal way by the composer, in that and other ways by the composer's peers, and in myriad ways by the composer's public. Music itself is a complex art form with wide-ranging social, cultural, intellectual and economic manifestations, not easily explained in any context.

In what seem to be sensible, general descriptions of their music, composers typically reply, "I compose mostly orchestral music," or "I compose computer music," or "I mostly compose choral music," or "I compose operas," or "I compose all kinds—chamber music, solo works, band, choral, electronic, etc." Pressing further, the questioner responds, "Oh . . . that's interesting, but what I mean is what kind of music . . . you know, jazz, rock, classical. . . ." Composers often must be tempted in such situations to answer that question, "What kind of music do you write?" with a *non sequitur* like, "Beautiful music, of course." Try it sometime!

To create their "beautiful music" composers must work continually throughout their careers to refine their understanding of the ways and means to create their music, intent on developing a distinctive profile for their portfolio of completed compositions. As their experience broadens and deepens, they understand and appreciate that the ways of etching that profile are as diverse as the modes of invention in music: music's forms, mediums and idioms, its notations, styles, and innovations. As we discuss in **MATERIALS OF INVENTION,** composers soon learn, when creating a modeling process for the time streams, the pitch space, the sound color image and the musical architecture of a piece, that all are conditioned and often determined by the medium chosen, the idiom used, the style expressed, and, however modest, the innovation developed. They learn that a deep understanding and full appreciation of the ways of making music—its modes and materials of invention—will aid immensely in modeling well-made, freely composed, artful pieces.

In painting and sculpture, the term *medium* refers to the materials and techniques actuating the artist's visual image: oil on canvas; charcoal on paper; an etched plate used to produce a print; carved wood; chiseled stone; cast bronze; and many more. Artists also use the term *media,* when referring to several different materials and/or techniques used in a particular artwork. The term *media* also refers to the universal means of mass communication in world society, including television, radio, newspapers, and so on. In fact, *media* has been so broadly applied in this sense that this originally plural form of medium, through repeated misusage in the "media," has come to have a growingly acceptable plural form of its own—*medias!* We do not intend here to spread even more confusion in the use of these popular terms. We will use *medium* for the singular form, *mediums* for its plural, and *media* only when referring to combined and interactive mediums in music. Clear? We hope so.

In music, the term *medium* embraces not only the materials and techniques of a composition—as in painting and sculpture—but its genres, idioms, and means of expression. **Medium** in music connotes the modes of invention, the means of communicating musical ideas and the methods of transmitting musical sounds. The performance, communication and transmission of music through its many mediums involves an ever-changing, always expanding range of characteristic musical expressions, gestures and meanings—its **idioms.** Composers freely explore familiar idioms, choosing stylistically to confirm some, refashion others or experimentally to invent wholly new characteristics of expression to form new idiomatic usages. These in turn can lead to brand new mediums or crossovers from one medium to another.

Medium and idiom have always been interdependent. But with the emergence of electronic and computer applications in the music of the second half of the twentieth century, their symbiosis has been greatly energized. Contemporary mediums, along with their distinctive but always evolving idioms, now include: music for voice and voices combined; instruments alone and combined; voices and instruments combined; large instrumental and vocal aggregations; electroacoustic and computer music mediums; environmental sound mediums; and—the most expansive and inclusive—combinations of all these mediums plus the inclusion of the theatrical, choreographic, graphic, plastic, cinematic and video arts. With such a range of mediums and idioms, it's no wonder that composers tend to specialize in one or another, realizing that even a lifetime of composing experience in only one medium and its idioms is barely enough to probe its potential for creating "beautiful music."

MUSIC'S LITERATURE

Composers, performers, entrepreneurs and audiences bring musical mediums and idioms into being. These mediums grow, continue, evolve, and even become musical institutions. Or they become a part of music's history when the music of that medium is superceded, its medium and idioms obsolete and no longer heard. Mediums that survive and flourish do so because their literature—the idiomatic music of that medium composed and already collected—is continually being performed, refined, enriched, and broadened. The string quartet, the orchestra, the band, the choir, the piano solo—these and many others form the core of music's traditional mediums, all with a literature rich with model compositions, the exemplary masterworks of music. Composers continually study, perform, and listen to music's literature, of course, out of their love for this music. They realize, too, that knowledge and assimilation of the best literature of the various mediums of music will make them more fluent as composers, learning the "language" of a medium. They, in turn, can compose works which add new idiomatic usages and "turn new phrases," as it were.

It is important for composers to know how a medium and its idioms has developed and continues to develop. With historical perspective, our sense of the evolution of its literature can help greatly in modeling our own pieces.

Equally as important as the knowledge of the literature and history of mediums of music is the appreciation and influence from the most recent works in a medium. We compose a piece. It is heard by other composers. By listening to and assessing the significance of the sounds and substance of the piece, these other composers are inevitably influenced, one way or another, by the experience of the music we compose. As composers, we often describe such experiences in literary terms, stemming certainly from our concept of the term literature as the "collected works" of any medium. We speak of a composer's "fluency" in, say, the harmonic "language" of a piece. We cite other works in the literature from which we feel the composer might have "derived" his modeling process. (The terminology of literature, in fact, goes all through music with metaphorical descriptions of its form and continuity—phrase, motive, subject, episode, climax, statement, exposition, recapitulation, denouement, and, in the authors' case, narrative modeling.) Thus, composers' works influence and are influenced by other living composers' compositions, and in the process cause a medium and its idioms continually to evolve.

MUSIC'S IDIOMS

All mediums are distinguished by their own set of idioms, their own characteristic musical expressions. These have developed because of the acoustical and physical nature of the instrumental and vocal mediums, their traditional performance context, and their flourishing literature. A *glissando,* for instance, is certainly idiomatic for the solo trombone or the violin. A *glissando* would not seem to be idiomatic for keyed woodwind instruments, though expert performers can, with practice, affect a credible succession of pitches sliding between the keyed, chromatic semitones of the instrument. Interestingly, however, even though a clarinet *glissando* might seem idiomatically "misplaced," calling for such a nonidiomatic performance technique on the clarinet can be quite effective in the right compositional context. Today, in fact, arising from its frequent use in jazz, the clarinet *glissando* could be said to be a nominal part of the professional clarinetist's idiomatic arsenal.

In a very real sense the medium of the modern symphony orchestra is, itself, a vast array of 1) the idiomatic usages of all the individual instruments; 2) the section performance idioms of like instruments; and 3) the full ensemble idioms of the orchestral tutti. Orchestration textbooks abound with examples from the literature of idiomatic—and non-idiomatic—orchestral scoring.

The idioms of the traditional mediums of music are rooted in their literature. In spite of, or more likely, because of this, "non-idiomatic" innovations continue to be introduced in new compositions for the traditional mediums of music. Many such innovations are introduced by composers or performers and, for various reasons, are never widely adopted by other composers or performers. Other new developments are introduced and, for various reasons, are adopted and adapted for use by many composers, changing quickly from the nonidiomatic status to idiomatic. In some instances, such innovations are so striking that they sometimes change from non-idiomatic to cliche, and, decades later, become accepted idiomatic practice! For instance, the American composer Henry Cowell in 1923 first introduced what he termed "the string piano" in a solo piano piece, *The Aeolian Harp.* In the score he indicated that the piano strings themselves are to be "swept with flesh of finger" of the right hand, while "all the notes in lower staff (are) to be pressed down without sounding." At other moments in the piece, individual strings are "plucked." Gradually, through the next several decades, composers began, more and more, to call for this somewhat controversial departure from traditional piano keyboard performance practice until, in the sixties, the inclusion of an on-the-strings passage in piano music was so common that it became a very tired cliché. Today, such performance techniques are considered a normal part of the idioms of the literature of mediums which call for the piano.

MUSIC'S MEDIUMS

It is clear that the mediums of music making are distinguished most often by how the instruments and/or voices are combined in performance, from a single performer with or without accompaniment (**excerpts 1–5**) to very large aggregations of hundreds of singers and instrumentalists. These mediums include solo and chamber ensemble, orchestral, choral and combined choral and instrumental mediums.

Mediums are distinguished as well by the musical purpose they serve or the performance context in which they appear, from music presented in concert halls or as sound installations to the theatrical/musical presentation of opera and music theater to vocal and instrumental music functioning as part of the liturgy and ritual of church music services.

Mediums are also distinguished by the significant scope, quality, and uniqueness of the literature composed for particular instrumental or vocal combinations, from the traditional chamber music medium of the string quartet (**excerpts 9** and **10**) to the much evolved twentieth century wind ensemble medium (**excerpt 13**) to the contemporary electroacoustic medium of computer music (**excerpts 6, 7,** and **15**) to the newest innovations of opera for television (**excerpt 16**).

Fine . . . but wait! At this point it may seem logical to develop carefully delineated categories of mediums. In so doing, we could learn of and appreciate the many and diverse performance resources available to composers today. This is what such a large task would involve: 1) make a comprehensive list of all the traditional mediums, each identified by its specific instrumentation; 2) add to this list all the new and emerging mediums and their characteristics; 3) group all the mediums, new and traditional, into logical categories; 4) discuss the history and development of each category and its most significant and flourishing mediums; and 5) cite and discuss important compositions in the literature of each medium and important recent development.

Many compositional issues are raised by aspects of the task as just outlined. Certainly, sorting and describing the mediums of music seems, in itself, reasonable enough. But what interests us most as composers about this secretarial task is not the doing of it but the compositional issues raised as a result of the planning and thinking involved in accomplishing the task. What is the most important thing for a composer to learn about the mediums of music? To know, for instance, that a piano trio is not a piece for three pianos but is a traditional reference to a piece for piano, violin, and cello? Having made that clear, it must then be suggested that the composer is, nevertheless, free to compose a piece for three pianos. Or could the issue of terminology be avoided simply by listing piano trio in a category called, perhaps, "chamber ensemble mediums," and the "nontraditional" piano trio in something called, "instrumental family ensembles"?

As we have continued to stress, and stress here once more, it is very important for composers to study model compositions in the continually expanding literature of the music of all mediums, traditional as well as newly developed. But, here, we also stress that this admonition should not, as a result, cause us as composers to march in lock-step with any arbitrary categorization of mediums of music, however logical, however solidly based in historical precedent, however precise and well-organized. We don't create free compositions by first consulting such a list. Lists of anything will influence how we model a piece: ranking, categorizing, small versus large, vocal versus instrumental, traditional versus innovative, old versus new, and so on.

How can we distinguish and study mediums, then? How and why do composers choose a particular medium?

A MEDIUM'S LITERATURE

To become better acquainted with how a medium develops and builds a tradition of idioms through a literature of successful pieces, let's take one medium as a case study. A full history and survey of the literature for any medium represented in our **PORTFOLIO** would be an extensive musicological undertaking, one which in the case of a venerated medium such as orchestra could take and actually has engaged whole scholarly books. Flute alone is a medium which has developed only in this century, and while there is already a very extensive literature for it, a few important pieces clearly stand out as models for the growth of idioms. Roger Reynolds' *Ambages,* the very first excerpt in our **PORTFOLIO,** draws from and at the same time contributes to this tradition.

In general, works for a single instrument other than the keyboard instruments—piano, organ, etc.—are mainly a phenomenon of the twentieth century. There are a few exceptions, such as J. S. Bach's beloved solo cello suites from the eighteenth century. They are designed, however, to simulate the contrapuntal textures of keyboard instruments such as harpsichord, and although they accomplish this with great elegance and power, they did not establish a vital tradition for further growth in the work of subsequent composers. What force or impulse gave the stimulus and impulse for recent composers to work with an individual nonkeyboard instrument and try to stretch such seemingly limited resources into the stuff of a viable medium? In most cases, it was performers of instruments lacking the grand literature of concertos and sonatas enjoyed by the piano and the violin who sought solo pieces as vehicles for their own marvelous instruments that had been slighted or ignored in traditional chamber music. They commissioned, invited, begged composers to write for them, offering fascinating and unique techniques they had discovered for their instrument. The list of performers who did this in the 1950s through the present is a kind of honor role of contemporary music pioneers—Stuart Dempster and, later, James Fulkerson (trombone), Bertram Turetzky (contrabass), Harvey Sollberger and, later, Robert Dick (flute), Jan de Gaetani (voice), Philip Reyfeldt (clarinet), to name a few.

Composers responded not only to the untapped musical potentials of these instruments but also to the real need for their music and the dedicated enthusiasm of these performers. Some composers also became excited about their own instruments, seeing how they could draw on the performance backgrounds they nearly all have. William O. Smith wrote for solo clarinet, for example, and played his own works, achieving an autonomy that heightened the intensity already inherent in that medium.

The inception of solo flute literature goes back a bit further to the beginning of the century. Each of the three landmark pieces we will consider likewise was commissioned by a performer. *Syrinx* by Claude Debussy (1913) was written for flutist Louis Fleury; *Density 21.5* (1936) by Edgard Varese written for Georges Barrère; *Sequenza* (1958) by Luciano Berio for Severino Gazzelone. *Sequenza* was particularly successful for Berio, so much so that it was followed by a whole series of Sequenzas for other single instruments. Each has become the quintessential avant-garde work for that instrument, exploring with powerful drama and coherence the most advanced performance techniques in its medium.

Even though these three landmark solo flute pieces are all by European composers, their influence on American music was strong. *Sequenza V* for trombone (discussed in chapter 2, **FORM MODELING**) followed from the successful creation of new idioms in the flute *Sequenza.* It was written for and, in fact, with considerable creative input from American virtuoso trombonist Stuart Dempster. The work was performed around the United States and became known to American composers and respected for its technical innovations and powerful new form. The three European flute pieces are significant in many other ways, worth studying in depth and detail. Obtaining a score of each piece is highly recommended, so that details can be understood in the context of each work's entirety.

This is the background and context of influence for a work such as Roger Reynolds' *Ambages.* Other American works, such as Charles Wuorinen's *Flute Variations II* (1968) and Robert Dick's *Afterlight* (1973), continued in an American vein to advance the medium, confirming and extending the idioms of their predecessors. But what are some of these idioms, and how can they be described?

We define musical architecture as the interrelationship of elements of musical structure—rhythmic, pitch space, sound color, and loudness patterns—as they form musical materials. An idiom is a particular architectural pattern, described by the specific ways these domains relate.

For example, *Syrinx* uses a particular gesture to come to the end of its first section, in which the flute has imitated the sound of pan pipes, in turn imitating the songs of birds with agile ornaments of a gently undulating line. Then a long note in a fairly high register (C-flat above the treble staff), approached by a lower and quicker note almost like a grace note, swells with a crescendo (in measures 6–7) as it is sustained. The function of this gesture, to pull back momentum and close the opening section, is achieved by relating the highest pitch heard thus far with the longest duration thus far. In its high register, the note's color is also outstanding, more so too because its color changes as the sound intensifies with the *crescendo* and then fades with a *diminuendo* a whole tone higher on D-flat. It is a simple idea yet an effective contrast, natural to the transparent character associated with the flute. The idea is hinted at again at the end of the entire piece as a swell and sustained "color note" now in the lowest flute register. It has become a subtle part of modeling the whole work's form.

Density 21.5 concludes its opening section much the same way. The sustained pitch is a bit higher (E three ledger lines above the staff in measures 13–14). It is approached by a more elaborate pattern of three shorter notes leading up to it through an expanded space of more than an octave. And it *crescendos* but does not fade, instead stopping abruptly at the peak of the *crescendo* for a dramatic pause. This powerful closing gesture is used again many more times including at the very end of the piece. It becomes a major motive or driving force in the work's material and form. What was largely a single effect in the antecedent piece, *Syrinx,* is now an important mannerism central to *Density 21.5's* coherence.

We leap much further in this evolution to *Sequenza,* some twenty-two years later. Single sustained notes, first in a low register then throughout the flute range, are the reverse in dynamic shape—an explosive attack, a quick dropback in loudness, then a sustained fade. Still the simple sustaining of a pitch allows its particular registral color to be absorbed. Now the elaborate dynamic shaping inflects that color, giving the rhythmically static event an active momentum even as it fades. Throughout the piece, this idea initiates

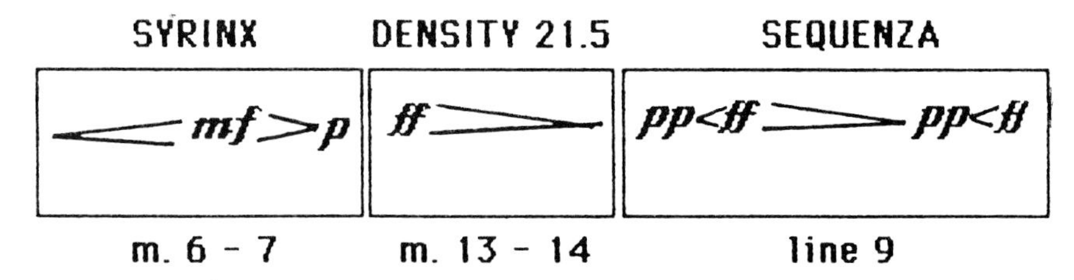

Figure 3.1 Development of the dynamically shaped sustained-note idiom

event streams; it has graduated from a cadential effect, then an important closing motive, to now the main impulse launching most of *Sequenza's* events throughout its form.

The seed of a much more obvious if possibly trivial idiom can also be found back in the same measure 6 of *Syrinx*. The note approaching that long sustained high C-flat is much shorter and not far from it in pitch space, a kind of auxiliary note much like a not-too-fast grace note. Describing a grace note architecturally is easy: a short sound very rapidly followed in time by a longer sound, the pitches usually also in close proximity. Later in *Syrinx,* grace notes actually notated as such begin to occur, and by the middle of the piece they permeate a repetitive, bird-like line.

Density 21.5 seems largely shy of this rather obvious flute idiom, using notated grace notes only twice (although once in a very bird-like fashion in measure 23). But a rhythmic cell opens the piece and becomes a strong motive threaded throughout the work's rhythmic fabric. Its pattern of two rapid notes, sixteenth notes, introducing a much longer sustained note of slightly higher pitch, F-sharp, resembles common ornamental patterns traditionally written as grace notes. Perhaps asserting this resemblance stretches a point, but the way this rhythmic motive evolves seems to bear out the interpretation. At the very middle of the piece (proportionally just where *Syrinx* broke out into a rash of grace notes!) the rhythmic motive occurs again as an even more rapid pair of thirty–second notes introducing a longer F-sharp (an octave higher than the original sustained pitch at the beginning). Even as the rhythm of this gesture is compressed in a more grace-note-like fashion, the intervals are expanded. Now the sustained note is approached by a leap from a whole octave above, at its compressed speed a rather gymnastic event. In the waning phrases of *Density 21.5,* the idea is truncated into a single grace-note-like thirty-second note leaping down a more moderate six semitones to an only slightly longer F-sharp.

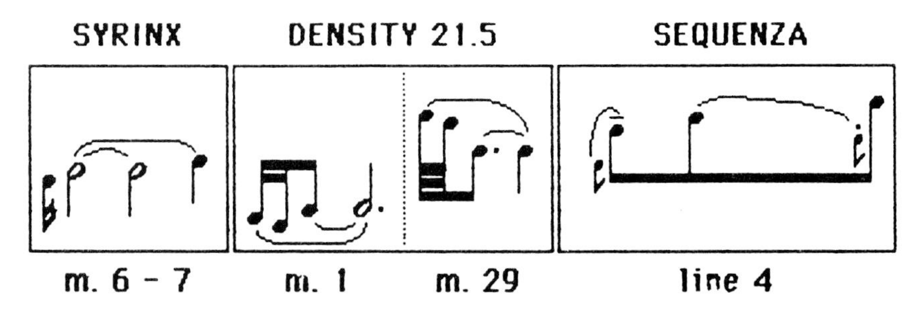

Figure 3.2 Growth of the grace note like rhythmic idiom

This developing grace-note idiom unquestionably matures in *Sequenza,* which abounds in grace-note patterns as a nearly ever-present component of rhythmic material. So varied and extensive are the notated grace-note patterns—from single grace notes to groups of as many as eight, and covering many intervals of pitch space from one semitone to as wide as twenty-nine semitones—that we might conclude these are no longer just ornaments but essential melodic materials. Again, the effect becomes a motivic mannerism and eventually an idiom inherent to the medium.

The solo flute medium is a fertile one, replete with such examples of developing idioms (possibly explaining why it has been so popular among late twentieth century composers). We will briefly mention one more found in these three landmark pieces. Figure 3.3 is a comparison of the first three pitches heard in each piece.

Figure 3.3 Comparison of first three pitches

The shape in pitch space of the *Syrinx* pitches can be expressed as [−1 +2 semitones]. If a shepherd's pan pipes were chromatically tuned, this close, conjunct pattern would be easy to play, much more so than leaping with the mouth between pipes widely separated in their attached line. *Density 21.5* begins with fairly low pitches but exactly the same [−1 +2] interval pattern! Surely Varese was very well acquainted with *Syrinx* and meant to pay homage to it with a thinly disguised quote. The interval pattern is later altered, developing into the pattern mentioned in the middle of the piece, a stretched out and straight plunge [−1 −12].

Sequenza begins with a more complex pitch shape. At first thought, this is an entirely different pattern, but it owes an ancestry to the opening of the two previous pieces. [−1 +11] still starts with a downward one semitone interval and still turns to go up beyond the starting pitch. And the three pitch classes used—G, G-sharp, A (see the definition in chapter 6, **PITCH SPACE**)—are adjacent in a contiguous segment of the chromatic scale, just as are the E, F, F-sharp of *Density 21.5* and the A, B-flat, B-natural of *Syrinx*.

All these similarities are hardly mere coincidence; they evidence the composer's awareness of and sensitivity to idioms, both those that are natural to an instrument's character and those that have developed in already established literature for the medium. They are the backdrop to the selection of materials for an informed, literate composition for solo flute such as Roger Reynolds' *Ambages,* **excerpt 1** in our **PORTFOLIO.**

To find our interval idiom, we must look just a little further into *Ambages,* to measure 3. No longer the pattern of the very beginning, the G, F-sharp, and G-sharp still acknowledge that interval tradition, the chromatic scale segment, the turn, one interval expanded as in *Sequenza,* but this time the downward first interval . . . [−13 +14]. Also like *Sequenza, Ambages* makes a florid filigree figure in grace notes spanning a space of fifteen semitones.

But these are only small details of *Ambages,* not main motivic material. And what has become of the dynamically shaped sustaining of a colorful pitch? The sustained note is now an opening gesture, its sense of color heightened by a *pianissimo* dynamic level, a circular mark calling for a "harmonic" tone quality (produced by using a fingering for the pitch, C, in a lower octave and overblowing to produce the higher C), and a specification for no vibrato to be used, *nv.* There is no dramatic *crescendo* or attack this time. There is a pitch bend, gradually raising the C up a full semitone to D-flat! Since this is accomplished by rolling the flute so its aperture (the hole blown across) changes its angle to the embouchure (the lips and their air stream), the tone quality dramatically mutates during the bend.

Only vaguely descended from the *crescendo* cadential gesture of *Syrinx* and *Density 21.5,* the pitch bent, color heightened sustained sound not only opens *Ambages* but recurs and evolves throughout the piece as a kind of theme. It also spawns many related events, such as the elaborate inflections of the repeated pitch class B in measures 13 and 14, introduced with a grace note, flutter-tongued, shifted up an octave, dynamically "sighed," changed to a harmonic bent to a noticeably lower pitch marked by "( )" above two of the notes. Sustaining and shaping a single colorful pitch has become more than an idiom in a tradition—it is now an innovation and a fascination at the core of this music's whole substance.

MODELING THE MEDIUM

The way we model the piece can be and often is derived directly from the medium. But the way we model should also cause us to choose one medium over another or, in fact, to create a brand new medium designed especially for the form of music we are modeling and want to create. Whether the medium is prescribed by circumstance or chosen freely, we always model the medium as part of the modeling process of the composition.

A complex array of constant and variable conditions affect the modeling of the medium of a piece. These are important to consider every time we begin a piece: whether the medium is freely chosen as an addition to our growing portfolio of performable compositions; whether we have been commissioned to compose a piece for a specific ensemble, occasion, or purpose where the medium is precisely prescribed; whether the work is to be a study or experiment, exploring innovative approaches to modeling form; or whether the work is, itself, a study in modeling a medium of performance.

The medium freely chosen—It would seem that when the medium is completely up to the composer to model that the only complications would lie in the pleasant task of choosing from among the vast array of possible mediums of making music—"whatever strikes the fancy," as it were. True, but since the medium chosen directly affects the form the piece takes, the composer should make such an important compositional decision a part of the modeling process. And even before that takes place, the composer has some very practical matters to consider.

What pieces has the composer completed already and in what mediums? What mediums remain and which would serve well to balance the variety (or even uniformity!) of pieces in the composer's growing portfolio of performable pieces? What performance opportunities for the piece are open, and what mediums do these involve? Do these performance opportunities involve professional, student, or amateur musicians? Will the work involve a text either as a vocal setting, a spoken narration or dialogue or function as a metaphor in narrative modeling? If no performance opportunities presently exist, what mediums seem most universally performable? What level of technical difficulty will make the medium most available? How much rehearsal time is available? Where might the piece be presented for the first and subsequent performances? The answers to these questions narrow the number of possible mediums open to the composer and, in very practical terms, determine the way in which the medium is integrated into the modeling process of the piece.

The medium prescribed—Likewise, it would seem that, when the composer has been commissioned—whether contracted, invited, or chosen—to compose a piece for a specific medium, nothing further needs to be known before the modeling process is begun, "cut and dried," as it were. Yes, but certain important information should be in hand.

What is the stated purpose of the commission? Is this the first such commission or part of a continuing series? Is the commission for an established soloist or ensemble in a particular performance context, such as a professional touring ensemble or a resident ensemble in a particular concert venue? Is the commission for a concert series with a range of possible instrumentations? If the commission is for a specific, organized, ongoing ensemble, what is their performance profile and history? Do they often perform newly composed music? To what extent do members of the ensemble consult with the composer about the nature of the commissioned piece? Where will the piece first be performed and how much rehearsal time will be allotted for its preparation? What degree of flexibility does the composer have to expand or limit the available performance resources? What is the maximum and minimum duration expected of the piece? Can tape music or other mediums be combined with the ensemble? Once more, the answers to these questions determine to a great extent the conditions affecting the integration of the prescribed medium into the modeling process of the piece.

The medium explored—In the discussion of John Cage's *Variations III* in chapter 1, **CONTEXTS FOR LEARNING,** we observed that Cage gave the greatest possible latitude to performers of the piece, and that included the choice of the medium. The performers, themselves, were free to explore all possible combinations in planning a performance of the piece. Anything short of this type of performance freedom involves some degree of decision making on the composer's part. Here, however, it is more a matter of knowing what questions to ask oneself about the nature of the mediums of music than what answers will be found. Exploring the nature of a medium involves thorough research, experimentation in a kind of performance laboratory context, and analysis of the effectiveness of the particular use of a medium. For instance, ad hoc improvisation ensembles, organized by the composer, can be an excellent resource for exploration into the characteristics of different combinations and their interaction.

The medium personalized—Composing is normally a highly personalized endeavor, ideally in the quiet and solitude of the composer's own studio. Only when the composer is working to invent material with, for instance, an experimental improvisation group or with other artists or with a team of programmers in a computer music facility does the composer work with others to carry out the modeling process of a composition. Thus, the composer's personal medium of in-studio music making is all-important.

The piano continues certainly to be the most accessible personal medium of the composer, whether working directly at the keyboard to hear the immediate sonic results of temporal modeling or using the piano to test materials conceived first in the mind's ear at the composer's worktable. The piano with its seven-octave range and its immediate means of easy sound production (one need only touch a key!) as well as the universal availability of the instrument makes the piano ideal as the composer's personal medium. It's always there. Music history confirms that the piano has been the composer's instrument of choice by the fact that legion piano compositions have been composed since

Bartolomeo Cristofori perfected his hammered-string keyboard instrument, the *gravicembalo col piano e forte*, in the early eighteenth century. Composers have all at some point or another in their career been asked to reveal their personal composing medium with the question, "Do you compose at the piano?" Composers, however, rarely limit their choice of mediums for finished pieces to the piano. Most, as our discussion thus far elucidates, model the medium for the piece based on many other factors, primarily concerned with the context of performance. There have been composers, however, whose special musical conception has resulted in the creation of highly specialized personal mediums of music making, sometimes so unique that only one composer and no other can compose for the medium.

Since the late forties, composer Conlon Nancarrow has devoted most of his career to painstakingly plotting the distance between carefully punched holes in the paper rolls necessary for the performance of his player piano pieces, which comprise almost all of his compositions. Complex cross-rhythms, different simultaneous tempi, and complex, "impossible-to-perform" textures are "played" effortlessly in this performerless medium adapted for personal use by Nancarrow. His compositional approach predates similar techniques in computer-assisted composition, which began to develop a decade later.

Similarly, but not so exclusively, John Cage, in 1940, transformed the modern piano into the "prepared piano" with the careful insertion of nuts, screws, rubber erasers, pieces of plastic and other objects at precisely measured points between the piano's strings, causing it to sound like a kind of multicolored percussion orchestra. Cage invented this personal medium because of his great interest in percussion music and its combination with the dance. That same spirit of invention and personalization is carried on today in the music created by "the musicians" of the Merce Cunningham Dance Company with which Cage was creatively associated as music director for four decades. "The musicians," all composer-performers, have, since the sixties, devoted much of their creative energies to inventing new personal music mediums, primarily live-electronic "black boxes" for their compositions with the dance. Besides Cage himself, these composer-performers have included such important innovators of personal mediums as Gordon Mumma, David Behrman, Takehisa Kosugi, David Tudor, and Martin Kalve. What began with the invention by Cage of the prepared piano has now become an ongoing tradition of inventing personal music mediums of performance, whenever music is created for the Cunningham company.

Composer Harry Partch determinedly and quite successfully began in the early thirties to design and construct, himself, an entire orchestra of unique plectra, reed, keyboard, string, and percussion instruments, all made to perform microtonal tuning systems extending to the division of the octave into a just-intoned, forty-three tone scale. Partch's personal medium included a whole repertory of music he composed for his orchestra, performed on the instruments by musicians he trained in the specialized techniques required. Performances by the group were rehearsed and conducted by Partch or his proteges, the largest mixed-media pieces requiring theatrical staging and direction as well. Wide recognition for his work came in the mid-sixties as his pieces began to be presented widely in important performance venues in Illinois, California, and later in New York. His influence spread among younger composers as an instrument builder, microtonalist, and, most important, as a model creator of a personal medium of music making. Partch's book, *Genesis of a Music* (1974), sets out in detail the theory, principles and aesthetics involved in the world of music he created for his own highly personalized, self-invented medium of music.

Figure 3.4 Harry Partch conducting his ensemble

Like Harry Partch, composer Salvatore Martirano designed a unique personal medium for use only by him, so personal that its name, the Sal-Mar Construction, is an acronym formed from the composer's name. Unlike Partch, the system, completed in 1971, is performed by Martirano alone and is completely a product of advanced electronic technology. During the seventies Martirano toured extensively throughout the United States with the system, not a small feat since the large console stands higher than the composer and as deep and almost as wide as an upright piano.

The electronic sounds of the Sal-Mar are produced with analog electronic modules controlled by digital circuits, these in turn activated by Martirano on a large, lighted touch-plate keyboard. The digital circuits were designed to interact in complex, relatively unpredictable patternings; responding, Martirano improvises interactively. Also an important part of the system is a twenty-eight speaker audio system which routes the electronic sounds in spatial patterns through the performance space.

Martirano developed the Sal-Mar at the University of Illinois, whose School of Music in the fifties began to encourage the development of personal mediums and innovative approaches to composition. Significantly, the first computer-assisted composition, the *Illiac Suite,* was composed there in 1955–56 by Lejaren Hiller and Leonard Isaacson. Hiller, a trained scientist, made the computer itself his personal medium of music making. He also founded the Experimental Music Studio during this time, a studio dedicated to the development of innovative exploration in electroacoustic music. Partch and, later, Cage were both resident composers at Illinois in the sixties. In 1968, Cage and Lejaren Hiller co-composed the quintessential mixed-media composition of the sixties, *HPSCHD,* combining computer music, seven amplified harpsichords, fifty-one channels of computer-generated tape music, and a sensory bombardment of five thousand slides and several films.

Partch's personal medium—an orchestra of instruments of his own design and fabrication—was unique in design and accessible only to him and his proteges. Nancarrow's personal medium—the player piano—was, decades ago,

Figure 3.5 Sal Martirano with his Sal-Mar Construction
Photo by D. Rohde-Tipei.

widely available but uniquely used by Nancarrow. Its disappearance as a popular medium later made the medium itself unique. Cage's invention—the prepared piano—was at first a unique adaptation, uniquely accessible, but, as other composers like Lou Harrison and Christian Wolff created their own versions of Cage's medium, it became the property of all composers, universally accessible. Interestingly, Martirano in 1983 turned his attention to smaller but equally powerful personal mediums, adapting the compositional algorithms developed on his Sal-Mar to a system comprised of a personal computer with a MIDI interface to and from digital synthesizer modules. Manifestations of these approaches to the creation of a personal medium for composing and performance continue today, more prevalent than before because of the wide availability, especially, of adaptable electronic and digital music systems.

ELECTROACOUSTIC MEDIUMS

It would seem that no new mediums surely can be developed, that every means of musical expression has already been modeled, that, indeed, we have too many and need no more! But as surely as old mediums of music have faded into music history books, new ones have continued to emerge. This is particularly true today in this age of computer and electronic technology. With the development of digital synthesizer technology in the seventies and the ubiquitous spread of affordable, portable versions of this advanced technology (the Synclavier, Yamaha, Kurzweil, Fairlight synthesizers to name the most prominent), individual composers have discovered the power such instruments have in creating highly personal mediums of music for their compositions, electroacoustic mediums which even rival the symphony orchestra in sound color potential and event stream patterning.

The term itself—**electroacoustic**—connotes the extraordinarily broad reach of these contemporary mediums into every kind of music there is today: any means to make music that involves electronic and/or digital technology with or without the involvement of acoustic sound sources. The computer music medium, a genre of electroacoustic music and the most ubiquitous, has, in fact, become a mature art form, itself the progeny of experimental music and high technology. Its conception and gestation in the late fifties, its birth and early growth in the sixties, its widespread development in the seventies has, in the eighties, become a powerful medium of contemporary expression. Like its precursors, musique concrète and tape music, computer music has been "a music in search of a folk," so to speak; mediums springing from technology—radio, film, video, computer graphics—have at first seemed out of place and strange, somehow alien to "real" art forms. Such machine-art seemed ridiculous mimicking our more familiar, well-established drama, painting, instrumental and vocal music. Now, we recognize the value of computer music as an important medium of music with its own language, rich in subtle, powerful, idiomatic expressiveness and appreciated by a growing audience. The practitioners of computer music are a diverse professional group: composers, acousticians, performers, psychologists, theorists, and computer scientists, and, among the newest generation, individuals whose talents integrate all these special arts and sciences.

While there is, then, an eclectic profusion of electroacoustic art music mediums today, there are, nevertheless, discernible "foci." These center mainly 1) on composers whose powerful influence on their fellow composers is sustained by consistently original work; 2) on the venues of presentation and recording, where newly created work can be heard and assessed by a discerning audience, informing and influencing present and future tastes; 3) on a wide range of institutional studio facilities throughout North America and Europe; and 4) on the now universal availability of personal electroacoustic digital music systems.

It is almost rhetorical to state that composers of electroacoustic art music are fiercely independent in this highly personalized medium. They pride themselves on a self-reliant spirit that owes allegiance to no one studio (unless they founded and/or direct it!), to no one electroacoustic system (unless they invented it!), to no compositional approach (unless they are perceived as being its original developer!), and to no one particular, official or unofficial group of composers in the field (unless it is convenient and/or necessary!). This fierce independence creates a highly competitive field, reflective of our modern society, creating the ferment necessary for innovation and excellence.

One such creatively independent composer-performer, for example, is Nicolas Collins, who lives in New York and, in a 1986 interview with Annea Lockwood (another important voice in electroacoustic music), put a prevalent attitude about composing electroacoustic music succinctly and powerfully:

> In terms of the materials I use, my approach has to do with notions of appropriate technology and recycling. It's a kind of ecological approach to materials and also subversion . . . subverting technology, using it for what it's not supposed to be used for, actually subverting musical materials, taking something normally used in one context and using it in another. . . .When I come up with an idea, I look

> around to see what approximates it, what's available. The commercial music industry is so huge, and electronics play such a large part in it that there's usually something around, something designed to fit the economic necessities of your average rock and roll band that can be modified . . . I think it's rather interesting that, whereas the avant-garde used to be at the forefront of sonic and technological experimentation, now, all of a sudden, the tide has turned. John Chowning develops FM synthesis out at Stanford, thinks about it, works with it for years, and then Yamaha produces an FM instrument, the DX–7 synthesizer, that sells millions, and suddenly the people, who are programming keyboards for rock and roll bands, are miles ahead of a lot of avant-garde composers in terms of innovative sound design. (1986 *New Music America* program book)

Collins' attitude of openly appropriating and freely processing available mass-culture sonic materials and digital music systems is typical of the new generation of composers of electro-acoustic music, including a Carl Stone in Los Angeles or a Jerry Hunt in Texas or Anders Blomqvist/Ake Parmerud in Stockholm or a Michel Waisvisz in Amsterdam. This independent, highly personal approach to both materials and systems is influencing the institutionally based composers as well. In a review of the 1985 International Computer Music Conference held in Vancouver, author Larry Austin observed:

> Composers are increasingly less institutional and/or studio-bound; they prefer powerful, dedicated, often portable computer music systems, both the turn-key, off-the-shelf variety and custom fabricated, microcomputer-driven systems. Of the fifty-three works involving computer control and/or generation of sound, twenty-nine were created in institutional facilities providing dedicated systems for software synthesis; fifteen were created with Synclavier, Fairlight, Buchla, or Yamaha digital synthesizers; and seven were created with personal, custom-fabricated systems, often performable in real-time. Thus, it is clear that, as computer music scientist James Beauchamp remarked to me, 'hands-off has become hands-on.' (*Perspectives of New Music* 23 no. 2, 1984, 253)

In spite of its diversity, quality and abundance, venues for the presentation, dissemination and recording of electroacoustic music are "few and far between" in the United States. The annual, always moving, always eclectic New Music America festivals include a concert or two of electroacoustic music, unfortunately often relegated to a less important afternoon concert slot. The only other national venue is the International Computer Music Conference, begun in the United States in 1974. It has grown in importance since then as the pre-eminent forum for this particular genre of electroacoustic music. At these conferences, lasting several days, several hundred conferees attend a succession of performances of their computer music, interspersed with scientific sessions reporting on a wide range of concerns from systems development to psychoacoustic research to computer-aided composition. But, since 1982, the ICMC has been held in European countries (Italy, France, Holland, and, in 1988, Germany) every other year, reducing by half the possible American composers and audiences able to present and appreciate new electroacoustic compositions on a large-scale basis. There are, of course, important smaller venues: Experimental Intermedia Foundation, Roulette, and The Kitchen, all in New York, but typical of the many and various new music series in museums and alternative spaces around the country. And there are the ad hoc festivals of electroacoustic music that are held in American universities, such as the Electronic Music Plus festivals, which are annually presented in various universities in the eastern United States.

How is it that electroacoustic music continues apparently to grow and flourish? Two reasons for this have already been alluded to. One is the fascination that composers have with charting their own course, building their own world of sound, and being independent of conventional mediums for composers (orchestras, chamber ensembles, opera, and so on) that for the most part are closed to all but the lucky and/or well-connected. With mass availability of economical systems, young composers can be independently creative! Another, more important reason is the astonishingly beautiful music that has been and continues to be created in this wonderful realm of the electrical. So many compelling pieces serve as models to emulate. A third and more obvious reason is that there are simply hundreds of well-equipped studios devoted to the study and creation of electroacoustic music in the universities and conservatories around the United States. It is, in fact, uncommon for young composers in the United States not to have studied electroacoustic music systems at some point in their education and rare, indeed, if they haven't made a tape piece.

Explorations into combined mediums often challenge composers specializing in electroacoustic and computer music mediums, for performers and ensembles have more and more come to appreciate the wide range of musical expression possible in such combinations. Much of the music of these technological mediums has been, until recently, primarily involved with the playback in performance of precomposed tape music. From the late forties to the seventies, such playback was most often on reel-to-reel stereo or quadraphonic tape machines. Beginning in the eighties with the introduction of the PCM (pulse code modulation) digital recording format and, in the late eighties the cassette digital recording, new "noiseless" playback more and more has become the norm in such combinations. Playback of precomposed music, whether tape or disk or newly developed reproduction systems, continues to be important in combining with other mediums, because of 1) its performance and rehearsal reliability, convenience and portability; 2) its capability of being precisely synchronized with performers through headphone click tracks, and 3) most importantly, the precision of compositional detail that can be achieved consistently by the composer with precomposed performance materials prepared in-studio. Indeed, the possibilities of combination of mediums of music is well-nigh limitless and offers the composer exciting vistas to explore as the modeling process for a piece is being created.

COMBINED MEDIUMS, COMBINED IDIOMS

After all, composing is combining. In creating their art, composers by definition are combiners of all the elements of music. This can include the combining of mediums and their idioms. In a sense, combined mediums and combined idioms could be said to exist anytime a composer calls for more than one performer or sound producing medium in combination. But we hardly think of, say, the string quartet as the combined mediums and idioms of the violin duet, the viola solo, and the cello solo. Rather, we thank Franz Joseph Haydn for "inventing" and composing for this now venerable combination, a chamber music medium rich with almost two hundred fifty years of literature that is still viable, performed, and growing. Nor do we normally think of opera as the combining of the musical mediums and idioms of vocal soloists, chorus, and orchestra with dramatic and choreographic art forms. We think of opera as an integrated medium of music with almost four hundred years of literature sustaining its distinction as one of our oldest and most important musical institutions.

What we do have in music are essentially two kinds of combined mediums: unchanging vocal and instrumental combinations that constitute our established, traditional combined mediums of music; and newer combinations of mediums that are, by their very nature, always in flux. The traditional combinations include opera; music theater, bringing together elements from music and drama that are distinct from operatic traditions; music for film and television; music for the dance; and concertos, combining a soloist or small group of soloists with orchestra. To these well known traditional combinations we add the now widely accepted combination of taped electroacoustic music with instrumental and vocal mediums.

Nontraditional combinations of mediums—open and determined by the nature of the piece—are variously referred to as mixed-media, multimedia, theater pieces, performance art, and intermedia, as well as happenings, environments, and installations. One aspect, more than any other, is common to most nontraditional combined mediums: a strong electroacoustic element coupled with new and usually high technology.

"Tape-plus-live" now has a firmly established literature. It was born in the early fifties with the then experimental combination of tape and large instrumental ensemble in Edgard Varese's *Deserts* (1950–54) and the collaborative experiment composed by the American tape music pioneers, Vladimir Ussachevsky and Otto Luening in their *Rhapsodic Variations For Tape Recorder and Orchestra* (1953–54). Such combinations are now so commonplace that composition contests for various instrumental combinations almost always list "tape" as an optional inclusion. In fact, the instrumentation or medium specified by composers after the title of a piece—"Name of Piece," for instrumental medium and tape—seems today not the declaration of some novel innovation in combining such mediums but simply a nominal indicator of musical forces.

The tape medium is now so comfortably combined with other mediums of music because of the intense interest composers have demonstrated in the creative applications of the technology of electoacoustic music mediums. They have advanced its idiomatic usage dramatically in the past forty years from the spliced-together recordings of percussion and factory sounds of the earliest versions of Varese's tape for *Deserts* to today's computer processed and synthesized samplings of digitally recorded vocal sounds—stretched, contracted, merged, and transformed with millisecond control over acoustic details of the sounds and their event stream patterns, as in the computer music narrative on tape heard in combination with the chamber orchestra in **excerpt 15.** It is unfair, however, to believe that Varese's sonic imagery for his tape was limited to the results he achieved with the limited tape music technology of the fifties. That is disproved by the fact that he revised and improved the tape at least three times during the decade following the composition of the instrumental music, which itself remained unchanged through this period. The seeming awkwardness at that time of the combination of the tape's sounds and the instruments was well understood by Varese; in fact, the mediums are never actually heard in sonic combination in *Deserts* but always in contrasting alternation of instrumental and taped portions of the piece.

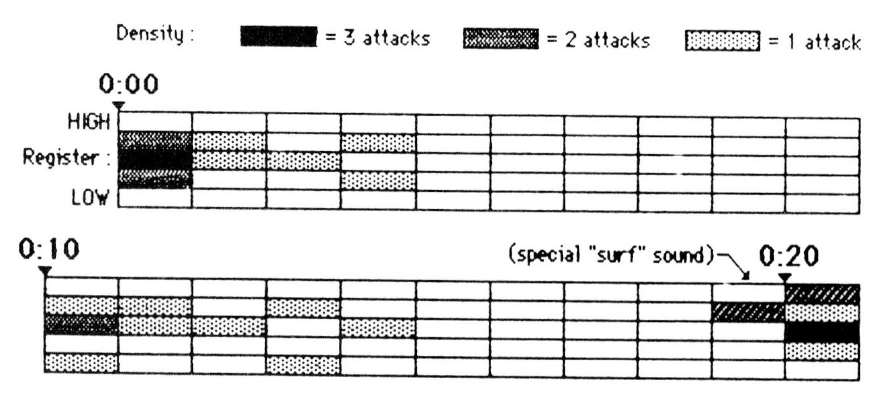

Figure 3.6 Notation of the tape part at the opening of *Peninsula*

CONVENTIONAL INSTRUMENTS WITH TAPE

"Electronic Music Plus," the name of an annual festival concert series already mentioned, expresses the common feature in an important genre of pieces combining conventional acoustic instruments with taped electronic sounds, truly "electroacoustic" mediums. The stimulating influence of electronic idioms on basic compositional thought is most evident in such pieces, which often extend instrumental techniques in response to that stimulus. When confronted with the thicker or longer or higher or more changeable complex sounds of which synthesizers and computers are capable, the instruments are found worthy of the challenge, extending beyond their own idioms to embrace these extremes and subtleties. Many kinds of interaction can then arise between the two unique mediums of instrument or instruments and of taped electronically produced sounds.

The most basic relationship is a simple **independence** of inherently different mediums, coexisting in time and sounding space, mixing to form a composite texture but not pointedly interacting. *Peninsula* (shown in **excerpt 7**) takes this approach, casually joining two distinct mediums. Precise relationships in time and pitch are not intended, as evidenced by the very general way in which the tape part is notated for the pianist, not showing individual sounds but only indicating changing densities of activity on the tape to help mark the large-scale passage of time (see figure 3.6). The piano and tape are two elements of an animated landscape, both simply within "view."

> Glacially-etched shorelines inspired sonic imagery for a series of pieces culminating in *Peninsula*. Mappings of these natural contours provide richly varied patterns as basic material for sculpting sound structures. In *Peninsula*, the piano explores some of the endless possibilities for articulating a spectrum of sonorities. The density of pointillistically separated synthetic sounds rises and falls in waves according to changing values also derived from the basic mappings. Larger confluences of waves are located in time by points of special significance in the mappings. The coexistence of piano sonority and synthetic sound is a metaphorical meeting of individually animated sonic environments. (from the composer's program notes)

In any coexistence, of course, some relationship inevitably arises. How the piano and tape colors begin to interact in a shared environment is examined more extensively in chapter 7, **SOUND COLOR.**

Karlheinz Stockhausen's monumental, pioneering work, *Kontakte* (1958) for piano, percussion, and four-channel tape, takes this basic premise but builds event streams in layers so dense that a sense of interaction, of actions and reactions, as in Newtonian physics, begins to develop.

Mario Davidovsky's landmark series of works, each for an instrument or instruments with tape, intensifies such interaction in time, establishing a tradition of **contrapuntal dialogue** between the tape medium and an instrument. The title of each piece, *Synchronism,* clearly implies the importance of precise rhythmic interaction, closely linking the "voices" of the two mediums in time. *Synchronism no. 1* (1963) for flute and tape is a pioneering work in this style, so influencial that it could have been mentioned in our survey of developing solo flute literature. It was not discussed then precisely because it is not a solo but a leap to another level of chamber music mediums, a duo, a conversation between equal entities.

The tradition is continued by Barry Vercoe, amongst many others, in his *Synapse* (1976) for viola and computer. It is chamber music in the most sophisticated sense. The computer at times accompanies the viola like an organ or harpsichord with chordal sonorities, at other times interspersing accents and trading melodic motives, all in a rhythmic counterpoint that requires extremely precise synchronization as well as "considerble virtuosity on the soloist's part." Vercoe's view of this medium is somewhat larger in scope—he calls the piece "essentially a small viola concerto"—but the interactive principle is the same, the notion of contrapuntal support of a soloist and a resulting dialogue.

Electronically produced sounds are not always "synthesized," made out of nothing by an abstract network of circuits or array of numbers. *Concrète* or recorded "real" or "natural" sounds are another traditional source, such as the surf captured and enhanced for the tape of Robert Erickson's *Pacific Sirens* (1969). In a kind of natural harmony, the unspecified group of instruments is integrated into the sound world of the tape as players are instructed to listen for tones in the wash of surf and use their own sounds to draw them out and eventually to elaborate them with improvisation centered around those tones. One medium merges with and adopts the substance of the other.

An even more profound **integration** can take place when sources of taped sounds include recorded sounds of the instrument itself. The computer sounds in *Peninsula* were made by digitally analyzing timbral qualities of acoustical instruments, mostly with percussive articulations, then modifying and resynthesizing them to build a pointillistic texture. One of these sound sources was a real piano note damped with a finger and struck forcefully with the ordinary hammer mechanism of the piano. This then produced one kind of resynthesized sound with a vague affinity to the color of the "live" instrument in the piece. Two other piano-and-tape pieces discussed shortly primarily or exclusively use piano sounds as models for designing computer-generated sounds. Such sharing of color sources is a powerful potential for integrating mediums, especially two such personalized mediums as piano and self-created electronic sounds.

Charles Dodge makes this integration with another rather personal medium. *The Waves* (1984) places a voice in an environment of singing sounds. Both the wave-like patterns of these sounds and their almost human color are derived from the voice of Joan LaBarbara and from a Virginia Woolf text vividly describing ocean waves.

> Dodge wrote the work for Joan LaBarbara, who performs to an accompaniment derived from the qualities of her own voice. Dodge prerecorded LaBarbara reciting the Woolf passage and performing extended vocal techniques (multiphonics and reinforced harmonics). The digitized voice is employed both as a sound source for computer extension and enhancement—primarily through filtering techniques—and also as a control for the frequency and amplitude of the purely computer-synthesized sounds. Dodge worked closely with the M.I.T. Experimental Music Studio's John Stautner to map and extract the voice's acoustical gestures (its pitch and features of its speech), and to use these in designing the work's synthesized and computer-enhanced sounds. (notes for the compact disc, *Music for Instruments* and *Computer,* M.I.T.'s Media Laboratory)

The piece melds voice and computer into a single integrated medium expressing exquisitely the imagery of the title and text.

William Albright's *Sphaera* (1985) for piano and computer employs all of these states, mixing them in a complex and parapatetic form. Although the computer sounds are modeled from recorded and then digitally modified piano sounds, they initially establish a character distinctly different from the "live" piano. Environments of very high sustained and low percussive sounds frame a wide-ranging piano part. Initially, the piano attempts exploratory gestures, testing the response of this inscrutable background. Dialogue quickly ensues, thrusts and paries back and forth, probes and responses through which the two entities seem to learn their common capabilities. Eventually, they engage in games of dancing mimicry, triggering each other with identical gestures such as skyrocket arpeggios or *glissandi.* The games end only when the computer recedes to the background, then surges back to overwhelm the piano with its greater energy. Who gets the last word, or do the two mediums revert to their original separate existences? Listen to the piece to find out!

Author Austin's *Sonata Concertante* (1983) also uses the computer to extend piano sounds both in register and in color. It too travels through **transforming states** of relationship between the real piano and its synthetic counterpart. But the journey is a longer and yet straighter one, transitions more gradual and methodical. An indifferent coexistence in the opening *capo* (the work's "head") takes some six minutes to thaw, gradually drawing the two forces together. Then in a four-minute *cadenza* they come together on hammerstoke chords, only to diverge repeatedly into interspersed improvisation and desultory pointillism. Finally, a *coda* fuses their efforts on the hammerstrokes for a powerfully integrated finish.

NONTRADITIONAL COMBINED MEDIUMS

As we have discussed, the context in which a piece is to be presented is an important factor in modeling its medium. That context is traditionally involved with the performance of a piece of music as one of several pieces that make up a program of what is referred to as "concert music." The traditional performance protocol for concert music is familiar, has remained virtually unchanged for three hundred years, and will no doubt continue into the twenty-first century. The audience gathers in a concert hall, is seated and awaits the appearance of the musicians. Provided with printed program listings of the composers' pieces to be performed and the names of the musicians, members of the audience exchange greetings and talk animatedly in anticipation of the evening's musical offerings. The house lights dim, the stage brightens, the audience hushes itself, all is quiet. The musicians emerge, the audience applauds, the performers seat themselves and tune their instruments. When conductors or soloists are involved, they emerge at this point, acknowledge the applause of the audience, and a moment later the music begins. At the end of the piece the performance is applauded, the performers acknowledge the audience with a bow, and, as every piece is presented, the same conventions of performer/audience participation in the music-making/listening ensues. There is, of course, an entire range of variations of this convention, from formal adherence to a strict concert protocol to chatty, informal concerts with a high degree of spontaneous interaction between the preformers and the audience.

Composers understand these time-honored rituals of presenting their music. In accepting the rituals, they work within the constraints upon their music that the rituals require: a concert music composition should normally be limited in durations to about twenty minutes and should reasonably conform to the concert ritual of presentation just described.

Nontraditional combinations of mediums, by and large, found their beginnings in the composer's vision of a piece which has demanded the breaking of many of the constraints of traditional concert music presentations. Since the fifties, the process of reexamining and changing the context for the presentation of music has gained credence and momentum as many composers have found themselves confronted with and reacting to the realization that 1) the traditional combined mediums essentially restrict the composer from expanding performance resources and compositional imagery to include other artforms with music, and 2) the development and widespread use of taped electroacoustic music—a "performer-less" medium—caused the composer to rethink concepts of presentation of such pieces. With the first "performances" of compositions for taped electroacoustic music alone in the traditional concert format, the composer as well as the audience was confronted with the paradox of placing a "performer-less" medium in a "performer-full" tradition.

Established tenets of the concert ritual were challenged. With no performer other than the technician controlling the tape machine and no musician performing the piece, with only the loudspeakers to look at and listen to, without a performer to acknowledge applause, how should the audience behave? Applaud the tape machine for its flawless playback? Where was the gracious performer to signal the composer to stand and acknowledge the audience's applause for the piece?

These uneasy feelings certainly were experienced in one of the first successful public concerts in the United States devoted entirely to tape music compositions, presented by Luening and Ussachevsky on October 28, 1952, at the Museum of Modern Art in New York. As *New York Herald-Tribune* music critic wrote: "It has been a long time in coming, but music and machine are now wed. . . .The result is nothing encountered before. . . .It is something entirely new. A genesis cannot be described." After 1952, both Luening and Ussachevsky continued to compose solo tape pieces from time to time, but their main compositional efforts were concentrated on the combination of tape with instruments or orchestra or tape music for dance, film, radio, television, or drama. As with many other composers in the electroacoustic mediums, they understood the tape medium as a powerful combining force with other mediums of music as well as other artforms.

At this point we stress, however, that while the medium of solo tape music compositions certainly has been an important factor in the development of nontraditional combined mediums, we should not conclude that the medium itself is incomplete and somehow flawed. Quite the opposite is the case. There is now a flourishing tradition of solo tape pieces, understood and appreciated for their substance and beauty. Audiences are now quite accustomed to the inclusion of a performerless tape piece in a concert of new compositions. In fact, audiences have learned that their aural acuity may be actually heightened by the absence of visual performance activity. We are, indeed, quite capable as listeners of cultivating a high degree of appreciation for the sonic imagery a composer projects in a fine tape music composition. We listen, perhaps closing our eyes, to concentrate more intently. Composers have learned, in fact, that darkness helps this process of concentration and often ask that the hall be entirely darkened as their piece is heard. Tape music is a very personal medium, both for the composer and the listener. Alone in the studio, the composer listens to the piece over and over as the materials for the piece emerge. Similarly, members of the audience, "alone" in the darkness, listen as they would to a recording in their home. We have come to accept this performerless medium in the concert hall almost as naturally as we accept the performerless mediums of radio and commercial recordings. James Dashow's *In Winter Shine* (**excerpt 6**), for instance, is as welcome by an audience in the concert hall as it is when it is heard in the playback of a compact disk recording in the privacy of one's home. This has come about, of course, because composers have made this very personal medium rich with a splendid repertory of master compositions.

In 1952, the same year that Luening and Ussachevsky were presenting in concert their first tape music compositions, John Cage was also exploring that medium (*Imaginary Landscape no. 5* and *Williams Mix* as part of the Project of Music for Magnetic Tape in New York with composers Earle Brown, Morton Feldman, David Tudor, and Christian Wolff). He was also collaborating with composer/pianist David Tudor and dancer Merce Cunningham to create the first composed "happening" at Black Mountain College in North Carolina in the summer of 1952. In a radical departure from concert protocol, Cage and his collaborators composed and performed what they termed a "concerted action," involving simultaneous combining of poetry reading, films, slides, piano music, phonograph records, dancing and lecturing. All together, their actions involved and confronted the audience with an experience that broke radically from concert traditions and accepted musical practice. These separate events in 1952—a tape music concert in New York and a "happening" in North Carolina—are often cited as seminal, influencing two generations of composers to explore the rich potential of nontraditional combined mediums.

In 1952, what Cage and his collaborators termed a "concerted action" came instead popularly to be described as a "happening." In 1980, composer Robert Ashley said of his *Perfect Lives* (live performance version 1977–83, all-video version 1984), "This is my idea of opera, or television, depending." Depending on how one perceives this nontraditional combining of mediums, Ashley's *Perfect Lives* could also be called a concerted action, electronic music theater, video art, performance art, opera for television, on and on. Labels fail. The live-performance version—combining narrator and actors, multiple video monitors of both live and prerecorded action, continuous piano and synthesizer music, tabla—seems more operatic, the all-video version more like televison. Ashley, in co-opting the traditional musical term "opera," simply means that *Perfect Lives* is storytelling, staged and set to music. "When the piecing together of imagery becomes so intense that one is aware of its rhythms, in effect the actions of the perceiving mind, 'opera,' or the communication of those rhythmic forms, arises naturally." (From *And So It Goes, Depending* by Robert Ashley, 1980)

Perfect Lives, in both versions, is presented in seven separate "songs," thirty-minute episodes in which, as the plot of the chant-like narration of its story unfolds, the characters are described in the prosaic language, music, and settings of middle-America. In **excerpt 16,** synopses and still video frames of the episodes describe the settings, the characters, the time of day, and the stylized positioning and motion of the television cameras visually tracking the action. The music is continuous and always focused on a kind of musical and poetic elaboration, both chanted by "R the singer" and played in the vernacular of various popular piano keyboard styles by "Buddy, the World's Greatest Piano Player" ("Blue" Gene Tyranny), all with choral punctuation by the male and female actors (David Van Tieghem and Jill Kroesen), all mixed in a montage of pre-recorded keyboards, synthesizers, percussion and voices. Critic Charles Shere wrote of the visual and aural impact of a performance of Ashley's piece, as follows:

> On-stage monitors showed prerecorded videotapes and the input of one live onstage camera, alternating between closeups of Tyranny's hands and views of Ashley . . . *Perfect Lives* is conceived as an opera for television, and its conceptual language is that of an age conditioned by television. The events of *Perfect Lives* are sung in static half-hour presentations; the audience's attention—in the touring version of the opera—is on figures which do not move. Ashley stands center stage, hands in pockets, shiny-silver-grey-suited, masked by dark glasses; "Blue" Gene's back is to the audience; the chorus, impassive in vaguely punk costume, remains alert but coolly immobile throughout the piece. Even in live performance, the visual connection between audience and performers is via television: those tapes and closeups on the monitors. Ashley calls these images 'isotapes': The image upon which the episode is based doesn't tell the story or have eventfulness. . . . Like a sporting event with its slow-motion replays, different camera angles, and stopped frames, *Perfect Lives* exists in real time as well as in television time.' " (*New Performance,* 3 no. 1: 1–7)

The essential role of Ashley's artistic collaborators is expressed most significantly in the music composed and improvised by pianist "Blue" Gene Tyranny and the visual imagery conceived for the video tapes by John Sanborn. In a very real sense, Ashley has carefully nurtured this multifaceted collaboration with other artists to model the form and continuity of *Perfect Lives.* In essence, he has composed a collaborative relationship among several artists to create a viable fusion of artforms. All eight of Ashley's "operas" composed since the first, *In Memoriam . . . Kit Carson,* in 1963 have involved intricate personal interaction among Ashley's collaborators. He speaks of this in relation to *Perfect Lives:*

> The nature of the collaboration in every aspect of the composition of *Perfect Lives* is that I could not do it alone. . . . It is, in my way of thinking, aesthetically impossible. It is required that *Perfect Lives* represent as many voices as it can sustain. Ideally, these separate voices should be as distinguishable as the technique will allow. Ideally, they should be without restriction as to their detail (amount). They are independent and simultaneous. The technique requires them to be synchronous. Otherwise, they are separate, private parts (joke). . . . In other words, the process of composing the details of the parts (characters) begins with the collaboration and agreement

> in the recording studio and ends (never ends) only in performance. This point is essential to the piece. I haven't composed melodies or harmonies or entrances or orchestration, because I have found that approach difficult precisely in the area of storytelling or "opera" in that the product of that approach is archetypically a revisionist history, rooted in memory and prejudice, and restricts the composer to speaking about the past only (or, apparently so, considering the contemporary repertoire). The idea of story telling modeled on the technology of the electronic media, a gathering of actualities, seems more relevant, bypassing the past, and interesting to me. . . . The techniques of the traditional role for the composer seem to me inextricably involved in maintaining the past as a field of understanding, i.e., "modernism." I find the idea of a single vision, the idea of the "auteur," incompatible with the demands of maintaining a mode of actuality. A technique of profound collaboration is essential. In the blizzard . . . the composer should rather be the instigator and the guide than the model and the definition. The idea of a profound collaboration suggests, to me, relinquishing every eminent domain in favor of actuality and relevance. So, by "collaboration" I do not mean just bringing together the various elements of nineteenth century music drama. I mean mutual involvement in the evanescent aspects of the materials, such as they are today.

When composers model nontraditional combinations of mediums with other artists, "mutual involvement in the evanescent aspects of the materials" becomes all-important if the form the piece takes is intended to be wholly integrated. Accidents do happen, but simply bringing together artists from different artforms to combine their efforts and create a piece does not guarantee a successful process. More often, such a piece doesn't achieve a cohesive form but remains, in performance, "mixed-," "multi-," and seldom "inter-" media. In fact, Ashley's insistence on using the term "opera" for the carefully integrated mediums of his pieces comes superficially, of course, from his penchant for the ironic but more, we believe, from his deep desire to associate his integrated, nontraditional combination of mediums with the likes of Monteverdi's *Orfeo,* Mozart's *Don Giovanni,* and Berg's *Lulu.*

IDIOMS AND STYLE

Musical idioms are ephemeral, always in flux. As in language, they come into usage, stay awhile, disappear perhaps, reappear, then die. Or, rather than dying away, they remain for long periods as a prevalent characteristic of a particular genre of music. We discussed earlier, for example, "on-the-strings" piano techniques introduced in the twenties by Henry Cowell, the ins and outs of their use by composers through the years and their final adoption today as a familiar idiom in piano compositions. As knowledgeable listeners to music, we are to some degree always aware of the presence or absence of such characteristic idioms. There is no music without idioms, just as there can be no music without a medium to hear it. As composers, we use idioms and sometimes even cause musical idioms to come into existence: the way we express these idioms in our music constitutes what we often refer to as our compostional style.

When beginning the collaborative effort to write this book on composing, we agreed at the outset that we should not—could not—make our text an exhaustive "compositional cookbook" of current styles, full of recipes for as many different kinds of musics as we could possibly explore and illustrate. Musical idioms are constantly changing, and our new composing cookbook would soon be old, languishing on a higher and higher shelf each year with other old cookbooks with recipes no longer exciting to taste, too much used, decades old. As we have written our book, interested colleagues in the field have asked, "How will you cover all the styles of composing?" or "Will it treat twelve-tone music?" Our answer often is, "We are writing our text much like we compose a piece, modeling the book on the way it seems to us that composers conceive and carry out the processes of musical invention, how composers decide to form their pieces rather than what style or system of composing they may seem to have adopted or even originated."

Still, our estimation of the worth in a composer's pieces very much resides in understanding and assimilating that composer's particular use of music's idioms, what style the composer has adopted, mastered, or virtually invented. In music, as in all the arts, our understanding of particular musics will probably always be described generically with such **stylistic labels** as pattern music, atonal, tonal, eclectic, chance music, neo-classic, new romanticism, new wave, post-Cagean, the vernacular, avant-garde, twelve-tone, the Polish school, sound mass, uptown, downtown, academic, minimal, maximal, experimental, on and on. Such labels serve as quick overall descriptions of whole bunches of pieces by different composers but are for the most part universally resented by composers when directly applied to their own music. Composers want a distinctive compositional profile for their music, labeled only by title and the composer's name and by the beauty of the art that has led to its creation. Composers want their music to be valued first for its worth as original art, not by what style the composer seems to be using to model the music's surface characteristics.

In works by a composer like Morton Feldman, one can find throughout almost all his mature works a consistent hallmark of his style—*Slow. Soft. Durations are free.* (**excerpt 4**)—truly a Feldmanesque idiomatic characteristic. In contrast, many composers invent new modeling processes for almost every piece or group of similar pieces they compose. This can result in as great a diversity of idioms among all of one composer's works as one might find among all of several other composers' works. Lukas Foss is such a composer. His works are rich with a diversity of idioms he assimilates from recent innovations by other composers, modeling them in original ways in his own works. His *Solo* (1981) for piano (**excerpt 5**) combines a stream of repetitive, eighth-note patternings of gradually changing pitch constellations of characteristic minimalist idioms with the jazz-like instruction for the pianist to sing—"Any register. Don't try to project; just sing as if to yourself."

While Foss and Feldman have distinctive idiomatic profiles for their music, other composers model their pieces through equally imaginative use of the medium with more familiar idiomatic characteristics. In *Wings* (1981), for B-flat clarinet or bass clarinet (**excerpt 2**), composer Joan Tower asserts her command of virtuosic clarinet idioms. This piece opens with rapid flurries of repeated figurations in the *dolce, chalameau* register of the instrument, rising suddenly to its highest register to sustain four piercing *forte* trills with accented eighth-note interjections. There is no mistaking that a metaphorical bird has suddenly taken flight. At *poco piu mosso* the bird asserts its command of the sky with wide swoops through the clarinet's range, testing the highest, lowest and every other vector of registral space between. The flight calms itself, gradually slower and quieter, until in the last staff line, long, low adjacent tones seem to glide to the flight's completion, but then end with a sudden, *forte* leap to the heighths. Tower knows the clarinet and its most virtuosic idioms, fluently incorporating them in her metaphor for a bird in flight.

Composer Andrew Imbrie is equally fluent in his mastery of idioms of the medium of the string quartet. His very first quartet was recognized for its excellence with the prestigious Pulitzer Prize. In **excerpt 10** from his *Fourth String Quartet* (1973), Imbrie explores the expansive sonic qualities of the cello in what he refers to as "Aria," invoking the idiomatic texture of a traditional, operatic vocal form to focus our attention keenly on the expressive cello line, quietly accompanied by the violins and viola. Also "crossing" idioms, composer Barbara Kolb invokes idiomatic instrumental writing in combining the soprano voice with flute and guitar in her *Songs Before an Adieu* (1979), **excerpt 8.** The soprano asserts her equivalence to the other "instruments" with Kolb's angular, exclusively syllabic setting of the e.e. cummings poem. She admonishes the soprano to "emphasize enunciation" for accented passages or "coordinate with flute and guitar" or to be "irregular and impulsive," all instructions out of character in a traditional singer/accompaniment relationship. Past mid-point in the piece, Kolb relieves this declamatory/instrumental style with the more traditional *"liberamente e molto tenuto"* (significantly in Italian!) and, at the end, "gently and mysteriously; reflective."

Thus, in looking at only a few of the excerpts in our **PORTFOLIO,** we quickly find a rich variety of idiomatic features among and contained in all the pieces. These range from the provocative invention of brand new, highly individualized modes of expression to the fluent virtuosity of more familiar idiomatic usage. In this and other chapters of *LEARNING TO COMPOSE,* salient idiomatic features illustrating important modes and materials of invention in the excerpts as well as many other works are discussed in detail. Studying how composers model mediums and their idioms to create their own style of composing helps us to become more fluent and inventive in creating our own distinctive musical profile. When someone asks, "What kind of music do you write?", you'll know how to answer.

INVENTION 3

Listen to some classical guitar music, recordings of which are readily available; it need not necessarily be recent music. Then study the two pieces in the **PORTFOLIO** which use guitar, **excerpt 8** and **excerpt 3.** Make charts of what you find: copy chords over onto your own staff paper, make a list of kinds of figures or gestures, another of notations special to the guitar.

Do some research into the instrument, its history if you're interested, but mainly the physical aspects of playing it. Draw a fingerboard chart of the six strings and the pitch each produces at each fret. Find a method book which explains plucking and strumming, damping and harmonics—or better yet, find a friendly guitarist to demonstrate these techniques. Go back to your charts and lists from the Carter and Kolb pieces, which now can be interpreted in such ways as actually plotting out chord pitches on a fingerboard chart.

Of all the idioms or ideas for a piece that should develop from this research, choose just two small items—say a melodic figure and a pair of chords, or a particularly colorful articulation of sound and a rhythmic arpeggio. On a separate sketch sheet for each idea, try to draw out as many different versions of your chosen "motives" as you can imagine.

Reflecting on all the potential material you produced in this fashion, begin to model a form for a solo guitar piece. That has already begun with modeling your medium but now must focus on specific images of space, time, and story (the spatial, temporal, and narrative modeling discussed in chapter 2, **FORM MODELING**) to establish an architecture, a trajectory, and a continuity for your piece. Don't try to follow the pieces you studied. They have already provided background stimulus which you have assimilated, but many paths are now open to make subtley or strikingly different images from the nature and idioms of the guitar.

INVENTION 3 VARIATION

Use the same process to start a solo piano piece. Study the pieces in the **PORTFOLIO** which use piano, **excerpts 4, 5, 7, 15,** and **16,** make charts and lists, listen to other piano music. But then in studying the physical aspects of playing, get access to a piano and approach it yourself as though it were an instrument you know nothing about. (This may have actually been true with the guitar.) Your experimentation could be confined to just the keys and the pedals. Or you might explore the inside, the strings as well, but with a cautionary note: don't put anything on the strings that won't come off easily and completely; and don't touch the dampers, whose sensitive alignment is critical to proper normal functioning of the instrument.

Again, out of this exploratory modeling of a medium and after selecting a limited palette of ideas, begin to model the form for a solo piano piece.

INVENTION 4

To a playwright, writing convincing dialogue is critical. One piece of advice experienced authors often give is to get to know your characters very well before writing their thoughts, actions, or speech.

Choose two orchestral instruments with which to have a dialogue. They should be different, not from the same family of instruments (woodwinds, brass, percussion, strings). Listen to some orchestral music which features these instruments and their typical characters. Then think about what character *you* would find interesting to ascribe to each instrument, not necessarily its typical character and perhaps even a contradiction of it.

Now invoking some narrative modeling, imagine a situation for a conversation between these two instruments. Write a paragraph for each instrument, describing it as a character with a role or attitude to portray in this dialogue. Use these descriptions to plan an architectural scheme of pitch registers, rhythms, colors and loudness balances for a musical setting.

INVENTION 5

The first step in modeling a medium is to gain access to the medium. It might not be fruitless but would certainly be frustrating to think about modeling in the orchestral medium if there were no hope of any access to orchestral performance. Get access to some electroacoustic device, one as common as a tape recorder or as sophisticated as a software synthesis system on a large computer. If you are not already familiar with the basic operation of this machine, teach yourself about it not only by reading instruction manuals and getting a demonstration from an experienced user, but also experiment with its capabilities.

This may be a tall order and take considerable time and effort. While you are learning the system, listen to these pieces as background studies: *Sud* by Jean Claude Risset; *Any Resemblance* by Charles Dodge; *Idle Chatter* by Paul Lansky; *Symphonie pour un Homme Seul* by Pierre Shaeffer. All of these are electroacoustic pieces using prerecorded sounds as their basic material.

Back to the machine you are now familiar with. Record an actual sound or design a synthetic sound resembling a familiar sound. It could be any kind of sound, but you might want to choose one with complex or subtle qualities. Experiment with ways of changing its timbre with the various means of transformation available in your machine. Save or store those transformed sounds which appeal to you and which extend the qualities of the original beyond reality—higher or lower, longer or shorter, thicker or thinner, darker or brighter, more resonant than the original sound would normally be.

Try out combinations and successions of these extended sounds. Practice those combinations which seem to work well until you are fluent with them. Now you have modeled your own personal medium with its idiomatic materials. To start a literature for this new medium, make a piece with it!

OTHER READINGS
Books:

Appleton, Jon and Perera, Ronald, Editors. *The Development and Practice of Electronic Music.* Englewood Cliffs, NJ: Prentice-Hall, 1975.
Bartolozzi, Bruno. *New Sounds for Woodwinds.* London: Oxford University Press, 1967.
Bunger, Richard. *The Well-Prepared Piano.* Colorado Springs: Music Press, 1973.
Dick, Robert. *The Other Flute: A Performance Manual of Contemporary Techniques.* New York: Oxford University Press, 1975.
Dempster, Stuart. *The Modern Trombone: A Definition of its Idioms.* Berkeley, Calif.: University of California Press, 1979.
Hitchcock, H. Wiley and Sadie, Stanley, Editors. *New Grove Dictionary of American Music* entries on "Electroacoustic music" and "Computers and music," London: Macmillan Press Limited, 1986.
Partch, Harry. *Genesis of a Music.* New York: Da Capo Press, 1949, rev. 1974.
Rehfeldt, Phillip. *New Directions for Clarinet.* Berkeley, Calif.: University of California Press, 1977.
Sadie, Stanley, Editor. *New Grove Dictionary of Musical Instruments.* London: Macmillan Press Limited, 1984.
Turetzky, Bertram. *The Contemporary Contrabass.* Berkeley, Calif.: University of California Press, 1974.
Vinton, John, Editor. *Dictionary of Contemporary Music.* entries on "Instrumental and vocal resources," New York: E. P. Dutton, 1974.

CHAPTER 4
DRAWING MUSIC

> Notation's ambiguities are its saving grace. Fundamentally, notation is a serviceable device for coping with imponderables. Precision is never of the essence in creative work. —Roberto Gerhard

What does notation mean to a composer? Visions of ink bottles, pens, score paper, long exhausting hours spent hunched over a drafting board laboring to draw elegant or even legible manuscript—or, today, hours of coding notes at a computer. But calligraphy, the technique of drawing or printing musical notation, is only the final step in a process. A vital part of musical creation, that process plays a role through nearly all stages of a compositional endeavor. It is the process of expressing and recording ideas, of conveying a work's substance and the means of its realization.

> Notation is designed to convey music by graphic means. The graphic signs and directions either symbolize pitches, durations, and other audible phenomena, or provide instructions for mechanical manipulations of musical instruments. (Stone 1974, 517)

The notational medium chosen to convey musical ideas strongly influences the nature of the ideas to be expressed. Although we often think of a piece as a pile of manuscript pages bound together, in this case (recalling the now cliché axiom of Marshall McLuhan) the medium is *not* the message. The score is not the musical entity but only a necessary conveyor of its identity. For two of our **PORTFOLIO** inclusions, Dashow's *In Winter Shine* and Ashley's *Private Lives,* a score was apparently unnecessary and so the composer made none at all, but they are still very real pieces! Nonetheless, the influence of notation on musical thinking is powerful and must be understood so that it can be incorporated into the creative process.

> In a literate age, music has a double character. Generalizing, we can say that we often find it easier to appreciate structural and intellectual qualities of a piece from a reading of the score, while the emotional impact is only made apparent in live performance. On the printed page, the processes of composition can be easily followed. We can refer backward and forward; parts can be simultaneously viewed, and where every detail is fixed, we can come to terms with music at our leisure. Often the processes of composition may be appreciated

> . . . almost without reference to the resulting sounds, and we can appreciate the excellence and originality of the organization. (Cole 1974, 123)

Notation should not be treated as a prescriptive padagogy, simply a pragmatic conformity to "get the job done." With an appreciation for the great diversity of notational systems and styles that can be adopted, and with a theoretical understanding of the basic representational and perceptual processes universal to them all, the composer can design notations best suited to the musical ideas being explored. In an interactive way, the nature of ideas can suggest suitable notations, but a notational system can in turn spawn ideas through a ready potential for certain patterns or configurations. For example, it would have been difficult for Morton Feldman even to conceive of the floating, timeless sense that lends sonorities such clarity in *Last Pieces* if not for a notation that could allow such qualities to exist. What he chose or invented as a notation is elegant in its simplicity (see **excerpt 4**).

Because of this intrinsically interactive relationship, as musical style and thinking have evolved, so have notational means of expression undergone innovation and experimentation. We recognize the dynamic, evolutionary quality of our musical heritage, constantly enriched as it has been by new ideas and an ever-changing diversity of explorations. It is no great leap, then, to realize that notational conveyance of our musical culture is as metamorphic as the culture itself.

Why do we need notational innovation? Some hints about the underlying purpose and function of notation can be revealed in answering that question.

TRENDS Important trends in contemporary musical style and thinking have shaped notational innovation, in fact demanded it:

- **Improvisation,** the interest in incorporating performer action and choice in the design of events (as in the flute and guitar parts near the end of **excerpt 8**).

> The performer's creative collaboration is essential. With understanding, he must read between the notes; establish the context in which signs are to be interpreted; and regulate all the minute variations of tone colour, articulation, and attack which can never be fully notated, and which are in many cases made intuitively rather than consciously. (Cole 1974, 129)

- **Timbre and gesture exploration,** the interest in discovering new ways of producing sound events.
- **Micro- and macro-composition,** extending the extremes of compositional specification and control to both minute details and to the broadest perspectives of conceptualization.

> Two technical reasons why a highly determinate notation is appropriate to our age: the extreme concentration of much contemporary music demands an equally detailed notation, which will account for the music's microstructure with a painstaking thoroughness; and secondly, there is the question of the intelligence, skill, and availability of the new generation of contemporary performers, which open up new possibilities of getting ever more exacting instructions carried out. (Cole 1974, 128)

New ways of expressing musical thought are needed to be more **accurate** or more **efficient** expressions of new ideas or to offer greater **potential** for the very kinds of ideas that can be imagined.

THEORY How notations work and what aspects of musical structure they represent can reveal a great deal about the foundations of musical thought. Basic human processes of perception and communication are at work in notations, deepening a sense of meaning in the ways we draw our music.

> Current philosophical trends, the new and expanding communication sciences, the need to discover how best we can talk to the machines which play an increasing part in our lives—all tend to focus attention on the process of communication itself, as something that can be manipulated to our advantage or disadvantage. Musicians have woken up to the significance of the notational link, and the possibility of acting on the whole complex of musical activities through the notation. There is a reversal of the traditional position, in which the notation is thought of as existing for the sake of the music. (Cole 1974, 131)

A notation is a communication or a record of musical ideas, expressing one or both of two things: instructions for certain performer **actions,** or some **quality** of a sound or pattern or complex of events. The graphic marks which carry out notational functions fall into three basic categories:

- **Symbol,** a mark with visual autonomy and distinguishable identity.
- **Field,** a set of lines or other delineators with significant spacings or dimensions.
- **Words,** expressing complex meanings through language.

The combination of symbol identities and their placement and orientation in delineated fields forms a multidimensional matrix of information about the complex of dimensions in a musical structure. Matters of shape, color, size, spatial connections and symmetry may be utilized to help delineate or clarify meaning.

Figure 4.1 is a hypothetical example which includes several idioms common to contemporary style for a solo string instrument, scored in a relatively conventional notation.

The **staff** is a field; the clef symbol is placed to center around and indicate the position middle C in that field. Of course, the vertical placement of note symbols, modified by accidentals, indicates pitch. Shapes of notes represent relative durational values in a time scheme indicated with numbers. Italic letters abbreviate Italian words for loudness; their placements below certain notes

Figure 4.1 Notation of a hypothetical passage for viola

indicate changing levels of relative loudness, along with the graphic lines of a *crescendo* (getting wider apart to show getting louder) and *diminuendo* (converging to show getting softer). Finally, many words supply other important performance information.

SYSTEMS It is useful to consult books about notation to see what has been devised and used to express the vast diversity of compositions in the last seventy years or, for that matter, in the last seven hundred years. By the way, to assume that the evolution leading to our "modern music" and modern notation has been some steady progress toward ultimate superiority would be to ignore the peculiar appropriateness of each adaption along the way. For example, the four-line staff and neumes of medieval Gregorian chant are not just crude ancestors of the modern five-line staff and beamed eighth-notes; they were entirely sufficient, elegant representations of their music's subtle and beautiful contours.

Figure 4.2 Sample notation of Gregorian chant

Indeed, since the universe of possible musical ideas and patterns is infinitely vast, no book can prescribe the precise means best suited to convey any particular idea. Through experience of reading and attempting to interpret scores and through, thoughtful examination of how and why notations work (or sometimes don't seem to work well), the composer can and must become his own notational expert, as intrepid in choosing or designing the means of conveying his music as he is about the musical conception itself. If factors of human perception and reaction, of musical training and expectation are taken into account, this self-reliance ought not be scorned as radical tinkering but respected as a natural part of creative exploration.

The notational innovations of contemporary music can be described in broad categories: extensions of traditional notation; space-proportional time notation; graphic (nonsymbolic) representations of texture and action; and musical "mobiles."

EXTENSIONS Traditional notation works through the chronologically ordered placement of notes signifying metrically proportionate time values in the field of a five-line staff. Many modifications of this basic symbol/field system have been explored and codified as common possibilities in contemporary music:

- **Microtonal specifications,** such as quarter-tone inflections of basic chromatic pitches. (See the pitch bend or *portamento* at the beginning of **excerpt 1.**)
- **Absence of bar lines,** allowing patterns of accent to flow freely without interaction against a regular scheme of potential metric accents. (See **excerpt 2.**)
- **Complex subdivisions of metric time values,** making groups of notes that interact in complex ways with each other and with metric divisions (see **excerpt 5's** quintuplets); "wedge" rhythms gradually expanding or contracting the number of beams within a group of notes to represent quick accelerations and decelerations (as seen throughout **excerpt 15**).

Figure 4.3 Modified notation of the viola passage

- **Timbre modifications,** symbols applied to conventional notes to designate alterations in the basic methods of tone production. (See the flutter-tonguing in **excerpt 1** and the multiphonic sounds for oboe and clarinet in **excerpt 12.**)
- Invented **action symbols,** representing (through a self-defining and often pictorial meaning) a performer's action rather than representing the resulting sound's qualities. (Some examples are the arrows indicating direction of strumming in **excerpt 3,** and the pictograms designating particular percussion instruments to be played in **excerpt 11.**)

In figure 4.3, all of these modifications are shown in a renotated and somewhat revised version of the viola music from figure 4.1.

> Avant-garde scores are full of special signs for new playing activities. Although new timbres are produced as a result of these activities, it is perhaps stretching a point to describe them as timbre notations, when the significance as often lies in the action itself. (Cole 1974, 79)

- Pitch approximations, note-stems with rhythmic information but no note-heads, allow for **improvised pitch** within a generally depicted contour; cluster symbols showing a vague range of possible pitches to be included in a very dense sonority. (See **excerpt 13.**)
- **Score designs** can be specifically tailored to represent antiphonal placement of performers in space (as in **excerpt 15**); scores with staff lines "cut-off" when an instrument is not active visually highlight changes in texture. (See **excerpt 13.**)
- **Box music,** collections of pitches and/or rhythmic values or fragments placed in boxes, provide source material for controlled improvisation within limits specified by an otherwise conventional notation. (See **excerpt 14.**)

Figure 4.4 illustrates these by again renotating our viola music of figure 4.1.

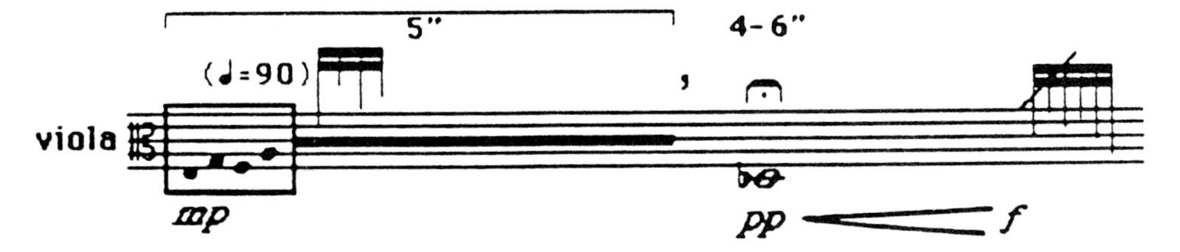

Figure 4.4 Viola passage with box notation

Many of these innovative extensions of traditional notation suggest to the inventive mind the possibility of a newly-defined system of notation based around a particularly useful innovation. In fact, the most successful new pieces

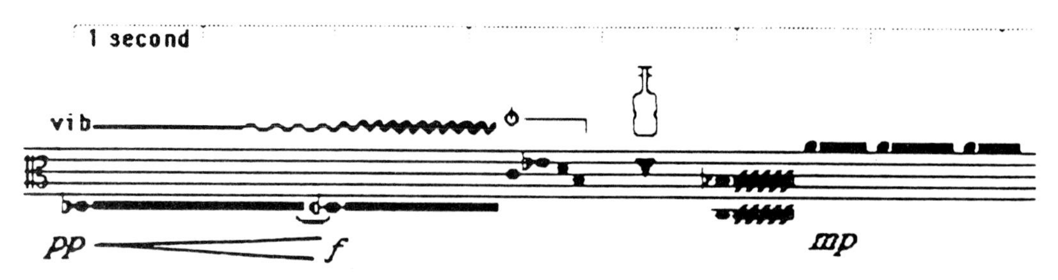

Figure 4.5 Viola passage in proportional time notation

utilizing notational innovations are those which treat the innovation in a thorough and systematic way as processes of intrinsic value. Here are some ways to assess the effectiveness of a notational system:

- The **suitability** of notation to musical idea. For example, ideally a field represents a density and distribution of possibilities in the range of some important musical feature.
- The degree to which a notation is **suggestive** in looks or form to its musical meaning.
- The capacity for **discrete** meanings avoiding undesired ambiguity.
- And the **conciseness, consistency,** and, thus, the **efficiency** of representations.

PROPORTIONAL TIME Representing time without pulse, meter, or note-value symbols can be accomplished using a simple, basic metaphor: durations of time are represented proportionally by **horizontal spatial extensity.** The width of a space on a score page marked by a beam, a box, or simply the empty space from one symbol to the next, is measured by eye (possibly with the help of a scale of measurement) and assessed as equal to, longer, or shorter than other surrounding spaces in some sense of proportion. This guides the relative assignment of time values of events by performers. **Excerpts 7, 8,** and **15** each utilize, at least in part, some proportional system to represent time.

The advantage of such a system is flexibility—performers are allowed to determine precise durations suitable with their performing actions and their instinctively fine sense of "temporal drama." The flexibility allows the composer, as well, to specify very subtle durational differences or highly dramatic ones in a clean way unencumbered by metric complications of subdivision brackets, ties, etc., and their labor of relating everything to an arbitrary pulse. Silences or pauses in actions show up, then, not as symbols—rests—but as clean, unmarked score space. This visually represents the basic duality of actions and sounds versus inaction and silence (see figure 4.5).

> Conventional notation has long been concerned with the exact synchronization of musical movement. The strict prohibitions of traditional harmony and counterpoint have made it essential that music shall move to a timetable, notes arriving and departing punctually so as to avoid all chance collisions. In new, permissive harmonic situations, parts may be allowed to run free, the principal question being, where, when, and how to bring them together again? (Cole 1974, 69)

Going one step further, the spaces proportionally representing time can be marked not by defined symbols but more intuitively by simple, suggestive drawings of texture or the character of activities.

GRAPHICS

> Musical textures and gestures are implied by means of graphic analogs: dense vs. empty fields imply sounds and activity vs. silence; bold vs. light imply dynamics; high vs. low imply pitches, etc. The length of the frame represents the duration of the passage. The choice of shapes is entirely free. Graphics defy standardization. Ideally they are unique for each composition since they, along with the instructions (if any) for their performance, are an integral part of the composer's creative vision. (Stone 1974, 522)

The simplest form of **graphic notation** replaces the traditional pitchfield of staves with bands of space vertically representing registral realms of pitch. Specific pitches and rhythms may not be of great significance but only the generic material of important textural configurations. Such direct representation of broad architectural configurations was chosen to graphically portray the event streams of *In Winter Shine* in **excerpt 6.**

Graphic means allow the notation to focus on the true musical significances without being bogged down, forced to specify detail. We can see the broad picture, less distracted by minute brush strokes (see figure 4.6).

> The notational system itself [can bind] the composer to certain patterns of thinking and compel him to issue orders in the form of 'this-or-that-level' for each separate step forward, when he may have already switched attention to aspects of musical experience that are only remotely connected with note-to-note relationships. These are the circumstances under which composers have begun to look for ways to free themselves from the discipline imposed by the stave; sometimes by taking new freedoms within the system, sometimes by doing away with the system altogether. (Cole 1974, 55)

Even with such differences in what is shown to be important, all of these innovative systems share one strong common feature with traditional notation: they all specify a discrete ordering of events shown in a left-to-right progress on a page.

But the sculptural **mobiles** of artists such as Alexander Calder suggest an exciting possibility of form: a set of material components "hung" in a floating system of suspension so that the parts can freely take on many possible relationships to each other in metamorphic flux. Musical materials can be thus "suspended" by breaking the customary assumption of left-to-right sequence in score reading. The result is often a menu-like page with boxes or segments of material which can be chosen in any order, or maze-like pages in which the many adjacencies of compartments suggest a variety of routes to choose.

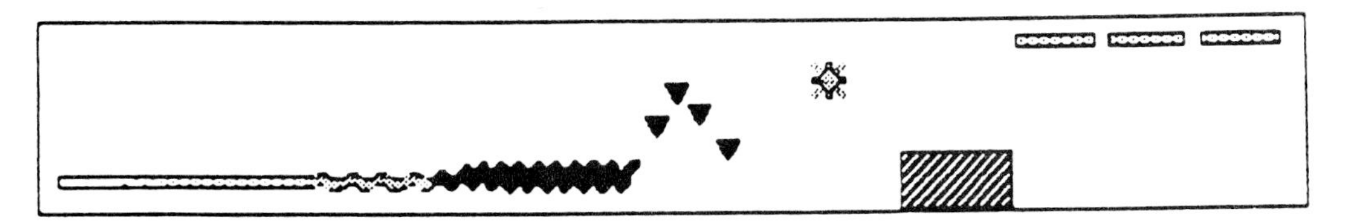

Figure 4.6 Graphic notation of the viola passage

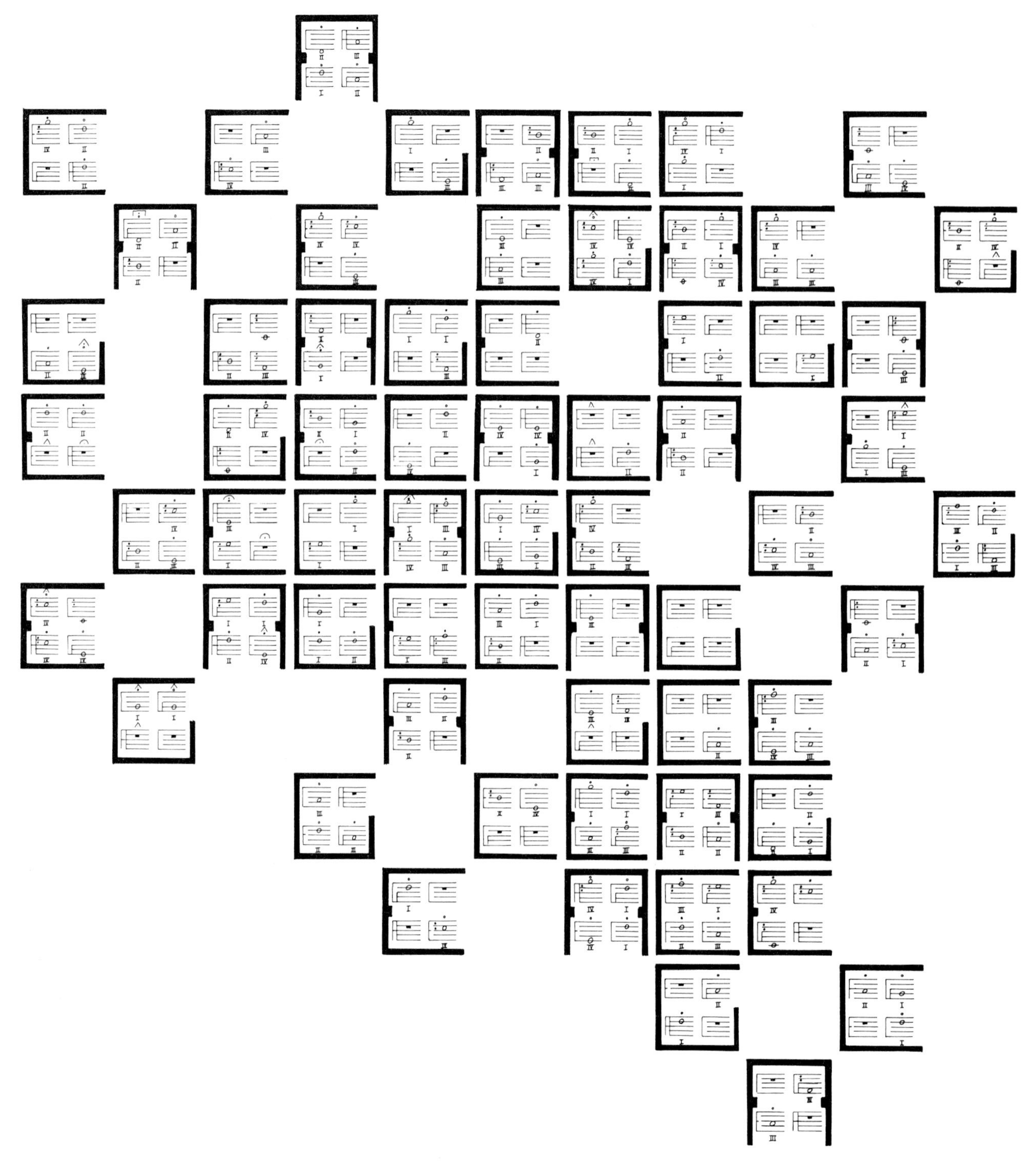

Figure 4.7 Full score in miniature of *art is self-alteration is Cage is . . .*

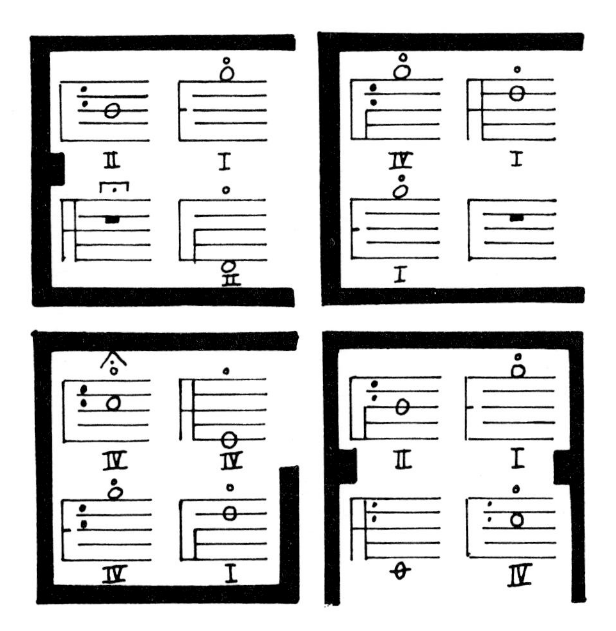

Figure 4.7a The score for (*art is self alteration is Cage is . . .*

Author Austin's work, *art is self alteration is Cage is . . .*, composed as a present for the seventieth birthday of John Cage, uses only pitch material based on the letters C, A, G, and E. Acknowledging Cage's fascination with multiple possibilities, the score is layed out in a huge field of squares, each a compartment of pitch material for contrabasses boxed by a bold, stylized letter C, A, G, or E. The eight players choose routes through this maze, moving to adjacent boxes in order to repeatedly spell CAGE. The game is fun and the sounds serene but by no means formless; the very format of the score embodies an intricate form containing all the possibilities.

SKETCHING TECHNIQUES

We can see that the best style or system of notation for a finished composition is the one best suited to the particular elements or interests that focus its form. In the same fashion, a process of sketching a piece records the stages of creative design of a composition. Of the many techniques just described for conveying ideas, sketching can utilize that which is best suited to the particular image that is being formed. Sketches should be custom designed so they convey to the composer the character and potential of thoughts as the composer reconsiders and refines them.

Because of this, the best means of drawing sketches of a piece may not be the same means best for conveying the finished work. The sketching process is most effective when it proceeds from the broadest, most general conception of image, intent, form—the macro-composition—gradually toward the more and more detailed aspects of material and structure—the micro-composition. This process of filling in form with detail should be well organized if the work is to achieve coherence in all its dimensions.

One traditional means of organization is a sketchbook, like that kept by graphic artists or the journals kept by authors and poets. The typical composer's sketchbook, though, is a bound book of staff paper. Of course, staves are a notational field designed to record the most precise details of pitch selection and order. Other ways of sketching more effectively address the broad initial concerns of image and form—texture, character of events, the flow and elasticity of time, the shaping of basic energy curves. Ways of sketching these thoughts might include: graphic **drawings** of textures; **verbal descriptions** of events in terms of energy or behavior; an outline describing the basic contents or shapes of successive large segments; simple, scribbled **energy curve** drawings highlighted by words describing emerging characters. Thus, custom-designed sketches of a piece might draw on the physical resources of plain or graph paper, lined paper for verbal outlines, and staff paper, which is good at first only for trying out cells or sonorities that might take on an important motivic role. A loose-leaf ring binder can keep all these materials handy and, better yet, would allow pages of sketched ideas to be grouped, reordered, supplemented, played with at will in search of a satisfactory coherence. The medium and the message, again the nature or means of the sketching process and the most crucial conceptions of a musical work, influence and even determine each other.

SKETCHING MATERIALS

Pitch/interval configurations, rhythmic patterns, lines, sonorities, contrapuntal relationships—will follow from such a coherence. Exploratory experiments, varying and developing small chosen bits of possible material, can spew out freely onto pages of sketch paper—more freely, in fact, if the planned coherence of form is embodied in other sketches of other format and purpose and does not rely at this stage on specific "notes" to convey itself. After a freely inventive exploration has generated rich splashes of material to choose from, a red pencil can come into play. As some of these materials emerge and their potential to become the generating basis of structures is established, they can be boxed in red, ready to serve the same role as boxed patterns in a score, providing the materials for improvisation.

As the student of composition is usually asked to show a teacher his sketches of a work in progress, we will without embarrassment provide for our readers and students a glimpse into our own typical sketching processes. Selected samples from the sketches of author Clark's 1984 chamber work, *Tropisms,* show the use of techniques and materials just described—verbal outlines and number patterns; graphic trajectory drawings (planning in this case the changing registers and then the rhythmic rates for each of the three instruments); then prolific pitch explorations with the boxed selection of patterns chosen as primary generators of the work's pitch language (see figures 4.8–4.8d).

We can also see a vague initial metaphor of organic growth develop by stages into an architecture for the contrapuntal fabric of the finished piece. A portion of the final score, proportionally notated for the three performers to read together, shows their dynamic relationships, marking explicitly the changing role of time leader.

Thus we have a plan of action—architectural drawings of form—and the materials with which to construct a realization of that conception, a notated score. Even at the scoring stage, if it has been preceded by an orderly and effective sketching process, the composer is not bound by the restrictions of working only "note-to-note" in a chronological tunnel but, by being able to glimpse the broad picture, can move freely from one part of a score to another, filling in details directly while following the various confluences of coherence.

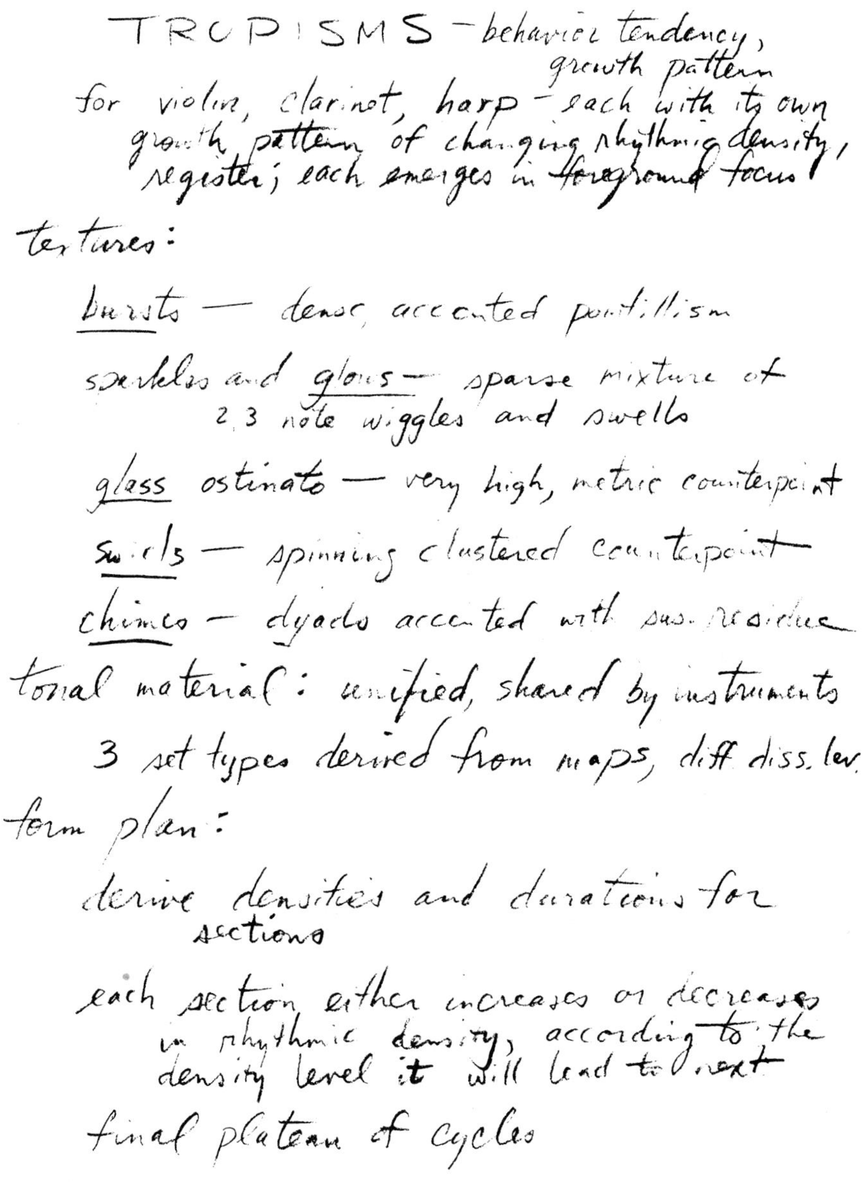

TROPISMS – behavior tendency, growth pattern
for violin, clarinet, harp – each with its own growth pattern of changing rhythmic density, register; each emerges in foreground focus

textures:

bursts — dense, accented pointillism

sparkles and glows — sparse mixture of 2,3 note wiggles and swells

glass ostinato — very high, metric counterpoint

swirls — spinning clustered counterpoint

chimes — dyads accented with sus. residue

tonal material: unified, shared by instruments

3 set types derived from maps, diff diss. lev.

form plan:

derive densities and durations for sections

each section either increases or decreases in rhythmic density, according to the density level it will lead to next

final plateau of cycles

Figure 4.8 Sample sketches of **Tropisms**

attack density ↓	VIOLIN	HARP	CLARINET
p. 1 60"	8↑-Low reg. CHIME	2–Low/Hi reg. CHIME	8↓-Med reg. CHIME
p 3 30"	10↑-Low	2– (chime)	6↓-M GLOW
p 4 60"	11↑-LMed SWIRL	2↑- SWIRL	4↓-MLow (glow)
p. 6 90"	13↑-Med (SWIRL)	4↑- (swirl)	2–L SWIRL
p 9 150"	16↓-M/Hi	7↑-→Med. GLOW	2↑↑-LMed (swirl)
p. 14 120"	11↓-Hi GLOW	12↑-Med SPARKLE	16↓-M SPARKLE
p. 18 90"	6↓-Hi GLASS	16↓-Hi GLASS	12↓-Hi GLASS
p 21 30"	3↓-Hi CHIME	10↓-Low/Med. CHIME	9↓-Low GLOW

3 attack density / ↓ : falling / Hi = register (rel.)

Figure 4.8a Sample sketches of *Tropisms*

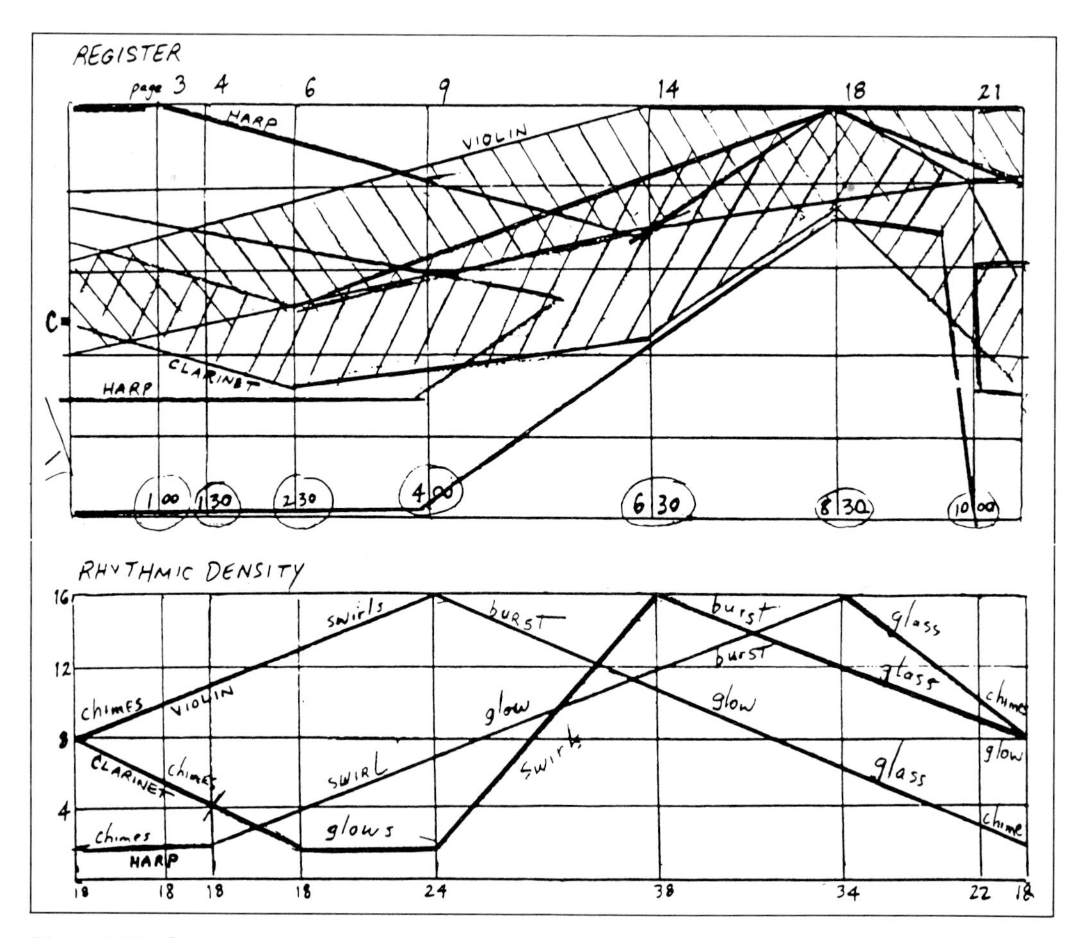

Figure 4.8b Sample sketches of *Tropisms*

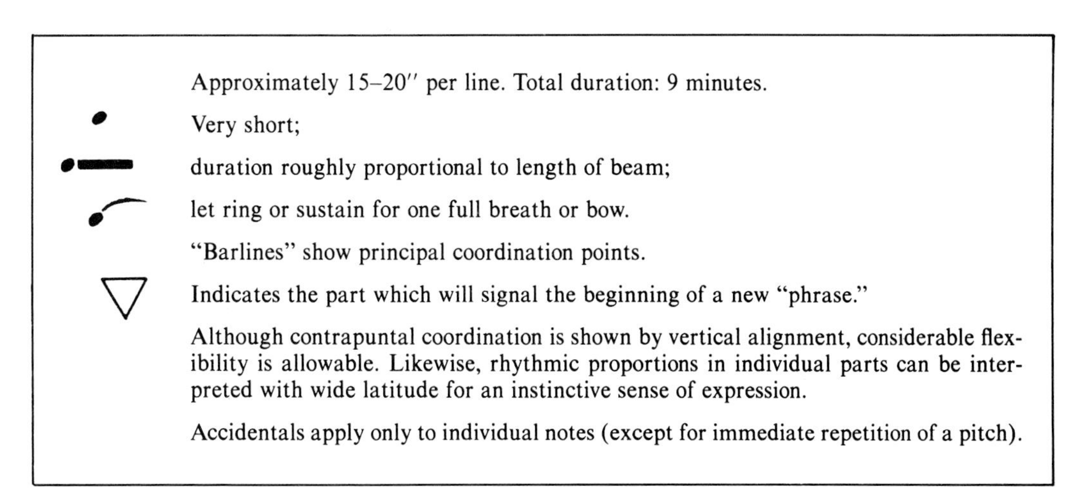

Approximately 15–20″ per line. Total duration: 9 minutes.

Very short;

duration roughly proportional to length of beam;

let ring or sustain for one full breath or bow.

"Barlines" show principal coordination points.

Indicates the part which will signal the beginning of a new "phrase."

Although contrapuntal coordination is shown by vertical alignment, considerable flexibility is allowable. Likewise, rhythmic proportions in individual parts can be interpreted with wide latitude for an instinctive sense of expression.

Accidentals apply only to individual notes (except for immediate repetition of a pitch).

Figure 4.8c Performance notes for *Tropisms*

Figure 4.8d Last page of finished score to *Tropisms*

INVENTION 6 Make a grid like this:

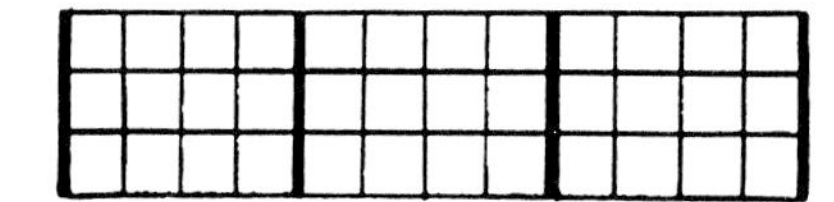

Each column will represent horizontally one second of time (grouped into units of four seconds like 4 4 meter). Each row of squares will represent a register of possible pitch activity—high, medium, and low.

In the squares, place numbers representing the number of sounds to be attacked or initiated during that second of time. This forms a basic sketch of rhythmic densities.

The sketch could then be refined and realized in a score containing rhythmic patterns in proportional time with registral contours shown graphically.

Or the attack grid sketch could be specified further and converted into an actual notation itself for improvisation by three instruments. Extra symbols can be invented and applied to the numbers, such as:

- bracket preceding a number means attacked simultaneously;
- tie extending into subsequent time squares for sustained duration;
- draw numbers darker and larger for loud, lighter and smaller for soft.

INVENTION 7 Draw a thick, bounded curve to represent registral contour and width as a changing function of time on a graph:

Then interpret this as a register graph, drawing over it (in blue pencil) a grid of lines dividing the vertical axis into seven bands representing seven octaves. Select pitches from the specified octaves to form dyads, two-note chords shown graphically as the upper and lower boundaries of the curve. Shade some areas of the curve to represent use of the damper pedal in a piano realization.

Divide the horizontal axis into segments of equal length, to which you can assign a time scale. Use the slope to suggest event rate—a steep slope in the curve might represent more rapid pacing, a relatively level "plateau" might be more placid. Experiment likewise with inflections of pacing of a conforming rhythm by association with other graphic aspects—slope of the ceiling or base, width of the registral band, presence or absence of shading. Transcribe the results into a piano score on a grand staff with time proportionally notated.

INVENTION 8 Select a conventionally notated score for keyboard instrument or for large instrumental ensemble, a piece emphasizing contrasts of texture. Draw a graphic representation of several segments of it. (This is a way to explore and better understand the possible connections between conceptions of texture and their realizations in finished and explicitly notated scores.)

INVENTION 9 Explore one or more of the pieces in the **PORTFOLIO,** studying and cataloging interesting notations used. Experiment, then, with some of the ideas found, renotating them in other ways and, thus, transforming their characters. Find a focus, a single approach to guide these renotations so that they will produce results that might go together as various materials for a piece of your own.

SCORES FOR STUDY AND LISTENING

Luciano Berio — *Circles* (Universal Edition, 1961)
Earle Brown — *Available Forms I* (Associated Music Pub., 1962)
John Cage — *Aria* (C. F. Peters, 1960)
George Crumb — *Makrokosmos I* (Edition Peters, 1974)
Jacob Druckman — *Animus I* (MCA Music, 1967)
Morton Feldman — *The King of Denmark* (C. F. Peters, 1965)
Lukas Foss — *Paradigm* (C. Fischer, 1968)
Mauricio Kagel — *Match* (Universal Edition, 1967)
György Ligeti — *Volumina* (H. Litoff's Verlag, 1967)
Kristof Penderecki — *Passion According to St. Luke* (Moeck Verlag, 1967)
Karlheinz Stockhausen — *Zyklus* (Universal Edition, 1961)
Iannis Xenakis — *Charisma* (Edition Salabert, 1971)
Roger Johnson, editor — *Scores: An Anthology of New Music.* New York: Schirmer Books, 1981
Larry Austin et al, editors — *Source, Music of the Avant Garde.* vol. 1–6. Sacramento: Composer/Performer Edition, 1967–72.

OTHER READINGS

Books:

Cole, Hugo. *Sounds and Signs.* New York: Oxford University Press, 1974.

Cope, David. *New Music Notation.* Dubuque, Ia.: Kendall/Hunt Publishing Co., 1976.

Heusenstamm, George. *The Norton Manual of Music Notation.* New York: W.W. Norton & Co., 1987.

McTee, Cindy. *A Music Calligrapher's Handbook: Tools, Materials, and Techniques.* St. Louis: MMB Music, Inc., 1987.

Read, Gardner. *Music Notation: A Manual of Modern Practice.* Boston: Allyn and Bacon, 1969.

Risatti, Howard. *New Music Vocabulary.* Champaign, Ill.: University of Illinois Press, 1975.

Stone, Kurt. "Notation." *Dictionary of Contemporary Music.* John Vinton, ed. New York: E. P. Dutton, 1974:517–526.

———. *Music Notation in the Twentieth Century: A Practical Guidebook.* New York: W. W. Norton, 1980.

Articles:

Behrman, David. "What Indeterminate Notation Means." *Perspectives of New Music* (Spring–Summer 1965):58–73.

Foss, Lukas. "The Changing Composer-Performer Relationship." *Perspectives of New Music.* (Spring 1963):45–53.

Martino, Donald. "Notation in General—Articulation in Particular." *Perspectives of New Music* (Spring–Summer 1966):47–58.

Yates, Peter. "The Proof of the Notation." *Twentieth Century Music.* New York: Pantheon Books, (1967):221–238.

PORTFOLIO

EXCERPTS OF SCORES BY AMERICAN COMPOSERS FROM THE SECOND HALF OF THE TWENTIETH CENTURY

A sense of musical continuity is of the utmost importance to the student of composition. We cannot learn from examples totally isolated from their contexts so that they have meaning only as specimens. That is why each score excerpt in this collection is an extended one, a full continuity within a piece, from presentation through elaboration to conclusion. Representing a variety of mediums, idioms, architectures, modes of invention, and each discussed from many angles, they are collected here to be convenient for comparison. Several chapters will compare their mediums and idioms and probe many other aspects of process in each composition.

These pieces were selected not only for their artistic value but because they include vivid examples of ideas, processes, relationships that are the essence of learning to compose. The selection is made difficult by the fact that there are so many fine compositions being made by American composers. Is this chauvanistic to restrict the selections to Americans? Yes! We are proud of the diverse accomplishments of our many professional peers in the United States. Fine examples from European composers could have been chosen, and many of their works are discussed in this book. They are certainly important to be aware of as part of the overall development of current musical styles and thought. But the American examples selected here serve just as well.

For that matter, why restrict the selection to music of the second half of the twentieth century? Does this advocate that "contemporary style," whatever that is, should be adopted and emulated by the developing young composer who reads this book? First, notice with even a mere glance at the excerpts that no single style is represented. In fact, quite the opposite. A wide diversity of styles is represented, although a truly comprehensive compilation of every conceivable style of music current in America is impossible! Second, you will find in reading this book and studying these excerpts as examples of concepts and processes that style is not the main point, anyway. **Style** in this sense is no more than a description of a musical work's apparent similarities to many other works. The compositional processes that produce results seen and heard in a finished piece are much more the focus of this study.

The composers selected are outstanding practitioners of our art. Although they are highly acclaimed and respected for their consistently fine work, they are, again, amongst good colleagues in a large company of professional composers and by no means intended to be an exclusive list. They do represent various geographic areas of the country (as the brief biographical information included here will show)—east coast, west coast, middle America. They represent both genders, and although there are still far fewer female professional composers today, those included here were included for the same reasons of interest, vividness, and thoroughness of their music, not primarily for their gender. Several generations of American composers are represented, some who through their pioneering work in early- and mid-century have become icons, others who bring to the collection a fresh view of the horizons of musical thought. There are teachers of composition as well as strictly professional practitioners.

What is common to all and to their personally unique musical works as exemplified here is a powerful understanding and command of compositional thought and processes. That is abundantly revealed by exploring their works in depth and detail. **LEARNING TO COMPOSE** does just that, examining each of the **PORTFOLIO** pieces from many angles in several chapters. Each piece will become familiar, but, of course, only an excerpt of the whole piece will have been explored. The fascination in this partial study should compel readers to seek a familiarity with each work in its entirety. And once the piece has become familiar as a stimulus and a guide to musical thought and compositional process, the whole score will be a handy reference source. For both these reasons the full scores of these pieces and others of great interest are an essential resource to the learning composer and should be acquired. Collecting a personal portfolio will involve a sizeable expenditure, but it is truly a wise investment. Think of the enormous expense and trouble composers of past centuries have endured in order to learn from the inspiring work of others; mass dissemination in our information-rich society is a blessing.

Hearing live concerts of music is also a worthwhile effort, but we are fortunate as well to have high-quality recordings available. We can listen to another's composition many times and deeply explore its aural dimension. We recommend and urge this, too, and list recordings available at the time of this book's preparation. But as acclaimed as these excerpts and their composers are or we think will be, new recordings are bound to become available too.

As mentioned in the *Preface,* the Inventions described in this book as exploration projects for the reader are not mere writing assignments. None leads to one "correct answer," and so sample solutions are not given, in order not to bias the student's creative response to possibilities. In a real sense, though, these excerpts of masterfully composed works, created in response to the recognition of provocative musical possibilities, are exemplary. Without seeking to copy these pieces as fixed models, we can draw from them valuable insight and inspiration.

EXCERPT 1

Title:	**Ambages**
Date of composition:	1965
Composer:	**Roger Reynolds**
Born:	1934 (Detroit)
Medium:	flute
Excerpt:	measures 1–18
Publisher:	C. F. Peters Edition, Peters No. 6829
Recording:	Nonesuch 73028

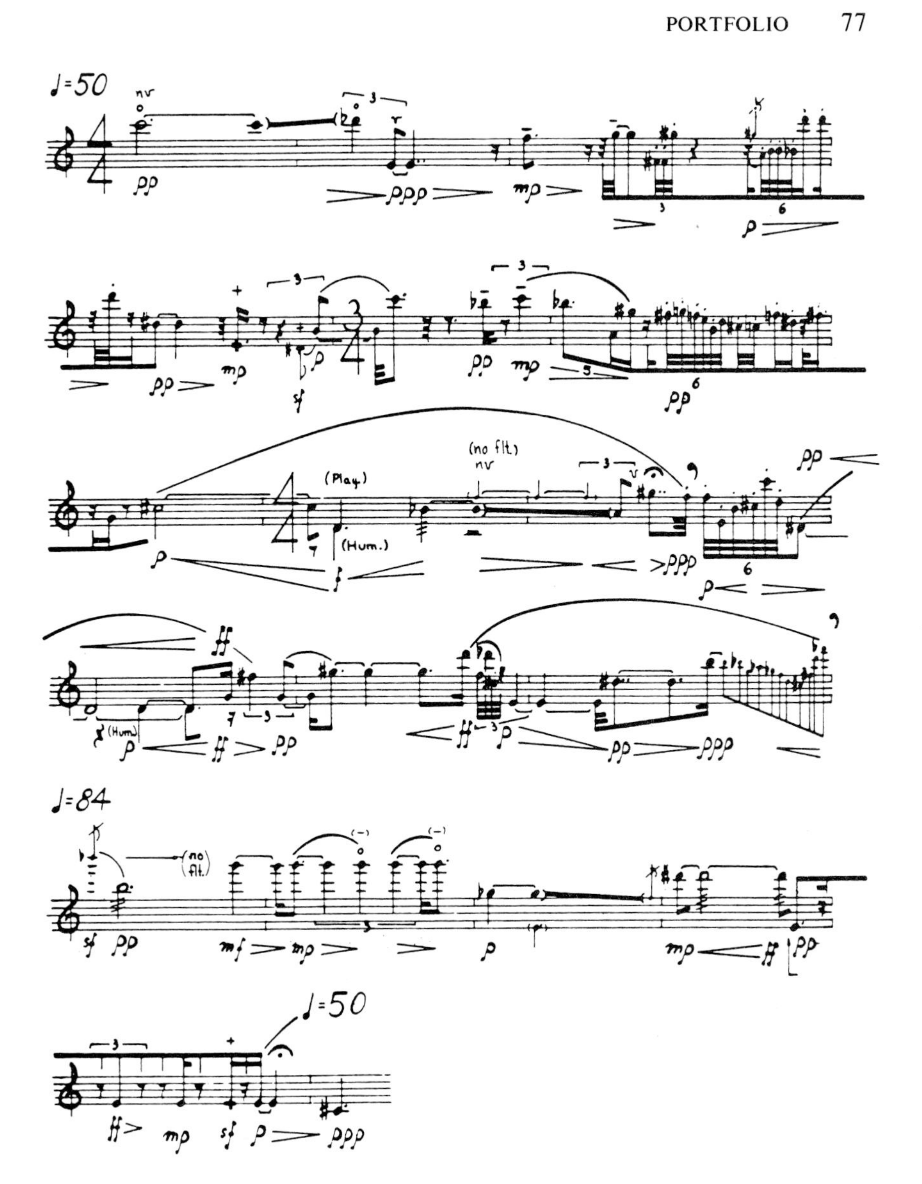
♩=50
nv
(Play)
(Hum.)
(no flt.)
nv
(Hum.)
♩=84
(no flt.)
♩=50

EXCERPT 2

Title:	**Wings**
Date of composition:	1981
Composer:	**Joan Tower**
Born:	1938 (New Rochelle, New York)
Medium:	clarinet
Excerpt:	from page 2
Publisher:	Associated Music AMP 7873–2
Recording:	Composers Recordings, Inc. CRI SD–517

mf dolce
cresc.
f
Poco più mosso ♩ = 112-118
ff
Ritardando to ♩ = ca. 80
dim. poco a poco
pp dolce
smooth
Poco rit. to ♩ = ca. 60
poco
pp sempre
poco cresc.
mp
pp
p
poco cresc.
mf
♩ = 44
pp dolce
p
mp
pp
ppp cresc. molto...
fff
p
fff

EXCERPT 3

Title:	**Changes**
Date of composition:	1983
Composer:	**Elliott Carter**
Born:	1908 (New York)
Medium:	guitar
Excerpt:	measures 39–54
Publisher:	Hendon Music, Boosey & Hawkes SRB–15
Recording:	Bridge Records 2004

tasto
vibr.
pont.
ord.
espr.
l.v.
leggero
espr.

EXCERPT 4

Title:	**Last Pieces**
Date of composition:	1963
Composer:	**Morton Feldman**
Born:	1926 (New York)
Died:	1987
Medium:	piano
Excerpt:	from page 2
Publisher:	C. F. Peters, Edition Peters No. 6941

Slow. Soft. Durations are free
PIANO
3. 25. 59

EXCERPT 5

Title:	**Solo**
Date of composition:	1981
Composer:	**Lukas Foss**
Born:	1922 (Berlin)
Medium:	piano
Excerpt:	from pages 28–29
Publisher:	Pembroke Music, Carl Fischer PCB–122

circa mp poco cresc.
gradually more pedal
mp cresc.
sempre poco cresc.
Optional:
sing A♮
B♭
(Any register. Don't try to project; just sing as if to yourself)
5 ♩ in 3/4
quasi f
f
più pedale
A
B♭
5 ♩ in 3/4
f
A
B♭
f

EXCERPT 6

Title:	**In Winter Shine**
Date of composition:	1983
Composer:	**James Dashow**
Born:	1944 (Chicago)
Medium:	computer music on tape
Graphic listening score:	Thomas Clark
Excerpt:	first four minutes
Recording:	*Music for Instruments and Computer* Experimental Music Studio/ Media Laboratory Massachusetts Institute of Technology

In Winter Shine by James Dashow
computer music on tape

graphic listening score by Thomas Clark

Time is shown horizontally with a scale of
approximately one minute per system.

Approximate registers of pitch space
are shown vertically in bands.

The architectures of event streams
are summarized graphically in rectangular blocks.

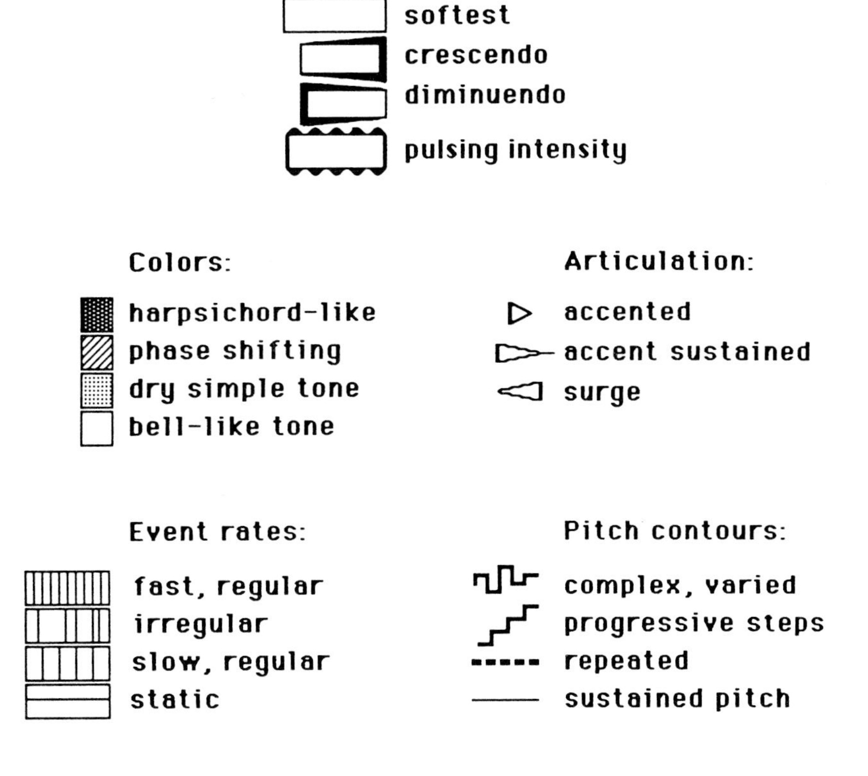

EXCERPT 6 Continued

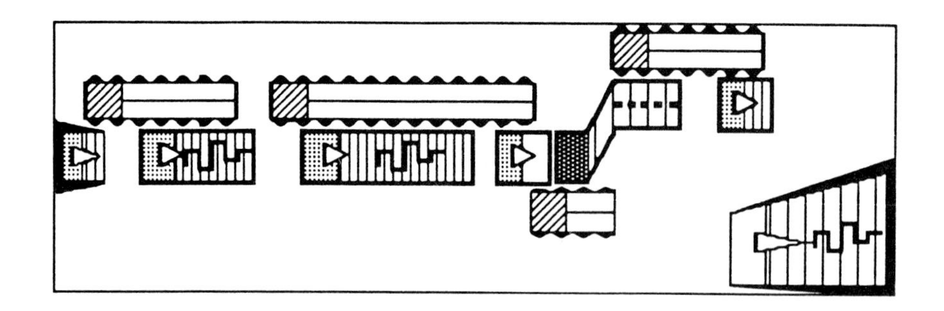

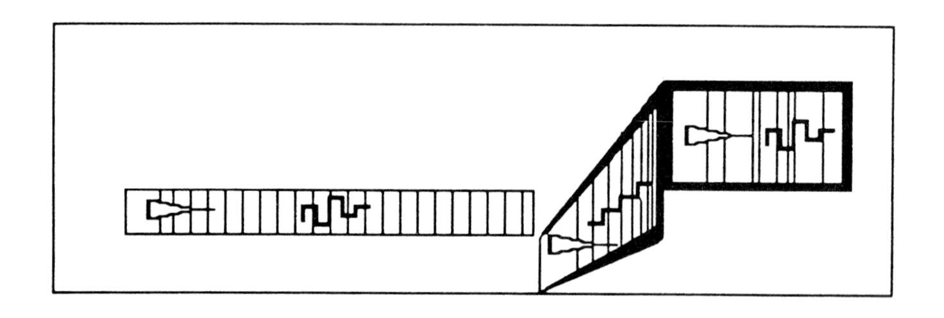

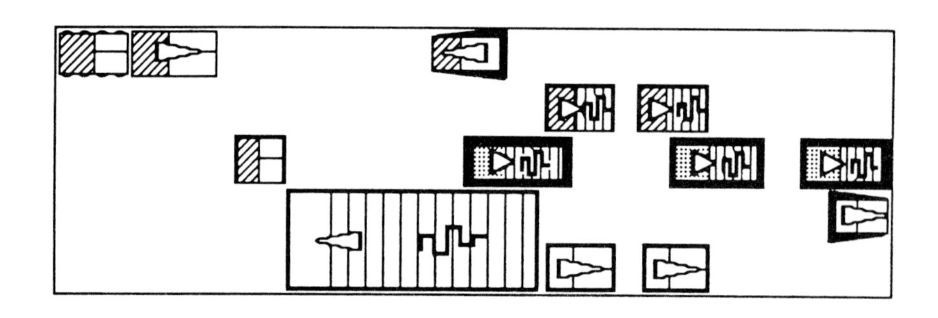

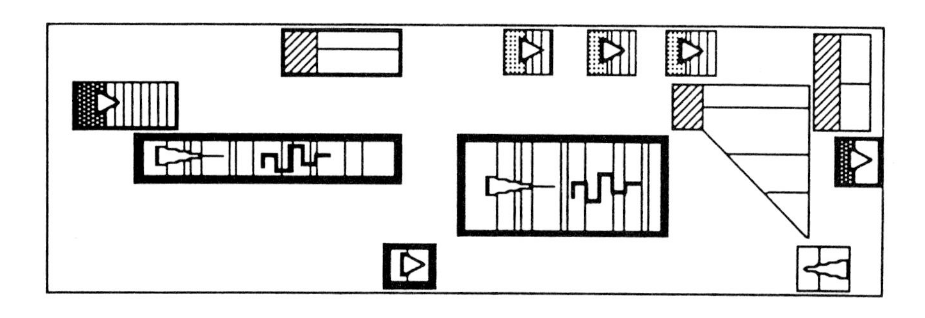

EXCERPT 7

Title:	**Peninsula**
Date of composition:	1984
Composer:	**Thomas Clark**
Born:	1949 (Detroit)
Medium:	piano and digitally resynthesized sounds
Excerpt:	first two minutes
Publisher:	American Composers Alliance
Recording:	CDCM Computer Music Series, Vol. 1 Centaur Records, CRC 2029 (compact disk)

f
f
mp
p (Hold until next marking.)
p
TAPE 0:00
= 3 attacks
Density = 2 attacks
= 1 attack
HIGH
Register
LOW
mf
p
p
Sus
0:10
(special "surf" sound)
0:20
p
mf
p
p
0:30

EXCERPT 7 Continued

1:30
1:40
1:50
2:00
SUS
(Middle pedal only)

EXCERPT 8

Title:	**Songs Before an Adieu**
Date of composition:	1979
Composer:	**Barbara Kolb**
Born:	1939 (Hartford, Connecticut)
Medium:	soprano, flute/alto flute, guitar
Excerpt:	beginning of second movement, "now i lay"
Words:	e. e. cummings
Publisher:	Boosey & Hawkes BH.BK. 822
Recording:	Bridge Records 2004

3''
freely
Soprano
Flute
Guitar
Now i lay with ev- ery- where
a - round (d) me the great dim deep sound of rain;
even 8th's, emphasize enunciation
molto legato
rit.
uneven 8th's; coordinate with flute and guitar
and of al ways and of

EXCERPT 8 Continued

freely
♩=108
life and day are on – ly loaned;
flutter
2"
accel.
where-as night is giv - en
irregular and impulsive
night and death and the rain are giv- en;
tr
sub. p
Vary articulation and dynamics, moving irregularly and impulsively in and out of cresc. and dim.
strum and arpeggiate; irregular and impulsive
gently and mysteriously; reflective
poco rit.
3"
4"
and giv - en is how beau - ti - fully snow

EXCERPT 9

Title:	**String Quartet in Four Parts**
Date of composition:	1950
Composer:	**John Cage**
Born:	1912 (Los Angeles)
Excerpt:	measures 199–220
Publisher:	Henmar Press, Edition Peters No. 6757
Recording:	Turnabout Records 34610

PIZZ.
ARCO
PIZZ.
ARCO
PIZZ.
ARCO

EXCERPT 10

Title:	**Fourth String Quartet**
Date of composition:	1973
Composer:	**Andrew Imbrie**
Born:	1921 (New York)
Excerpt:	movement III measures 1–21
Publisher:	Malcolm Music, Shawnee Press
Recording:	New World Records 212

Aria (♩ = 100)
arco
flaut.
ord.
dolce
poco cresc.
dim.
ord.
ff

EXCERPT 11

Title:	**Soundscape**
Date of composition:	1978
Composer:	**Dary John Mizelle**
Born:	1940 (Stillwater, Oklahoma)
Medium:	percussion ensemble
Excerpt:	movement 3. *Wood*
Publisher:	Lingua Press P.O. Box 3416, Iowa City, IA 52244
Recording:	Lumina Records L–002 236 Lafayette St. No. 4, New York, NY 10012

Wood:

= log drum (4 pitches) = twigs (many) broken with a twisting motion

= slit drum (4 pitches)

= wood block (8)

= temple block (8)

= maracas (2 or more ta ed together)

= cabaza (1)

= claves (2)

= slapstick (1)

XYL = xylophone (1)

= gavel and block (1)

= wooden headed drum (1)

= rachet (1)

MAR = marimba (1)

= marimba wind chimes (1)

= bamboo wind chime (1)

= wood bell or Japanese wood blocks (mokushō) (2 pitches)

EXCERPT 11 Continued

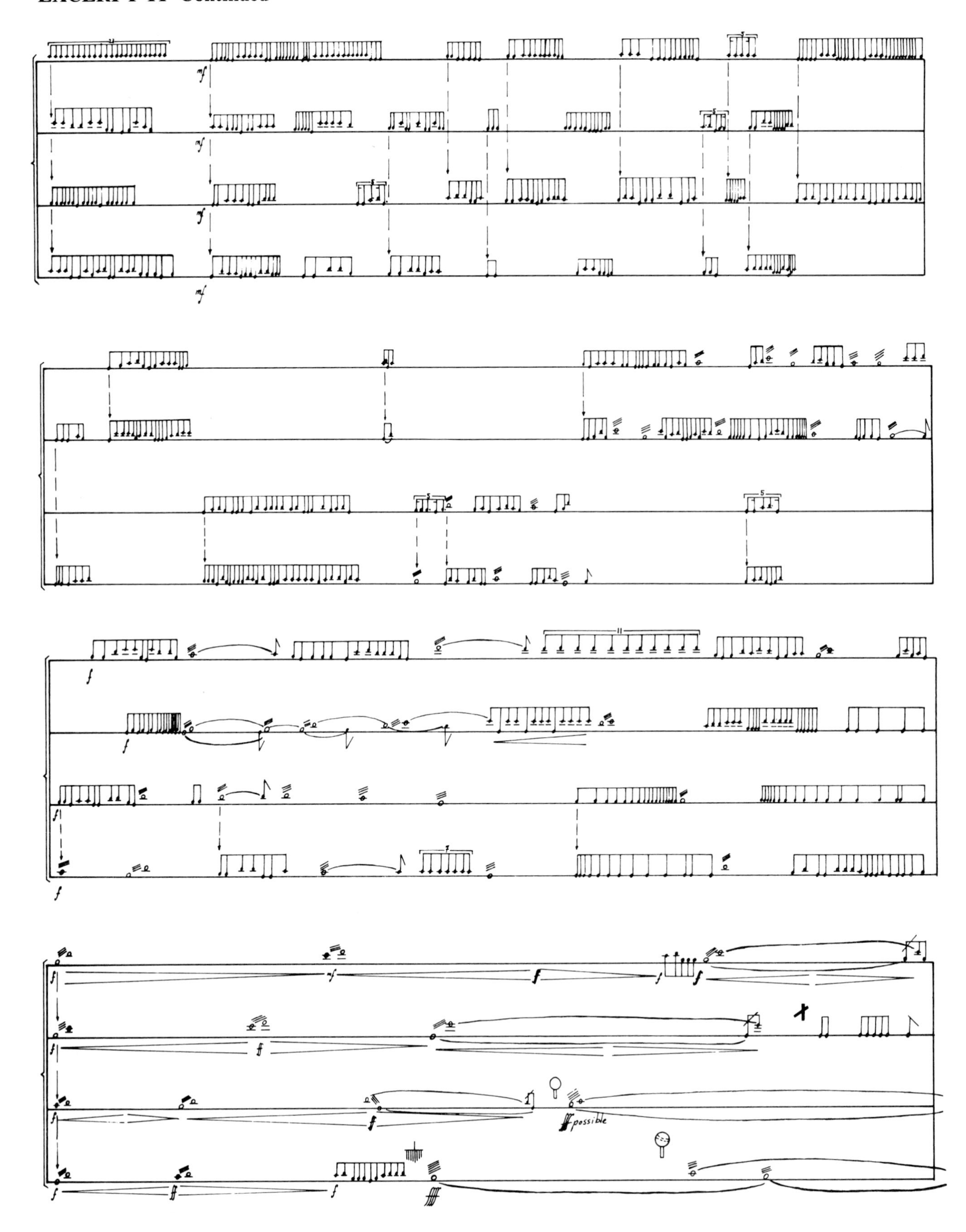

MAR
mp
sfzp
rall.
roll on different areas of head
l.v.
XYL
accel.
sfzp
rall.
pulses
possible

EXCERPT 11 Continued

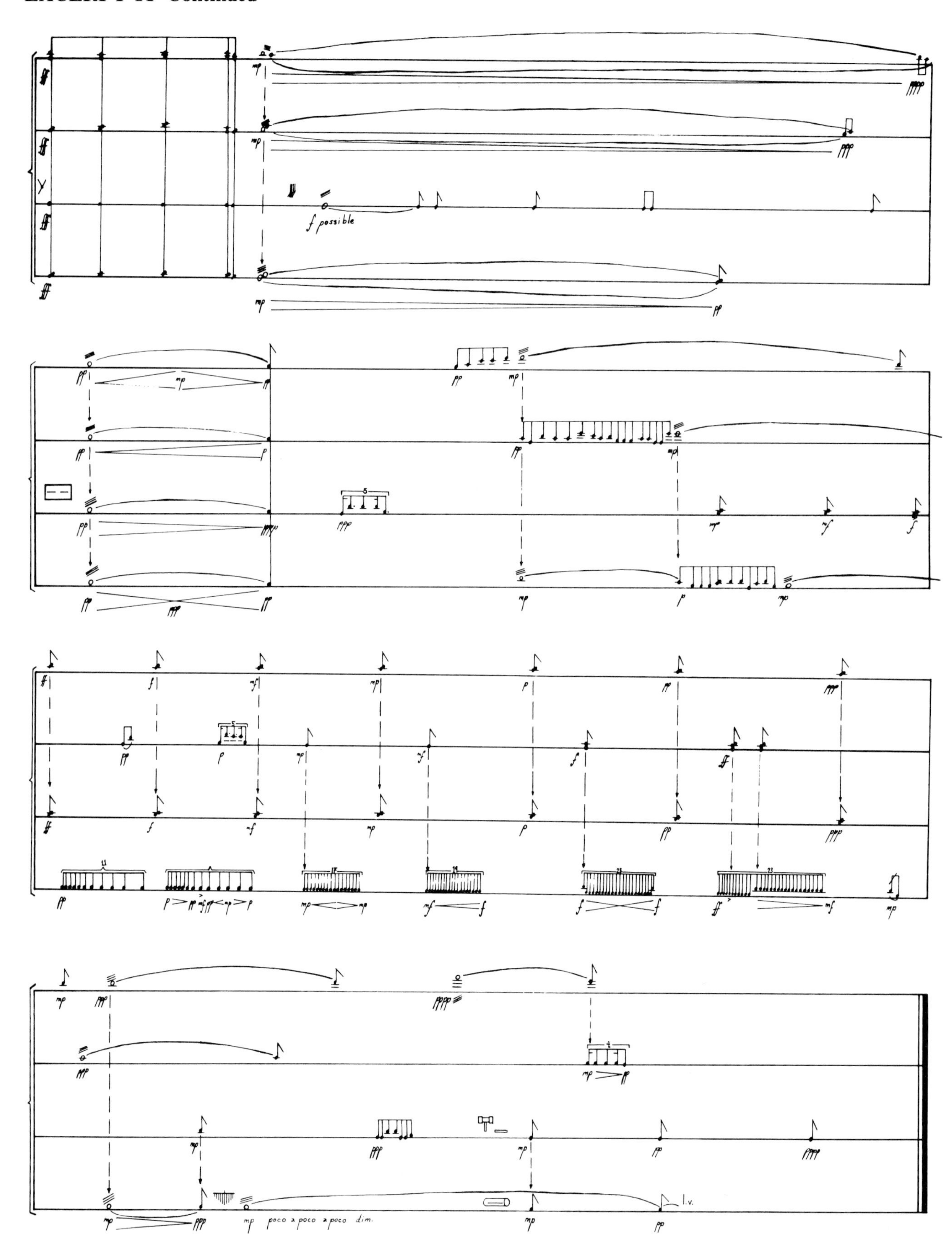

EXCERPT 12

Title:	**Parallel Lines**
Date of composition:	1979
Composer:	**Morton Subotnick**
Born:	1933 (Los Angeles)
Medium:	piccolo, ghost electronics, nine players
Excerpt:	marks 114–124
Publisher:	Theodore Presser 114–40268
Recording:	Composers Recordings, Inc. CRI S–458

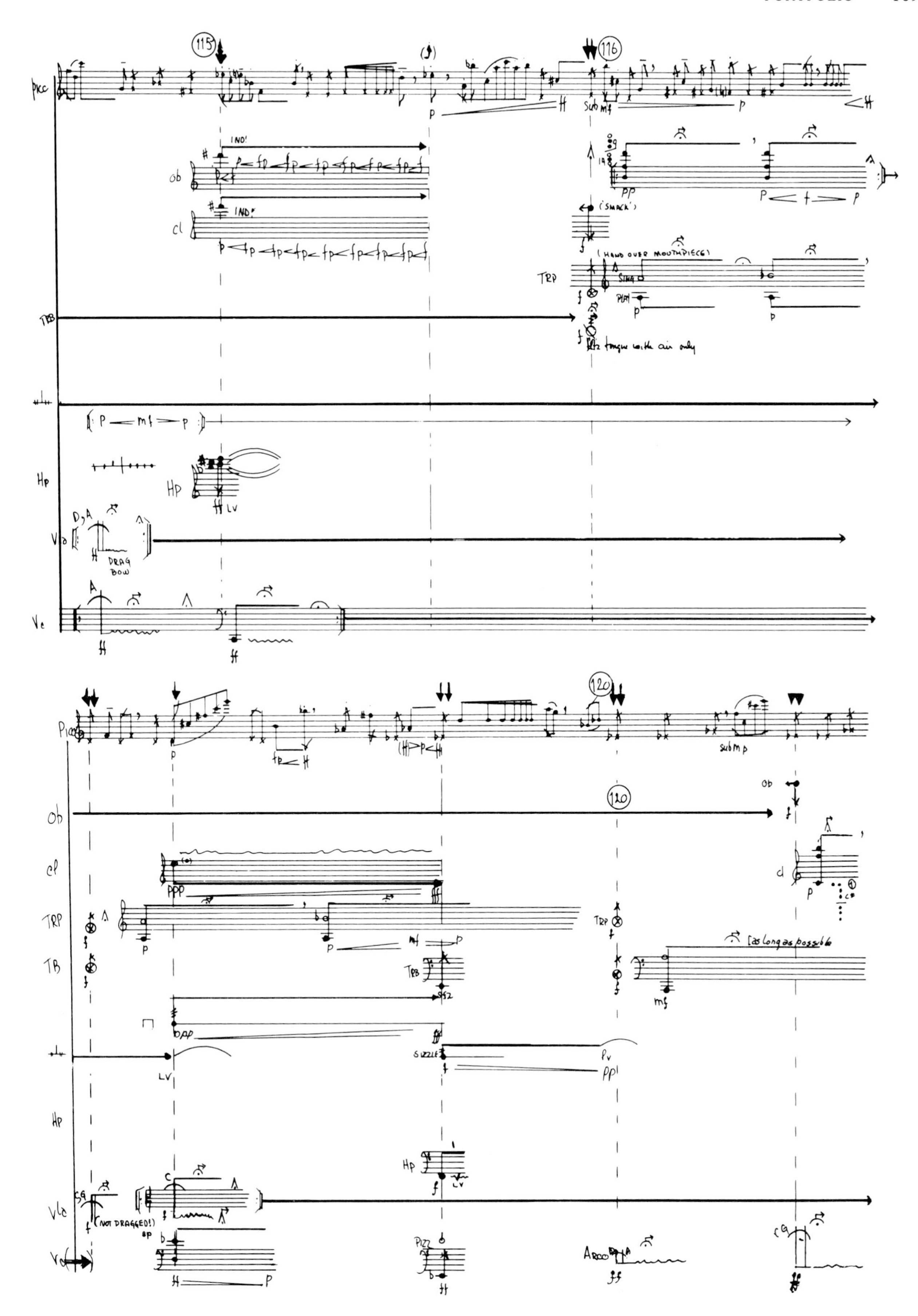
115
116
120
Picc
ob
cl
TRP
TB
Hp
Vla
Vc
IND!
('SMACK')
(HAND OVER MOUTHPIECE)
SING
PLAY
flz tongue with air only
DRAG BOW
(NOT DRAGGED!)
PIZZ
ARCO
sizzle
LV
sub mf
sub mp
[as long as possible]

EXCERPT 12 Continued

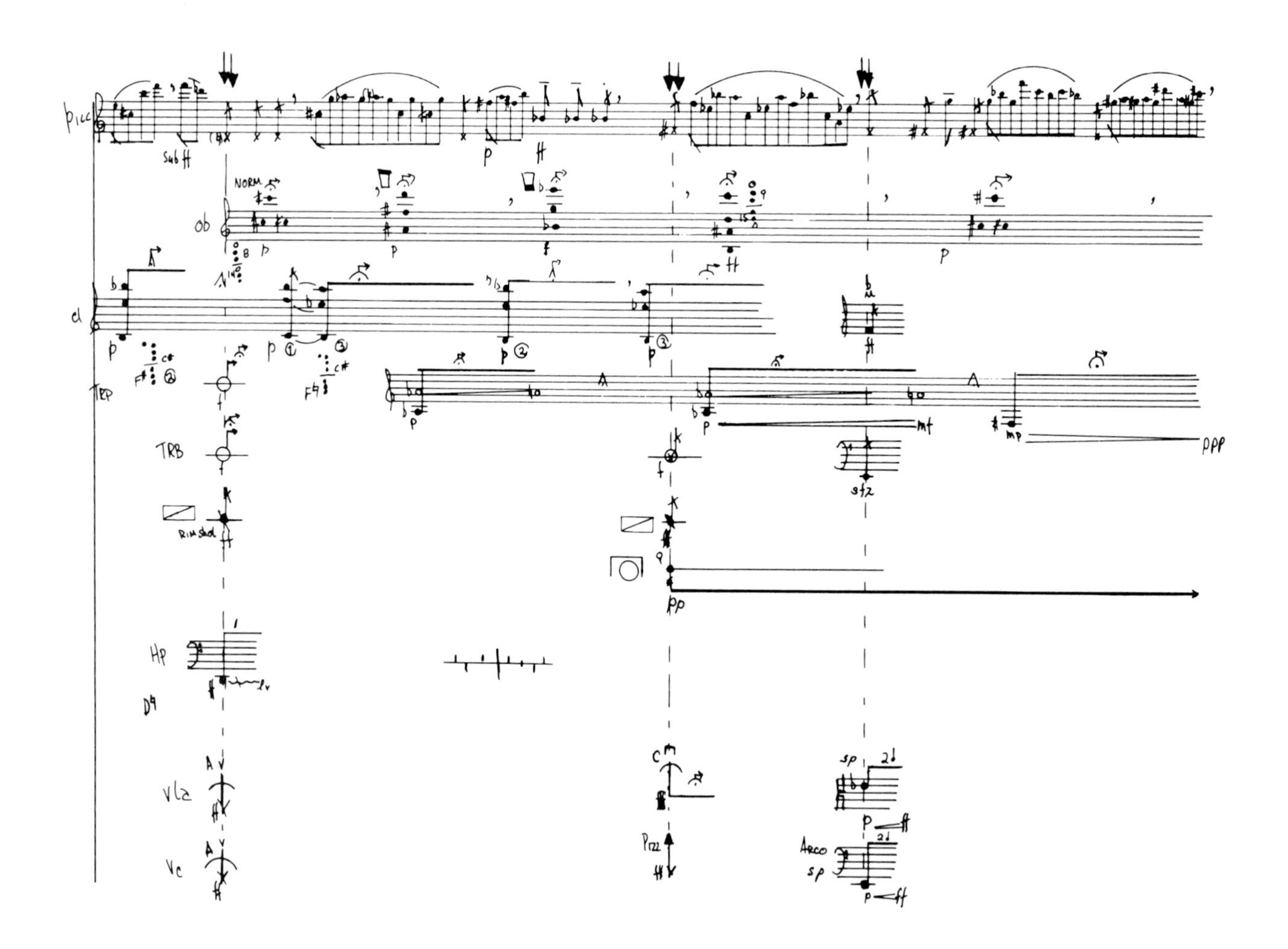

EXCERPT 13

Title:	**And the Mountains Rising Nowhere**
Date of composition:	1977
Composer:	**Joseph Schwantner**
Born:	1943 (Chicago)
Medium:	band
Excerpt:	measures 37–43
Publisher:	Helicon Music, European American Music

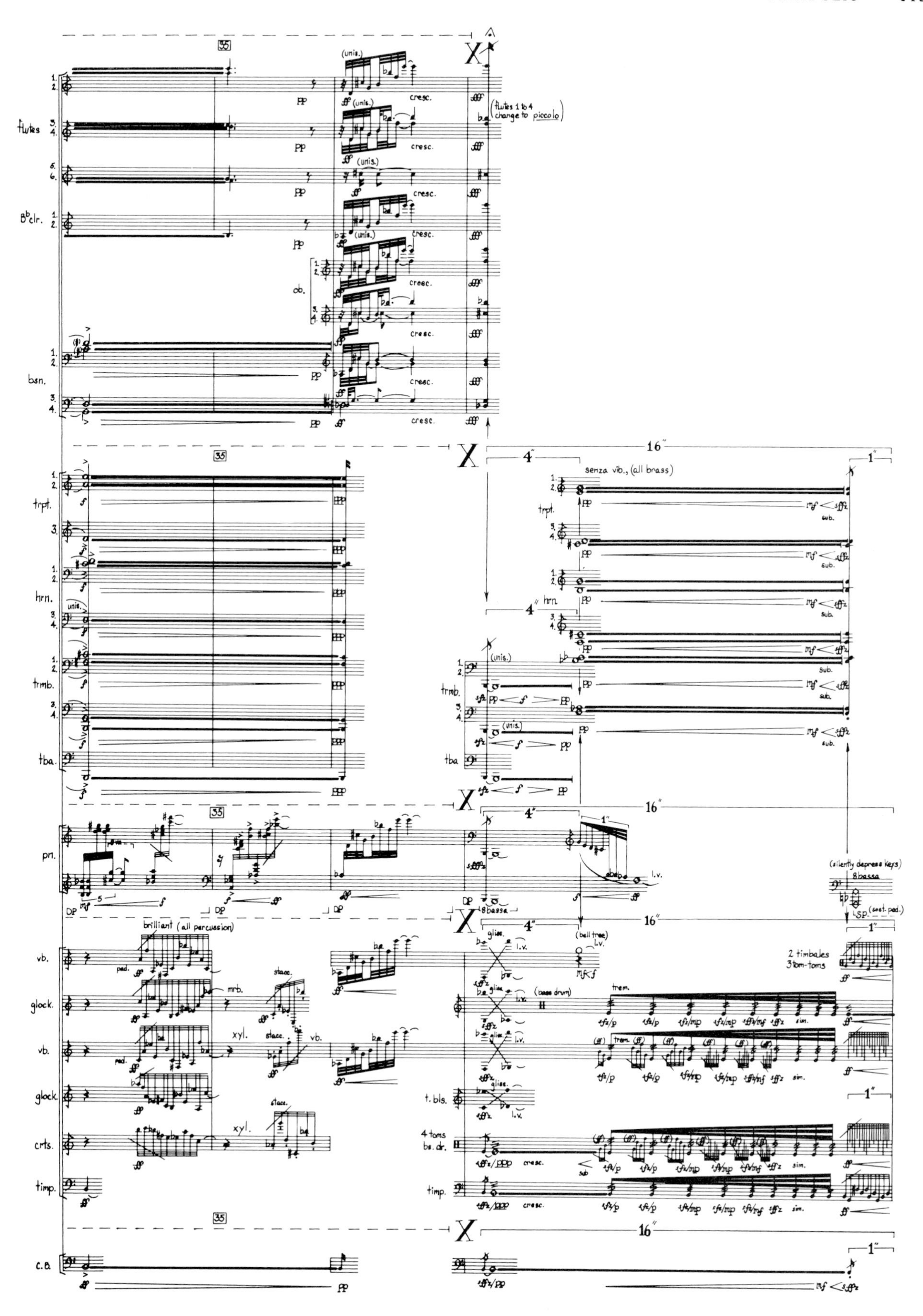
flutes
B♭ clr.
bsn.
ob.
(unis.)
cresc.
(flutes 1 to 4 change to piccolo)
trpt.
hrn.
trmb.
tba.
senza vib., (all brass)
16″
4″
1″
sub.
pn.
(silently depress keys)
8bassa
l.v.
(sost. ped.)
brilliant (all percussion)
vb.
glock.
crts.
timp.
mrb.
xyl.
stacc.
gliss.
(bell tree)
(bass drum)
trem.
t. bls.
4 toms
bs. dr.
2 timbales
3 tom-toms
sim.
c.B.

EXCERPT 13 Continued

EXCERPT 14

Title:	**Windows**
Date of composition:	1972
Composer:	**Jacob Druckman**
Born:	1928 (Brooklyn, New York)
Medium:	orchestra
Excerpt:	marks 29–31
Publisher:	MCA Music
Recording:	Composers Recordings, Inc. CRI S–457

Fl.
Picc.
Ob.
Cl.
B.Cl.
Fg.
Cfg.
begin with 3 figure
Cor.
Tr.
Trbne.
Tb.
Arpa
D♯E♭ G♭
Pno
to Org
Viol.
Vla.
Vcl.
col legno
Solo
Cb.
gli altri

EXCERPT 14 Continued

EXCERPT 15

Title:	**Sinfonia Concertante: A Mozartean Episode**
Date of composition:	1986
Composer:	**Larry Austin**
Born:	1930 (Duncan, Oklahoma)
Medium:	chamber orchestra, computer music narrative
Excerpt:	marks Q4–S5
Publisher:	American Composers Alliance
Recording:	CDCM Computer Music Series, Vol. 1 Centaur Records, CRC 2029 (compact disk)

Ob.
Cl.
Hn.
Bsn.
♩=60 (without conductor)
Fl.
lontano
pp sempre
Harp
DCB/EFG#A
Cues
15.01
15.08
15.14
15.15
15.22
Tape
<15.05> Le Gros is so happy with the symphony that he says it is his very best. <15.11> The andante, however, does not please him. <15.16> He declares that it has too many modulations, and it is too long. <R-3>
fell
for there is a time for everything
Vln. I
a niente
Pno.
Vln. II
Vla.
Cello
Tpt.
mute
Timp.
non-trem
Bass
pizz.

EXCERPT 15 Continued

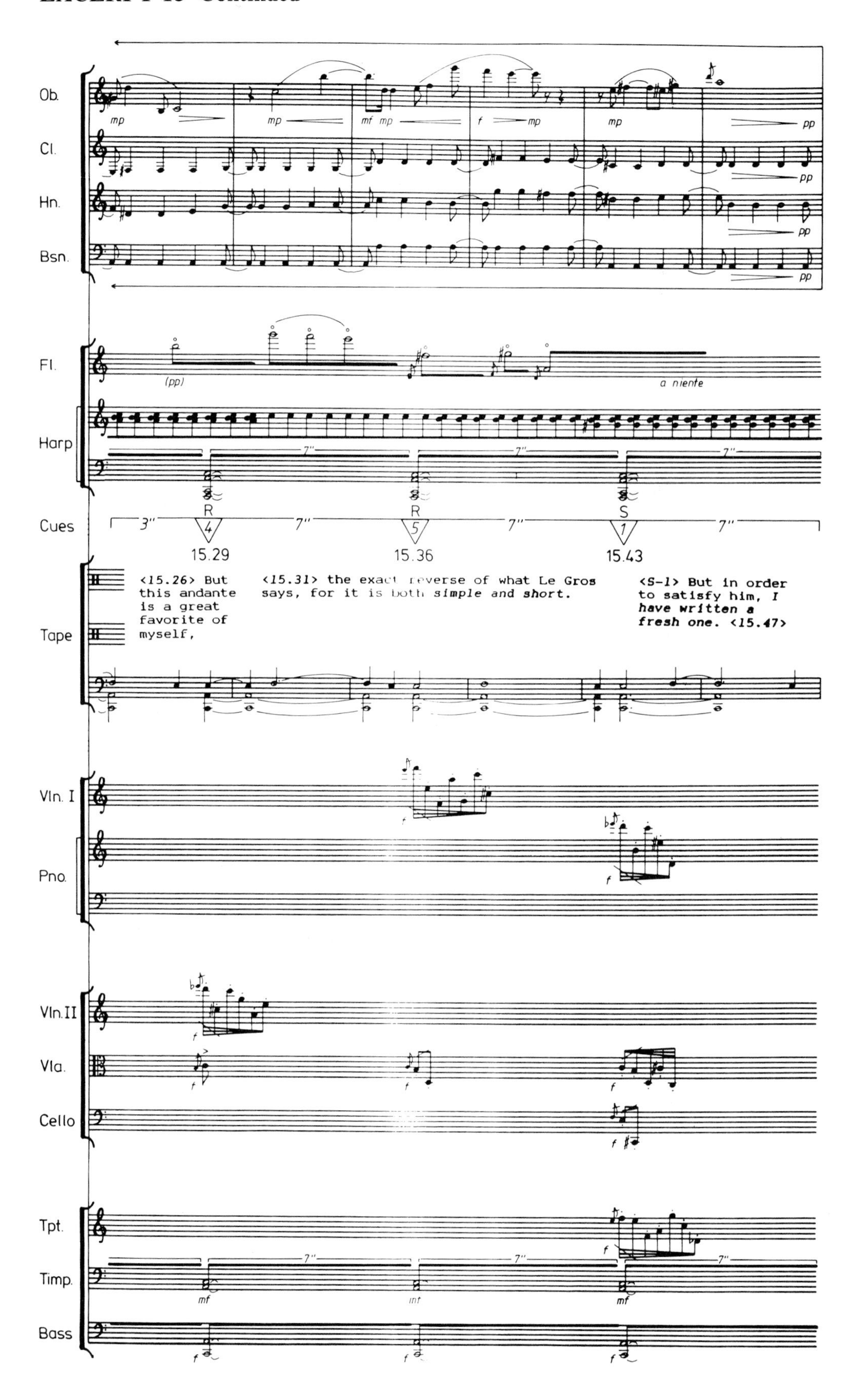

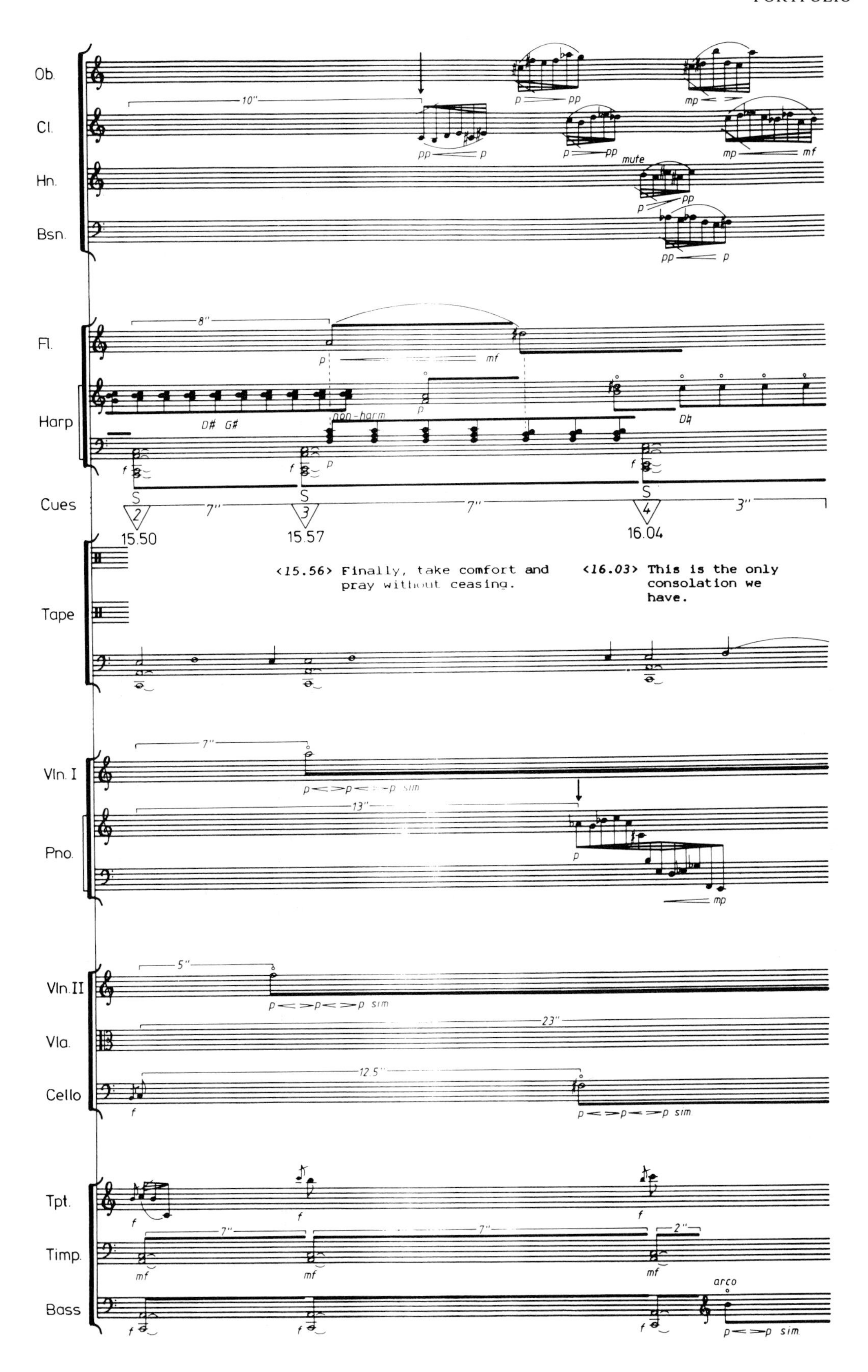
Ob.
Cl.
Hn.
Bsn.
10"
p pp
mp
pp p
p pp
mute
mp mf
p pp
pp p
Fl.
Harp
8"
p mf
D# G#
non-harm
p
D♮
Cues
S
7"
15.50
15.57
16.04
3"
Tape
<15.56> Finally, take comfort and pray without ceasing.
<16.03> This is the only consolation we have.
Vln. I
Pno.
7"
p p p sim
13"
p
mp
Vln. II
Vla.
Cello
5"
p p p sim
23"
12.5"
f
p p p sim
Tpt.
Timp.
Bass
f
mf
2"
arco
p p sim

EXCERPT 15 Continued

Ob.
Cl.
Hn.
Bsn.
f cresc ff
♩=120
Fl.
Harp
G#
Cues
T
5''
10''
5.5''
16.195
16.245
16.345
16.40
Tape
<T-3> Adieu,
mon Pere,
Wolfgang
Amade
Mozart
A— dieu mon Pere
<T-4>
Vln. I
Pno.
Vln. II
Vla.
Cello
Tpt.
open
Timp.
Bass

EXCERPT 16

Title:	**Perfect Lives**
Date of composition:	1977–84
Composer:	**Robert Ashley**
Born:	1930 (Ann Arbor, Michigan)
Medium:	live television, video tape, live and prerecorded music, actors, and speaker
Excerpt:	photographic images from the seven parts
Publisher:	Robert Ashley
Video recording:	Lovely Music, 10 Beach St., New York NY 10013

Descriptions of the seven songs of ***Perfect Lives,*** presenting aspects of the plot, characters involved, and the elements of the setting, the assigned hour, the "pattern" and camera motion.

1. **The park**—Portrait of a traveling man, perhaps the singer "R" himself, and the landscape of a small-town park. 11 a.m. Low horizon.

2. **The supermarket**—Portrait of the Old Man and the Old Woman—who live at the old folks home but who have a strange "arrangement"—in the landscape of a large Midwestern supermarket. 3 p.m. Lines converging in distance.

3. **The Bank**—Portrait of Gwyn and Ed, the elopers, and the captain of the football team—Isolde's younger brother who has worked at the bank since his graduation—in the geometrical landscape of the bank. 1 p.m. Grid.

EXCERPT 16 Continued

4. **The Bar**—The Perfect Lives Lounge, furnished with its television sets and its cocktail-lounge piano. A portrait of keyboard stylist Buddy, and his encounter with Rodney in the vertical landscape of the bottles and men at the bar. 11 p.m. Vertical lines.

5. **The Living Room**—The Sheriff and his wife solve the mystery of the missing money. 9 p.m. Equal vertical volumes.

6. **The Church**—The further adventures of Ed and Gwyn who meant only to elope but stumble into the landscape of a small-town ritual. Contains an important sermon on agriculture and geometry. 5 p.m. The rose window.

7. **The Backyard**—Portrait of Isolde, the oldest of the sheriff's kids, nearing thirty and still unspoken for, a woman who thinks in numbers. A mysterious epilogue in the twilight of the backyard. 7 p.m. The doorway.

MATERIALS OF INVENTION

CHAPTER 5
TIME STREAMS

Music makes time audible and its form and continuity sensible.
—Suzanne Langer

Music exists in time and its substance is the articulation of time. We sense this articulation both consciously and subconsciously. Consciously, our perception of time traces a course of experience and expectation through the changing context of each time-articulating event as it transpires in a piece of music. Subconsciously, we feel a sense of motion, a kinetic quality connected with the motions and cycles of our own bodies. Dancing, sleeping, walking, climbing, falling, staggering—these are all familiar kinds of motion with a sense of time that can translate into musical rhythms. Their various qualities—of speed, of smoothness, of repetition, of flexibility—are the qualities we build into rhythmic patterns to give music a sense of motion.

The great importance of time in the image of a musical work, especially in contemporary styles, is suggested by the number of pieces referring to time in their titles: Wuorinen's *Time's Encomium,* Crumb's *Echoes of Time in the River,* Penderecki's *Dimensions of Time and Silence,* Stockhausen's *Zeitmasse* (translated simply "tempi" but suggestive in German of "time masses"), *Timepiece* by Lawrence Moss, or *Time Cycle* by Lukas Foss. *Time Cycle* is for orchestra and soprano singing texts drawn from four writings by different authors, each with time as its central theme or image.

It is hard, almost impossible, to conceive of time unfolding as one continuous stream without variation, an incessant, continuous flow. **Clock time** is a uniform system for measuring the passage of time, but even it is meaningless without changing events to measure. In fact, units of clock time are modeled on the universal events of cyclic change, such as one day, the average interval of time from one dawn to the next. An hour is just a handy division of that time span, arbitrarily divided into parts by the useful dividing numbers, two and twelve. This shows that time is sensed on a hierarchy of levels, each marked by recurring events—each second our heart beats, each day we sleep, each year we plant crops or go to the beach or catch the first snowflake. Time exists as we sense it articulated on many levels by changing and cyclically recurring events.

In composed music, a time stream is set in motion and its flow controlled by changing sound events, so that there is more than just a succession of pulses—there is an ebb and flow of **rhythm.**

> When we hear a piece of music, processes of alteration follow each other at varying speeds. We experience the passage of time in the intervals between alterations. (Stockhausen, 1955)

Continuity in the unfolding of events in time requires memory to appreciate, referring back and comparing new events with previous ones. A coherent stream of relationships is created by the similarities and entirely repeated identities, the contrasts and even stark contradictions to prior events. Continuity need not mean large doses of sameness; recurring use of bold contrast could as easily operate as a continuity, with great momentum of change. In fact, a metaphor is quite apt: musical recurrence and contrast is like physical inertia and momentum. **Momentum,** the extent of contrast or alteration of patterns—the flow of the stream—is manifested in qualities of mobility and stability. This provides the basis to understand more specifically and to control expansion or compression processes.

> In any temporal form, repetition both extends and articulates matter. Its essential function is not to produce symmetry or closure, but rather to establish an identity, an element, which thereby differentiates itself and persists in time, remaining somehow constant under change. Reiteration emphasizes differences; it focuses attention on small-scale detail, on "texture." Recurrence emphasizes similarities and articulates more far-reaching relations of over-all structure. (Patricia Carpenter, "The Musical Object." *Current Musicology,* no. 5. [1967]: 79–80)

To achieve rhythmic continuity, the composer must have strong intuition for time, a sense of eventfulness. There must also be a good grasp of the mechanics for relating events, coherent in time when their minute features of rhythm form simple relationships. Compositional fluency depends upon understanding the details of well-designed event streams.

DURATION

Elements of rhythm can be measured in time, creating a stream of **durations.** Durational patterns arise from sound events in many ways. First, we perceive the length of a sound as it relates proportionally to previous sounds. Its duration may relate as well to an implied regularity of time division, a sense of **pulse.** Second, a less obvious but much more significant kind of duration is the **time span** from the beginning of one event or pattern to the beginning of the next—whatever is perceived as the next in succession, a comparable event. Durations formed in this way are not always entirely filled with sound; they include the "windows" of a musical architecture—pauses, interruptive rests, quiet recollections of previous events. We can see examples of this in **excerpt 3** and **excerpt 1;** a more important set of durations than the very short note values of the actual sounds are the time spans from the attack of one note to the attack of the next. These durations are similar but varied (see figure 5.1). Each duration of a sound event may also include a following rest or silence, as these examples both do. Generally, the proportion of a time span not filled with sound is thus a degree of isolation, a disconnectedness of sounds. When pervasive, such separateness of sounds in time is often called **pointillism,** after the century-old technique in oil painting of dots of color separated on a canvas.

Independent successions of events may also coexist in time, forming a counterpoint of event streams with overlapping and coincident durations.

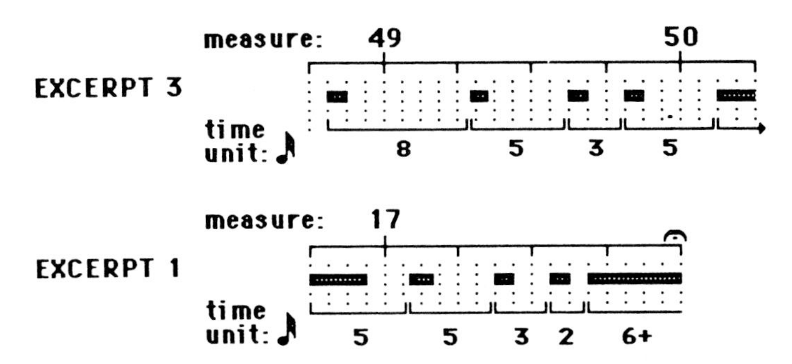

Figure 5.1 Time spans in pointillistic rhythms

> It is not the case that, in time, we hear one thing at a time. A conception of space in which things are spread out one at a time in a line is the conception of tactile space. We *hear* many things at once—one *time,* it is true, at a time. (Carpenter 1967, 73)

The patterns of durations in each strand of a counterpoint interact, sometimes coinciding, at other times independent. In other words, there may be **alignment** of their points of change in time or **divergence** of timing or, commonly, a mixture of these configurations. We can understand some of the intricacies of such interaction by drawing a time graph of a contrapuntal example, illustrating how the beginnings of notes "line up."

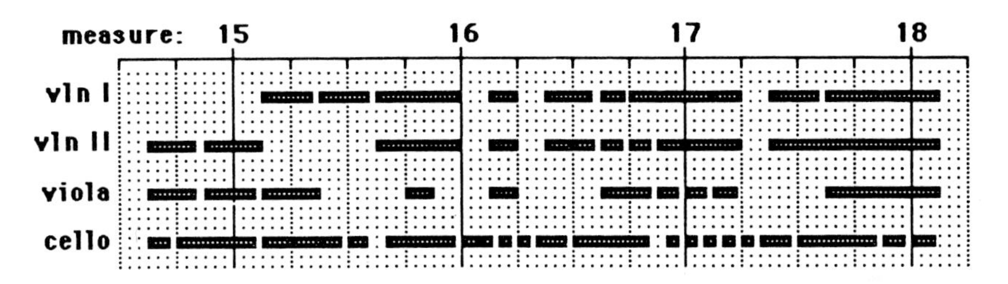

Figure 5.2 Time map from excerpt 10, event streams of each instrument

Rhythmic patterns can also relate to a **meter** in a kind of counterpoint between the explicit and the implicit.

> The meter is a fixed and steady abstract norm against which the rhythm, the constantly changing acceleration and slowing, syncopation, anticipation, shift of stress, and so on is counterpointed. (Barney Childs. "Poetic and Musical Rhythm." *Music Theory: Special Topics* 1981.)

This factor was also represented in the time graph in just this way, visually portrayed as a calibration of the background time measurement over which rhythmic patterns are drawn. All the moments at which some sound begins, **initiating time points,** mark off durational units of rhythm on a surface level. (Because of their critical role, these beginnings of notes are drawn bolder than the ends.) They are like fence posts in time, although they might make a highly irregular fence!

We can literally see the fence posts in **excerpt 11,** the third movement of Mizelle's *Soundscape* for percussion. In the second score system of the movement, dotted vertical lines marking moments of coordination between beginnings of grouped notes draw a broadly varied rhythm with their spacings.

Durational successions have other identifiable rhythmic properties, an understanding of which is critical to the comparison and differentiation that makes potentially coherent streams. The most important of these durational properties have to do with how connected they are in sound, how similar they are in length, and how simple or complex their proportions. Since these properties need not remain fixed, they may undergo processes of change as time streams are expanded, compressed, interrupted or fragmented.

ACCENT AND RHYTHMIC STRESS

Although duration is the most basic property of rhythmic elements in streams, other factors also contribute to a sense of rhythmic character.

> . . . perceived, accentuated patterns of motion from event to event in a string of sounds and rests, each event in the string having a certain moment of beginning, fixed duration and relationship to the accentuation of the whole. (Yeston 1976, 36)

The perceived prominence of individual elements due to various kinds of stress differentiates their roles. Goals of motion may be perceived, rhythmic focal points created by means of these **stress factors.**

The most obvious stress is by **loudness**—notes marked with an accent or events occuring at specified dynamic levels greater than preceding events. For example, the first cello note in measure 19 of **excerpt 10** stands out boldly with both an accent mark and a *ff* level in contrast to the softness of the other strings. The E-flat and G-sharp played simultaneously by violin 1 and viola at the end of measure 17 also have accent marks and jump suddenly to the louder level of *mf.* They also reinforce each other by their simultaneous attacks. This **textural stress** is closely related, the greater strength or mass a sound may have by containing a larger aggregate of pitches or an event by containing more instrumental colors or more activity. In figure 5.3, textural stress is identified by counting at each point in the composite rhythm how many instruments are initiating a note at that moment.

The second part of the third beat in measure 16 is texturally stressed, one of the few moments in the passage when as many as three of the four instruments attack notes at the same time. Here, increased loudness contributes stress as well, emphasizing that moment in the rhythmic flow.

The role of meter in the formation of rhythmic stress is somewhat abstract and, in a way, complex. **Metric stress** is the rhythmic prominence a sound or event exhibits when its point of inception coincides with the beginning of a metric time unit. As suggested earlier, **meter** is an underlying implied hierarchy of conforming time divisions. On the many hierarchical levels that this regulated time sense may operate, the beginnings of its equal units of time become points of focus for potential stress.

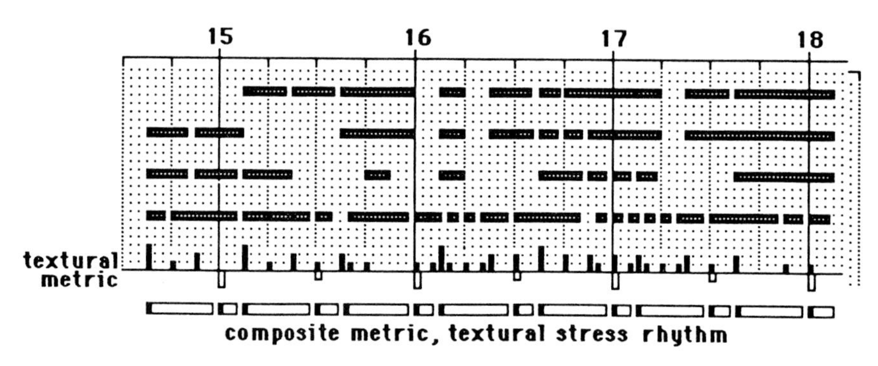

Figure 5.3 Composite rhythm, textural and metric stress rhythms

> Meter is not simply a matter of regularly recurring dynamic intensification. It is a set of proportional relationships, an ordering framework of accents and weak beats within which rhythmic grouping takes place. . . . It constitutes the matrix out of which rhythm arises. Meter establishes a structured continuum of accents. (Cooper and Meyer 1960, 96)

Extremes of register have an impact as stressed focal points in pitch space. In linear patterns, changing the direction or the rate of upward or downward registral motion makes contours. The simplest **contour stress** occurs with a sound or event at the turning point of a line, a change in registral direction, thus becoming the highest or lowest sound or event in its vicinity. Sounds or events suddenly much higher or lower than those preceding may possess contour stress even if not ultimate turning points in a registral curve. At the same moment of textural stress in measure 16, registral or contour stress emphasizes all the pitches, violin 1's A-flat, violin 2's B, and viola's C-sharp. In measure 17, the cello line is shaped rhythmically at both ends of its pitch space, reaching high G (in tenor clef) after the second beat, then plunging to low E at the end of the measure.

The most basic property of a rhythmic element remains its duration. One of the most persuasive factors differentiating elements is what is called **agogic stress,** the prominence of a rhythmic element due to its longer duration than recent previous elements. As with all other stress factors, there can be an infinity of shadings of relative agogic or length stress. The placement of agogically stressed elements in a rhythmic stream is important insofar as they are understood as interruptions in rhythmic flow or as goals of motion, the moments when motion in an event stream temporarily ceases.

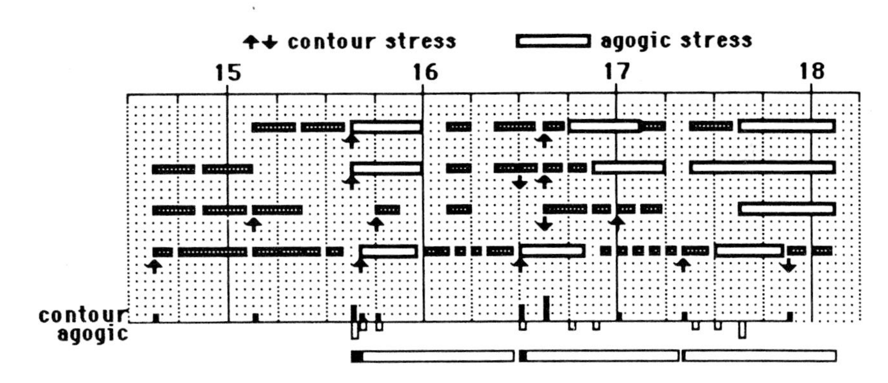

Figure 5.4 Contour and agogic stress in excerpt 10

Within a stream of rhythmic elements, some will stand out because of one or a combination of these stress factors. Elements stressed in comparable fashion and strength form a distinct pattern, a stream in itself consisting of the durations between their incidences. (Inevitably, all rhythmic phenomena end up being understood in terms of durations, articulated divisions of time!) A **stress rhythm** can be decisive in forming rhythmic character, more so than the surface stream of sounds and silences, especially when the surface is relatively conformed and undifferentiated.

TEMPORAL RELATIONSHIPS AND PROCESSES

Rhythmic motives, essentially characteristic stress rhythms, can be used to model coherent streams of events. On a surface level of sounds and silences, however, even within such motivic continuity a variety of individual durations can create a basic elasticity. Expressing **rhythmic range** as a comparison of the longest duration to the shortest duration in a stream is a simple way to appraise the variety of durations. In succession, durations can be more particularly compared.

> Rhythm is the preparation of one event by the last—the way in which one wave or one gesture, for instance, arises out of another. (Carpenter 1967, 80)

Trends form by the comparative differences of longer, shorter, or equal durations in a stream, and the speed of rhythmic events changes. Note that we are not speaking of **acceleration** or **deceleration,** which are gradual changes in the rate of what is perceived to be the relative regularity of a **pulse,** nor even of sudden changes in tempo. Changes in the spacing of initiating time points for actual sound events may not be as obvious looking at a score but are more directly responsible for rhythmic change.

Both rhythms in figure 5.1 show a **compression,** initiating time points getting closer and closer together. The concept of pacing can be understood quantitatively. As distinguished from tempo (the rate of implicit, regular divisions of time), **event rate** is the irregular, fluctuating speed of actual events. Here is a simple mathematical expression for **rhythmic density:**

$$\text{event rate} = \frac{\text{number of events}}{\text{total duration of the stream (in beats or seconds)}}$$

This provides the basis to better understand and control expansion or compression processes. For example, the composite rhythm in figure 5.3, actually shown by its line of textural stress marks, changes from as few as only one rhythmic event per beat to as many and as rapid as four per beat.

One approach to rhythm and temporal process relies on basic variation procedures to drive temporal processes of change. When rhythmic patterns are spun into motion by continual repetition, contrapuntal interactions of rhythm can be intricate and yet gradually absorbed through the repetition. The repeated patterns can be of different lengths, so that their repetitions have different cycles and their interactions continually change phase relationship. In this way, all their possible combinations in time are presented in kaleidoscopic succession. Steve Reich is one prominent proponent of this recently popular approach to temporal processes, sometimes called "pattern music."

Like complex phase relationships, patterns can evolve in time individually by being gradually transformed. Often, compression or expansion of time is brought about simply by **truncating** or **extending** a rhythmic pattern. As an example of producing temporal compression by simple variations in a single repeated pattern, examine the first five measures of **excerpt 5** from *Solo* by Lukas Foss (figure 5.6).

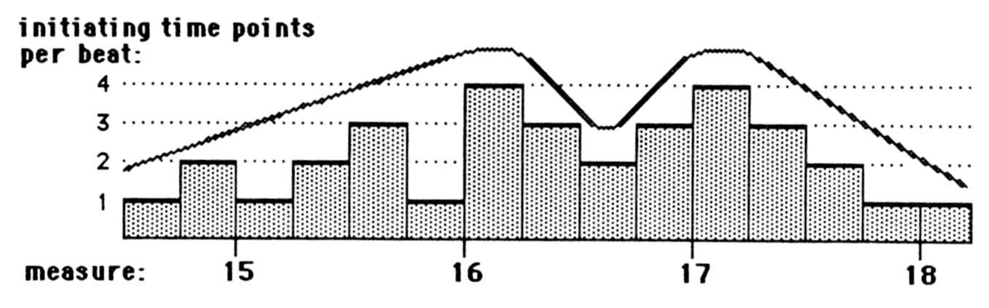

Figure 5.5 Event rate of composite rhythm in excerpt 10

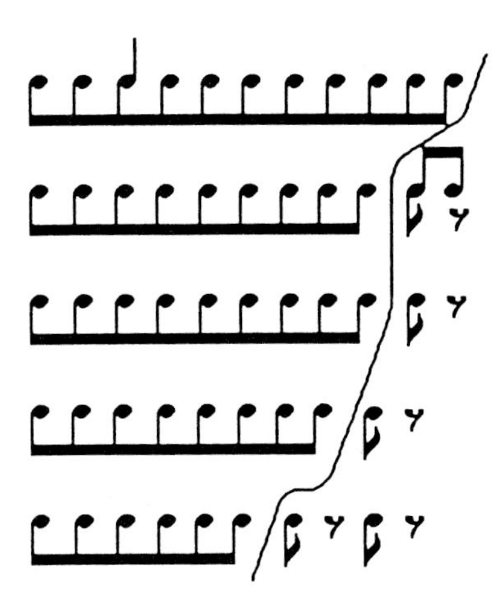

Figure 5.6 Successive truncations in the first five measures of excerpt 5

A quantitative comparison of any two successive durations in a stream forms a **proportion.** Ratios of two durational values range from the simplest, a one-to-one equality, to such irreducible ratios of primes as 7:5 or 1:13. A ratio's complexity, how big its numbers are, is one way to appreciate the **complexity** of a rhythmic proportion.

Rhythmic complexity can be thought of in another way. We perceive and understand proportions of time by subconsciously identifying a kind of atomic subunit of time that is a common factor in successive durations. The magnitude of the largest possible whole subunit common to two durations therefore represents the complexity of their proportion; the shorter the perceived subdivision of time needed to grasp the proportion, the more intricate or complex it seems. Thinking in terms of common subdurations suggests that rhythmic trends can be compressions or expansions of what might be termed a perceptual subpulse.

An idiom typical of contemporary rhythms pits different subdivisions of a beat against each other to create very small time differences, with resulting rhythmic intricacy. Measures 16 and 17 of **excerpt 10** pit triplets in the cello part against duple divisions of beats in the other instruments. Time particles no longer than one-sixth of a quarter note are thus forced into the resultingly complex composite rhythm. This kind of complication is more extreme with other special subdivisions of metric units, such as the quintuplets found in measures 14 and 16 of **excerpt 5.** In this passage, the length of measures is changing at the same time that very slightly different durations are created by special quintuple subdivisions of basic time units. A time graph of measures

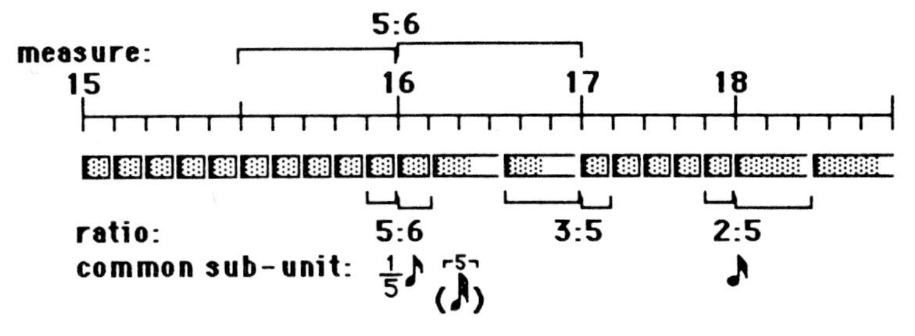

Figure 5.7 Complicated changes of meter and subdivisions in excerpt 5

15 through 18 illustrates visually the complicated and subtle stretching of measure 16 on levels both of short surface durations and of longer metric groupings of time.

Proportional complexity and simplicity might, then, be understood in either of two ways, the magnitude of arithmetic ratios or the intricacy of common perceptible subunits. By comparing and assessing proportions and subpulses, temporal trends such as **complication, simplification,** and **continuation** can be understood, especially over broad musical time spans such as the various sections of an entire piece.

The composer can think, then, in terms of temporal processes—compression, expansion, continuation—while determining the durations of single **sounds,** whole **events** consisting of successions of sounds and silences, and **event-complexes,** even longer segments of a time stream. With an architectonic or hierarchical model of time, each level of time, from surface to deep structure, contains **elements** which form into **streams;** on the next broader or deeper level these streams in turn become the elements of yet longer streams.

For example, the second movement of Kolb's *Songs Before an Adieu* in **excerpt 8** begins with three events, each aligned in the three parts. (They are centered around the pitch, D, as well as being aligned in time.) These three notes, time points, are rhythmic elements in a brief event stream announcing the beginning of the song. As an introductory, fanfare-like event, the group of three notes is antecedent to the following stream of sounds, suddenly decorated by rapid filigree figures in the flute and guitar. Together, these two event streams, the former halting and stark, the latter running and decorative, form an event-complex. In turn, this event-complex is the introductory element of the event stream for the whole movement, presenting the basic rhythmic and textural material for the rest of the song.

Event streams normally follow one another in time. The different ways they may do this or otherwise relate can be understood in four categories, kinds of **linkage:** separation, conjunction, integration, and elision. *Soundscape* (**excerpt 11**), with its sparse notation focused on rhythm and texture, will provide some visually clear examples of these relationships.

Conjunction the simplest linkage, is possibly the most common, with a stream as it ends being immediately followed by the start of a new stream.

Separation involves a pause, a rest, or another not closely related event interrupting the connection between the end of one stream and the beginning of another.

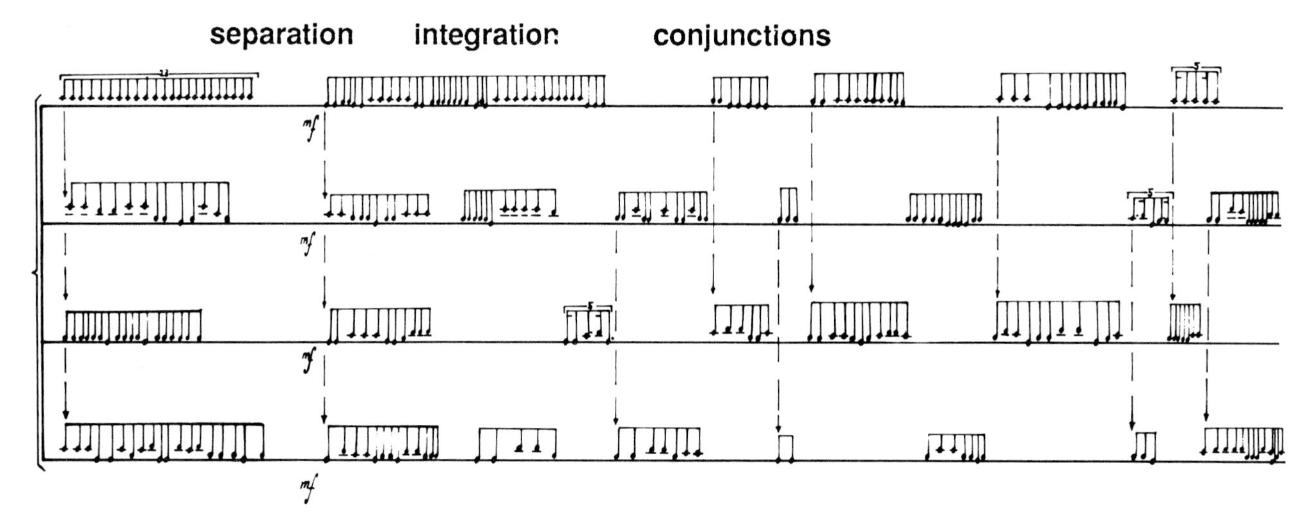

Figure 5.8 Relationships of event streams, second system of excerpt 11

Integration shares a segment of time in which final elements of one stream overlap and coexist with initial elements of another stream. The integration may be brief and make a casual link or so extensive that it can be thought of as complete contrapuntal merging of the streams. (Counterpoint will be discussed again as an important aspect of texture in chapter 8, **MUSICAL ARCHITECTURE.**) The fourth system of **excerpt 11** extensively overlaps rhythmic groups, increasingly integrating their streams of sound. This more connected rhythmic flow makes a transition leading in the next system to the next section of the movement, which is dominated by the continuous sound of extended tremolos.

Elision involves one actually shared element, event, or time point that can be understood as the final element of one stream and simultaneously the initiating element of another. In the third system of **excerpt 11,** one of the third percussionist's rhythms, a quintuplet figure, culminates in a tremolo at precisely the moment the fourth percussionist starts a seven-note rhythmic group.

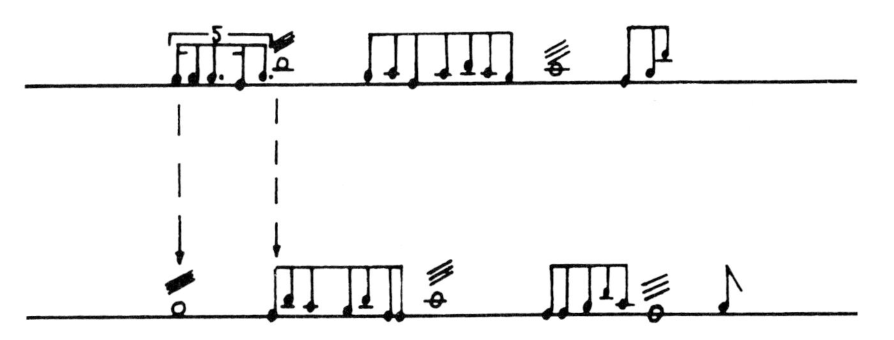

Figure 5.9 Elision of event streams in excerpt 11

CHANGE THROUGH TIME

Processes of change can be enacted by very gradual, subtle degrees, by lurching, rapid increases or decreases, even by abrupt reversals of the processes themselves. We can think of a vague notion of **rates of change** created by temporal or rhythmic trends.

Perhaps more significant is the rate at which trends are reversed, terminated, interrupted, replaced, the **elasticity of change.** A profound notion, this would be mathematically rather complex to measure. A perceptual approach may be more comprehensible, as described in two different ways:

> Experiential time is dependent on the density of alteration. The degree of information is greatest when at every moment of a musical flow the momentum of surprise is greatest . . . experiental time is in a state of flux, constantly and unexpectedly altering. (Stockhausen 1955)

> "Time" might be said to move "faster" or "slower"—if there is silence after a musical event the attention stays with that event, allowing itself perhaps to wander from it, to ruminate about it. If, on the other hand, events succeed one another rapidly and seem to be "unrelated", as say the spatters of "grace notes" in a Stockhausen

> piano piece, attention is so densely challenged that it may back off a step, so to speak, and regard the notes as a single cluster, a group event. (Childs 1977)

From the smallest, most detailed level of rhythm to the broadest levels of time and large segmentation, streams of durations form relationships of magnitude and proportion giving rise to trends or processes of change, the elasticity of which is the most profound quality of the unfolding of events in time. We can think of the unfolding as an energy curve, waves of rhythmic momentum with ebb and flow and possibly splashes or glassy calms.

> Certain vital moments in a piece of music serve us as focal and organizing, events which in the immediacy of the new so jar our expectation and so alter (and reilluminate) our sense of what we have heard that we regard what we are subsequently hearing in a changed fashion. (Childs 1977)

All of the qualities of rhythm we have been discussing influence the curve, weighing toward one side or the other of a basic polarity, **momentum** and **inertia.** Here is how the various possible qualities of many rhythmic factors participate in this system of polarity:

MOMENTUM—INERTIA
high event-rate—low event-rate
proportional complexity—proportional simplicity
elasticity—conformity
elision, integration—separation, conjunction
contrapuntal divergence—alignment

Composers often think in these terms and, in fact, as part of a sketching process often draw an energy curve. It is the lifeblood of form, the way in which time is shaped through change. This is a natural way at early stages of creation to think of a composition and to begin to form its character. It probably reflects the way we will listen to the finished piece and understand its broadest sense.

Returning one final time to our exploration of *Soundscape,* we cannot, of course, show the energy curve that Mizelle might have originally drawn or simply thought of at an early stage in its composition. Instead, however, some of the temporal factors we have discussed can be broadly analyzed and express a reasonable facsimile of the work's basic scheme or form with respect to energy levels and momentum of temporal processes.

In figure 5.10, we can see one description of the work's central scenario, its temporal form. Its trajectory is a complex wave form, increasing gradually

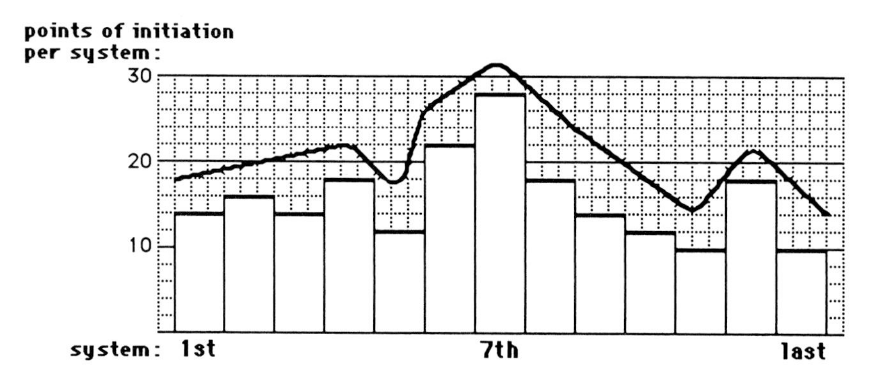

Figure 5.10 Broad event rate and trajectory of excerpt 11

in activity, backing off momentarily before surging to a peak of continuous activity in the middle of the movement. Gradually relaxing, a low point of energy is reached near the end, interrupted by one last modest surge of rapid, isolated note groups before quietly concluding.

> We will begin listening for similarities and relationships, later for divergences from a familiar and established ordering. For we will most probably attempt to order the increasing totality of what we have heard, and are hearing, as it happens. (Childs 1977)

A piece of music is "a moving object," so to speak, and before we can determine its mass of material content, we must design and understand its intended trajectory through time.

INVENTION 10 Construct a basic rhythmic event of three to six elements related to a notated pulse (say quarter notes). Note its character in terms of agogic stress—where is its longest duration, at the beginning, the end, or somewhere in between? Make variants of this basic event, stretching and shrinking the rhythmic range. Make other variants by compressing and expanding its event rate, using smaller or larger values which maintain the same relative proportions or still present the agogic stress at the same location in the event.

Choose several of these variants and experiment with ways to elide them in pairs; find one or two elements at the end of one which can also serve as the start of another. Now find ways to elide the pairs to make a whole connected string of variants. Contour might now be introduced by drawing notes on a one-line "staff," above or below and touching it, or above or below and separated from it. This gives five increments of register, like an ever-changing arpeggio of a five-pitch chord.

Bar lines may also be drawn preceding any note with metric stress (whose beginning coincides with the beginning of a pulse unit of time) but no more often than every two beats. Notice, then, whether or not the pattern of durations of measures thus made is conforming or elastic.

In selecting variants and constructing event streams, plan a particular unfolding scheme and try to select variants or alter them even more to realize that scheme of change. Here are some example schemes:

A compressing event rate along with a shrinking rhythmic range;
An arch form of compressing and then eventually expanding event rate;
A compressing rhythm of accent and contour stresses;
An expanding metric stress rhythm.

INVENTION 11 Write out a long stream of conforming values, say eighth notes, with no bar lines and all of one repeated pitch on a staff.

Place accent marks over some of these elements in an unpredictable pattern. Think of each accent as starting a substream, then make each substream with a different number of notes, odd numbers followed by even, numbers with no common integer factor.

Now apply another elastic pattern of stresses by changing occasional notes to a higher pitch. Some of these contour stresses may correspond to the accented notes, but some should not.

Analyze the composite rhythm of the two stress patterns as they interact. Think of this as a kind of hidden counterpoint under a uniform duration surface, and use this point of view to suggest other similar designs.

INVENTION 12 A stream will be constructed consisting of a succession of bursts of rapid, short conforming note values, each followed by a rest, a silence.

First, plan a scheme for the lengths of time from the onslaught of one burst to the onslaught of the next (what Yeston might call a "middleground attack interval"). The scheme can be expressed as a series of numbers for the clock time (in seconds) of the successive durations.

The scheme may involve gradually expanding durations, gradually compressing durations, or a more elastic alternation of individual expansions and compressions of the rhythm between beginnings of events.

Then, for each duration in this stream, determine how many short sounds will comprise the burst. An event duration can be nearly full of or almost devoid of sounds. This aspect of rhythm should be designed in relation to the kind of large-scale rhythm already planned, either expanding, compressing, or elastic. For example, an expanding event-inception rhythm might be coupled with an elastic pattern of changing extents to which the event durations are filled with rapid sounds. Or a very elastic event rhythm could be coupled with a consistently expanding or contracting pattern in the number of sounds per event.

Draw out the realization of these interacting patterns on a time-proportional grid (with a scale such as 2 cm = 1 second), representing sounds by dots each placed in height on the graph according to a sense of pitch register. The results could be readily improvised with a piano (without or with pedal), a collection of percussion instruments, or even an ensemble of players of various instruments, each of whom would execute the number of note-dots shown for each burst in a kind of "tutti" sprinkle of sound.

INVENTION 13 To make a stream, choose a meter with an even number of pulses per measure. In that meter, design two separate one-measure patterns: one which is relatively conforming in surface durations with an accent to provide some differentiation and interest; the other which is highly elastic in surface variety. Place its agogic stress to fall at a different point in its measure than the point of accent in the conforming measure.

Now choose a meter with one less pulse per bar than the original meter. In this shortened measure, write the two basic events, making whatever shortening adjustment seems best to fit within this shorter measure.

A two-voice canon can now be constructed. Start the original meter and its first event simultaneously with the shortened measure of the contrasting event type. Each voice will continually alternate event types after this simultaneous but opposing beginning.

Barlines can either be independently drawn, being careful of vertical alignment to mark time correspondences, or else express the odd-measured events in the even-measure meter with whatever ties are necessary to get these events across the "foreign" barlines.

As each voice continues alternating event types, the rhythms of each may be varied by such simple means as gradually inserting short notes into the elastic rhythms and replacing notes of the conforming rhythm with rests.

When both voices are simultaneously to begin an event, let that moment be cadential, a final arriving sound of longer duration in both voices. (This will occur at a mathematically predictable moment, according to the phase relationship set up. For example, six–beat and five–beat patterns will synchronize again after thirty beats or five of the sextuple measures.)

Any kind of varied noncanonic pitch contour may be applied to the results.

OTHER READINGS

Books:

Cooper, Grosvenor W., and Leonard B. Meyer. *The Rhythmic Structure of Music.* Chapter I "Definitions and Principles." Chapter VI "Rhythm, Continuity and Form." Chicago: University of Chicago Press 1960.

Kramer, Jonathan. *The Time of Music.* New York: Schirmer Books 1988.

Lester, Joel. *Rhythms of Tonal Music.* Carbondale: Southern Illinois University Press 1986.

Yeston, Maury. *The Stratification of Musical Rhythm.* Chapter 4 "Structures that Arise from the Interaction of Strata." New Haven, Conn.: Yale University Press 1976.

Articles:

Childs, Barney. "Time and Music: a Composer's View." *Perspectives of New Music* 15 no. 2: 194–219.

Elston, Arnold. "Some Rhythmic Practices in Contemporary Music." *Musical Quarterly* 42 no. 3: 318–29.

Erickson, Robert. "Time-Relations." *Journal of Music Theory* 7 no. 2: 174–92.

Rowell, Lewis. "The Subconscious Language of Musical Time." *Music Theory Spectrum* 1: 96–106.

Smither, Howard. "Rhythmic Analysis of 20th Century Music." *Journal of Music Theory* 8 no. 1: 54–88.

Stockhausen, Karlheinz. "Structure and Experiential Time." Trans. by Leo Black. *Die Reihe* 2(1955): 64–74.

CHAPTER 6
PITCH SPACE

When we hear a tone's pitch, we perceive it as being metaphorically high or low in a kind of sounding space. Acoustically and physiologically, we are perceiving the rate of periodic cycles of sound producing that tone's pitch: the greater or lesser the cycles' frequency rate, the higher or lower the tone's placement in our imagined **pitch space.**

The study of musical structure has always been concerned in particular with the dimension of **pitch.** Thanks to the thoughts of music scholars over hundreds of years, we have now an exceptional understanding of and appreciation for many intricate subtleties in tonal systems, relating pitches in schemes such as scales and triads. So, too, for many composers, choosing and combining pitches is an extremely important part of their work and their style. Great effort may be expended in creating, placing, and manipulating pitch combinations in original ways.

For many, this is probably a visual process, at least metaphorically. A space is pictured in the mind—possibly with the aid of a real spatial object, a keyboard. Designing ways to arrange that pitch space is like imagining a building or the outlines of a drawing. Interval structures are registral patterns of space made by choosing and ordering pitches. They create an important part of the sound character of a composition, its **pitch language,** a term used here in a general sense to mean any coherent quality of patterns in pitch space. Modern musical practice has established an accepted precedent for the freedom to explore fully all kinds of patterns possible in the pitch universe. But *coherent quality* suggests that along with that freedom there must be an intelligent approach to building some syntax of related patterns.

Spatial features of pitch patterns become vividly important in the composer's mind when designing the pitch language of a new piece. Inventive processes of some sort must be at work; identifying some of the more basic of those processes is essential in learning to compose in pitch space.

TUNING

First of all, the composer must have some notion of a kind of space to work in. How large is the space? Where in the whole universe of pitch are its ceiling and floor? And how will the space be divided? What measuring stick will mark the increments or small steps in space? The usual answer to this last question, most often arrived at by tradition without conscious consideration, is a division into octaves with each octave divided into six equal "tones" or twelve **semitones.** The octave is indeed rather universal, recognized in most cultures and most historical periods of music as the most primary **interval** or division of

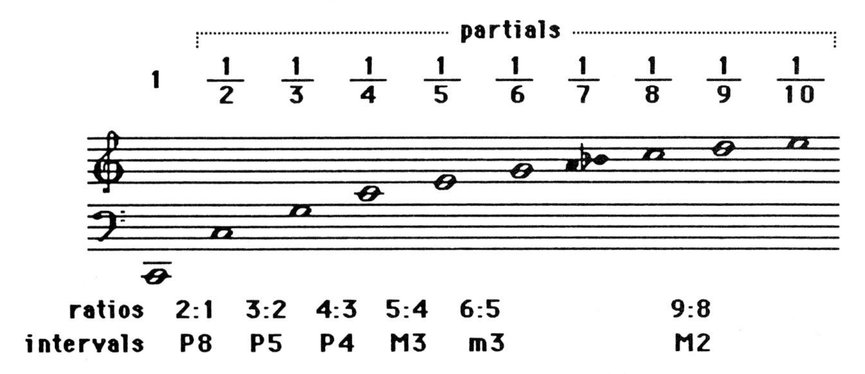

Figure 6.1 The overtone series of partials and ratios

pitch space to make a smaller segment. As the Greek philosopher and theorist Pythagorus recognized, it is based on the simple ratio of 2:1, so that a vibrating string or air column in a pipe, if shortened to one-half its original length, will make a pitch one octave higher but with a very similar sound. The evolution of a system for dividing octaves into twelve equal parts is a complex story both historically and mathematically, the result of which is the tuning of all modern pianos and other keyboard instruments.

Pythagorus discovered that the octave's 2:1 ratio was just the start of a series of divisions of a vibrating string into parts. Each simple whole-number ratio in a series produces a musical interval. This series produces the same intervals that relate overtones, the components of a sound resulting from the simultaneous vibrating not only of the whole string or air column but more slightly in several parts. As they are subliminally perceived, partial vibrations play an important role in our perception of tone quality or musical color, sometimes called **timbre.** Figure 6.1 shows the most important lower part of the series, which actually keeps going up into smaller and smaller intervals with higher number ratios. The seventh partial is marked doubly in black because its pitch is actually between the two indicated pitches of our modern chromatic scale.

Invoking only the simplest two intervals, the octave and perfect fifth, a tuning system can be devised. Start from a base pitch, going up successively by the 3:2 perfect fifths until twelve pitches in all have been produced. Then use 2:1 octaves to bring them all into one octave of pitch space. *Voila!*—a tuning scale.

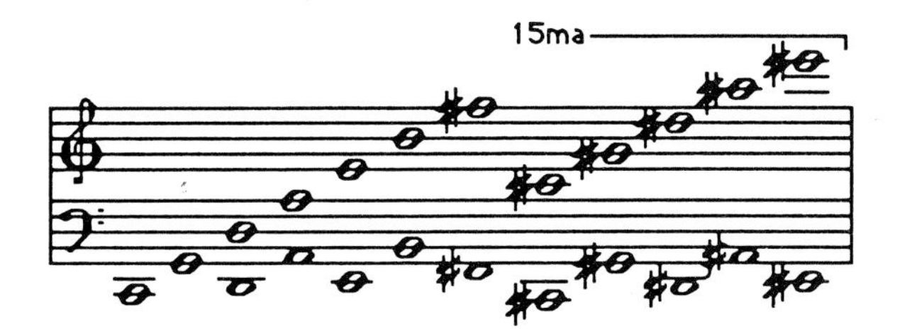

Figure 6.2 Tuning system with a cycle of true perfect fifth intervals

But there is a problem—going up one more 3:2 perfect fifth from the last pitch tuned, the E-sharp, doesn't bring us back to a pitch octave related to our original base C—it's too high. The discrepancy, called a *comma,* prevents the system from ever closing precisely. In fact, with historical dismay, we find that the intervals other than the perfect fifths around any pitch are all different sizes than those surrounding any other pitch in the scale. We have too many interval sizes, many of which do not match any size interval in the overtone series, the acoustical basis of our pitch sense.

Historically, the solution to this lay in tempering the perfect fifth, shaving it a bit smaller than an acoustically pure fifth to shrink the comma out of the system. Then all the intervals are very slightly out of "natural" tuning but completely consistent surrounding any pitch of the scale. The ratio of the resulting basic semitone interval is roughly 1.06 to 1.

It is in this system that the vast majority of composers and music scholars of the Western world think. However, some bold innovators, mostly Americans such as Harry Partch and, more recently, Ben Johnston, have explored other ways to tune a system of pitches, dividing octaves into more than twelve increments. The boldness of their innovations is exemplified in the fact that they were forced to invent entirely new notations and even new instruments to write and play their "microtonal" music. As discussed in chapter 1, **CONTEXTS FOR LEARNING** and in chapter 3, **MEDIUMS AND IDIOMS,** this is a part of the composer's compelling urge to control the parameters of his own creative design.

Our discussion of pitch space will focus, however, on the mainstream, equal-tempered twelve-tone tuning, the basis not only for chromatic tonality and so-called "twelve-tone" music and "atonal" music but also for other current modes of pitch organization with familiar or synthetic scales.

SCALES

Scales are the basis of most harmonic languages, an embodiment of all the interval potentials of a pitch organizing system. A scale is an abstract collection of pitches constituting the resources for building lines and chords. Octave related pitches (or, for that matter, enharmonically related pitches like D-sharp and E-flat) are considered members of the same **pitch class,** so that a collection's pitch classes can be represented within one octave of pitch space, usually in ascending order. By octave equivalence, in turn, the scale extends beyond this octave as far up and down as desired in pitch space. When pitches are collected—arranged close together within an octave in ascending order—the successive intervals from one pitch to the next form a **scale pattern.** It does not show all the intervals in a collection, only those on the "surface," but provides a simple recipe for constructing the scale.

When we say "scale," we usually think first of the common major and minor scales traditional to western music for almost four hundred years. They are the descendents of the church modes used for many hundreds of years before their rise to exclusive use. All the church modes and major and minor scales are seven note scales classed as **diatonic** because there are two basic building intervals in their collections, the wholetone and semitone.

Some scales have a focal point in the interval structure, a place for a pitch we are accustomed to understand as the center for the entire configuration of all intervals in the scale. If such a **pitch center** or tonic, as it is traditionally called, exists in a scale, its location is usually shown at the beginning and end of the scale. Figure 6.3 is an example of a scale used in Joan Tower's *Wings* **(excerpt 2)**.

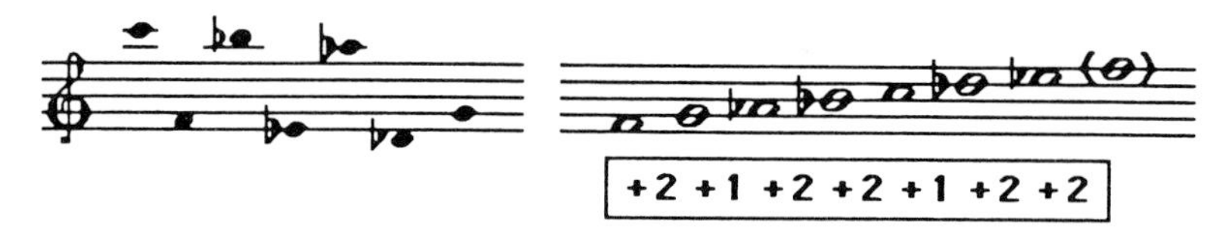

Figure 6.3 Scale collection in line 5 of excerpt 2

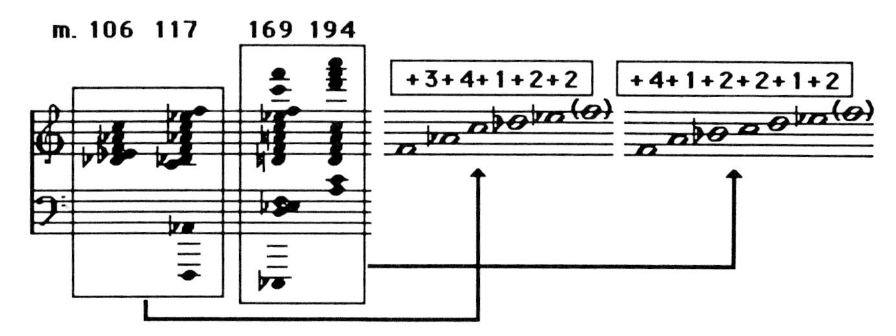

Figure 6.4 Scale collection in John Adam's *Harmonium*

The pitches used in the middle of the second movement of John Adam's *Harmonium* (1981), for orchestra and chorus, reveal two scale-like patterns. The first looks like an incomplete minor scale, the second like a mixolydian mode missing only one pitch class, G. As the scales in *Wings,* both show F as their pitch center.

SETS We usually think of scales as collections of a particular size, seven pitches per octave like the diatonic scales or thereabouts. But the pentatonic scale has only five notes per octave and the octatonic scale has eight (thus its name). If we broaden the notion of a scale beyond these traditional limits of sizes and names, we can use the same collecting and cataloging procedures to understand any size group of pitches. A **set** is just that, the abstract representation of the fundamental interval structure of a pitch collection of any size. Just like a scale, this representation uses octave equivalence to place representative pitches within a space of one octave arranged in ascending registral order. This way, even though a collection of pitches may not come from a commonly named scale, its octave-recipe scale pattern can still be identified and its interval configuration understood and related to that of other pitch collections. For instance, the chords in figure 6.5 from **excerpt 4** may look completely unrelated but can be derived from the same set.

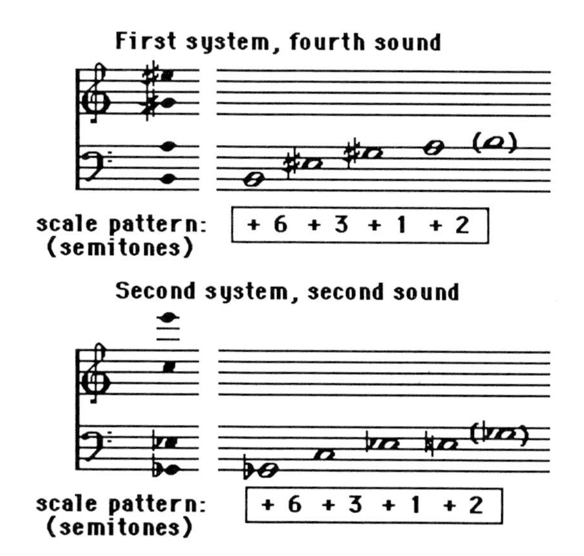

Figure 6.5 Comparing pitch class sets of two chords from excerpt 4

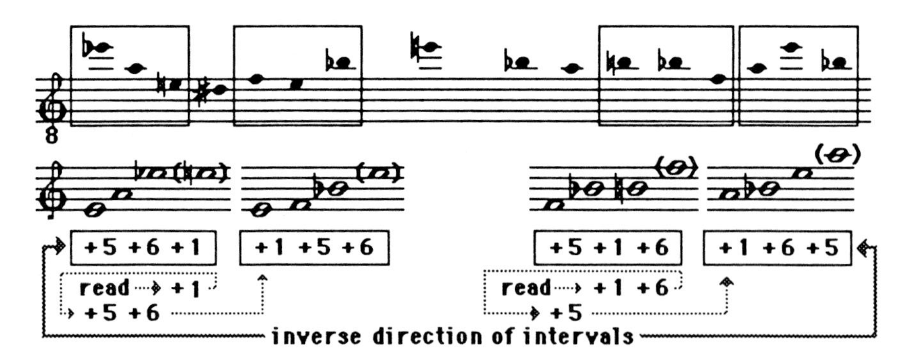

Figure 6.6 Related sets in the guitar line, first system of excerpt 8

A scale pattern expresses only one arbitrary octave of a scale or set collection. Octaves are really circular in nature like the face of a clock; finishing one octave, a pattern starts over in the next. Choosing to place a different pitch at the start (the bottom) of a representative collection will simply **rotate** the scale pattern which expresses it. Collections that seem distinct may actually just be different rotated versions of the same set.

To see this relationship, consider the sets formed by some of the guitar's pitches near the beginning of **excerpt 8,** as shown in figure 6.6.

The first and last of these sets show a more significant difference; they have the same scale pattern in reverse direction. This indicates an **inverse** relationship, an interval set configuration turned upside-down.

Scales and sets, then, are ways of segmenting pitch space by a one octave pattern that marks pitch points in all other octaves. They are broad patternings of the universe of possible pitches, selecting some and excluding others according to a spacing guide, all to limit resources for building actual pitch patterns.

CONSTELLATIONS

With this as an abstract background, we can start to think about actual strings of pitches (lines) and stacks of pitches (chords), particular patterns of pitches selected from a source scale or set and actually placed in pitch space. To invoke a metaphor, we will call such a particular pattern in registral space a pitch **constellation.** It differs from a scale and set in acknowledging specific octave places and distances in pitch space rather than abstract, octave-condensed interval potentials. A constellation is a real and specific pattern segmenting a particular chunk of pitch space.

Although primarily a registral phenomenon considered "out-of-time," a collection of pitches forming a constellation may be musically manifested in any time order—as a chord or simultaneity, or as a simple or elaborate arpeggio, as a segment of a line, or as a combination of pitches presented by different contrapuntal parts in a close context of time and texture. (More will be said later about ordering a line of pitches in time from successive constellations.) A pitch may play a role in more than one constellation; thus, constellations may intersect as well as join. In figure 6.7, taken from the first seven measures of **excerpt 3,** a line is seen to be comprised of several successive constellations, some intersecting.

Pitch constellations have both a registral order and a time order. The pitches in a constellation may be simultaneous or successive in time. Their registral order is identified by arranging the pitches from lowest to highest (even though they may appear in some other time order) but *not changing any octaves.* Measured simply in semitones, the resulting registral succession

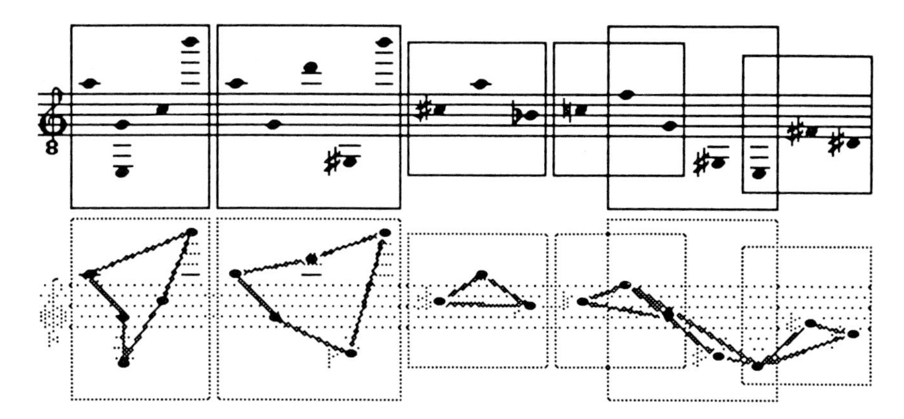

Figure 6.7 Pitch constellations in m. 39–45 of Carter's *Changes*

of intervals might be thought of as an ascending arpeggio of a chord, an **interval stack.** Intervals are best measured by the number of semitones for several reasons.

Traditional interval names are based on thinking of examples of intervals at particular locations in major and minor scales; this may be cumbersome and irrelevant if those scales are not really in operation organizing the pitches and intervals. Traditional interval names also make bad arithmetic precisely because they are not measurements of pitch space at all but names of sample scale segments. Stack a P5 (a "perfect fifth") on top of another P5; the resulting combined larger pitch space is a M9 ("major ninth") . . . P5 + P5 = M9! But measuring the intervals in semitones, 7 + 7 = 14. Much cleaner as well as mathematically sensible, the semitone-sized identifications are much easier to see forming, matching, and changing interval patterns in various interval stacks being related.

Now in figure 6.8, we can examine the interval stacks found in the three successive pitch constellations of figure 6.7.

The interval sizes shown in the stack are not all the intervals present in a constellation, only the intervals between pitches closest in space. The larger hidden or underlying intervals are important but easy to identify.

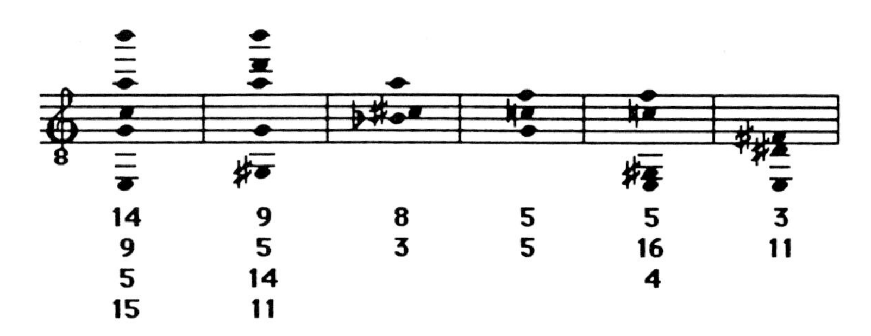

Figure 6.8 Interval stacks of pitch constellations, m. 39–45 of *Changes*

INTERVAL FRAMEWORKS

Because of its acoustical importance already discussed, the octave often serves in harmony as the interval at which to duplicate pitches in other registers, making a large sonority. It is, in fact, the interval traditionally used to project a scale or set throughout a whole pitch space. In interval stacks, however, other intervals can also serve in this way, especially those near an octave in size—10, 11, 13, or 14 semitones. Such intervals are crucial in determining the general aural quality of a constellation. A stack's framework is revealed by adding adjacent interval sizes, bringing to the surface its larger underlying intervals.

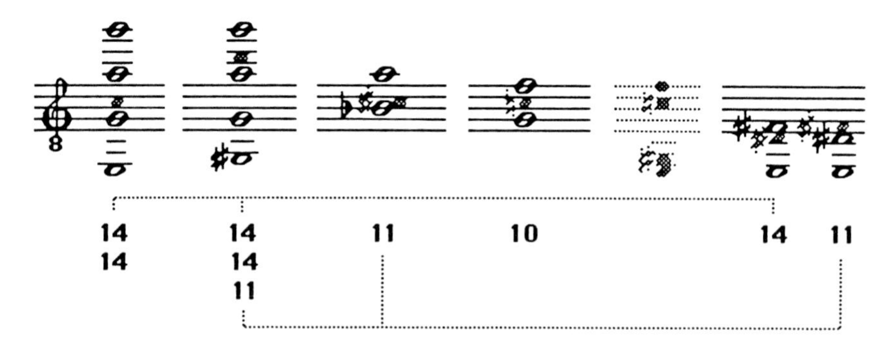

Figure 6.9 Frameworks of interval stacks

Doing this, in figure 6.9, to the interval stack of each constellation in our preceding examples, we find that 14-semitone intervals and 11-semitone intervals are common to the stack frameworks of the first three and last constellations.

INTERVAL QUALITIES

Now that we are conscious of these "hidden" but important intervals, we can begin to recognize some of the interval qualities that make the various characters of constellations. This will be important in selecting source interval stacks and guiding their coherent transformation. The acoustical simplicity or complexity and a possible symmetry of intervals are some considerations.

When two pitched tones sound in the same air, their waves—very fast compression waves of air—interfere with each other. The more similar the lengths between the waves, the stronger the interference. Similar wave lengths means similar frequencies and correspondingly close pitches. Thus, two tones close together in pitch space make an acoustically complex interaction. A tone close in pitch to a strong overtone such as the octave second partial of another pitch has a similar effect though not as strong. Basic three-note constellations whose interval stacks contain the most acoustically complex intervals only one semitone different in size from an octave or unison—1, 11, and 13 semitones—have an acoustically complex quality of dissonance or tension. They can be considered members of what we will call **interval quality GROUP 1.**

Finally, those basic interval stacks with no intervals close to an octave or unison make a final **GROUP 3** with familiar qualities associated with their identities as **triads** of various sorts.

Interval stacks with none of these intervals (1, 11, or 13 semitones) but containing an interval two semitones different in size from an octave or unison—2, 10, or 14—comprise **GROUP 2.** Those intervals possess some of the tension of the elevens and ones, but their brightness is warmer, more rounded.

Any basic three-pitch constellation containing an octave, 12 semitones, or a multiple of octaves, has a special quality. The pure and simple but hollow interval of the octave and the focus it places on its two pitches affects the constellation's consonance and balance. Such a constellation will have a special character within the interval quality group determined by its other intervals.

For examples of the contrasting natures of the three interval quality groups, we can return to the string of pitches in our first example of constellations, figure 6.7. Nine consecutive pitches from measures 42 through 44 of Carter's *Changes* form three three-pitch constellations, each with an interval stack belonging to a different interval quality group.

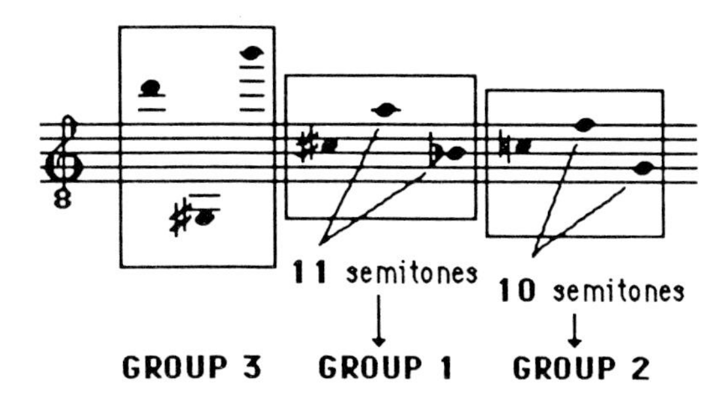

Figure 6.10 Interval qualities contrasted in pitches from excerpt 3

Play them on a piano both melodically while holding down the damper pedal and as chords; compress the first one by lowering the D and B an octave and raising the G-sharp an octave to minimize its difference in overall pitch space; you should still hear quite distinctly the three very different qualities.

Any constellation of three pitches can be placed into one of the three groups as a very general appraisal of its sound quality. But what about larger constellations of more than three pitches? Four pitches, for example, make a total of six intervals, only three of which would show in the interval stack. Now appraising the constellation's general sound quality is not so simple. But the quality groups for basic interval stacks of three-pitch constellations can still be used. Think of a larger interval stack as a pattern of interlocking basic stacks showing two intervals each but sharing one interval with the next basic stack. Then the group number of each basic stack contributes to a collection expressing interval qualities in the larger constellation. For example, at the beginning of the sixth system of **excerpt 8,** Barbara Kolb's *Songs Before an Adieu,* the guitar repeatedly strums a five-pitch chord in the less ordinary order of highest pitch to lowest (actually an upward motion on the instrument's strings). It is shown here in the octave it will actually sound, since guitar music is always written an octave higher in order to use only the familiar treble clef.

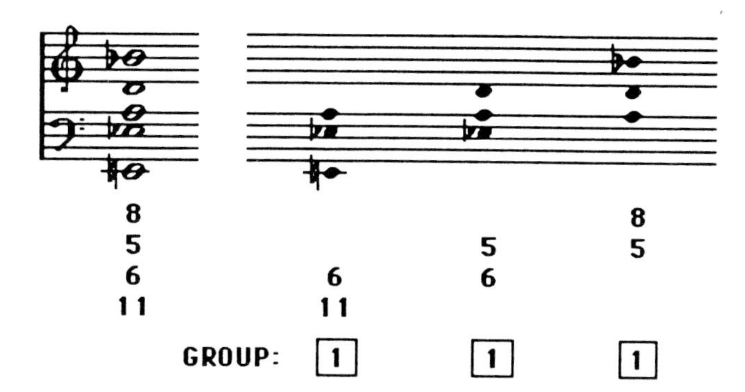

Figure 6.11 Guitar chord, beginning of sixth system of excerpt 8

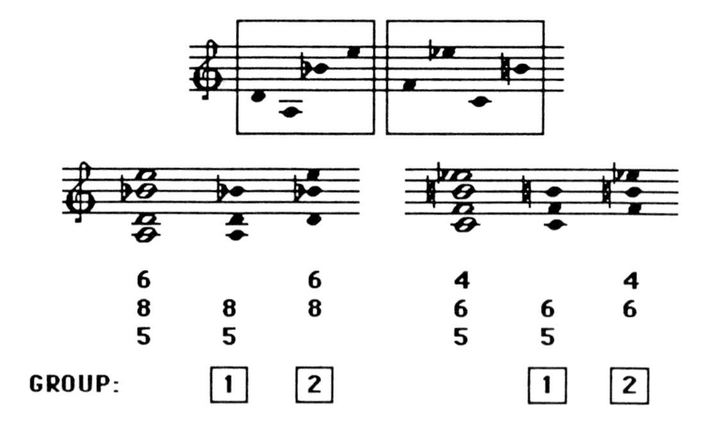

Figure 6.12 Vocal pitches, beginning of sixth system of excerpt 8

As a whole, this five-pitch constellation has interval combinations predominately of one quality, GROUP 1. The combination of basic stacks in a larger constellation might be mixed in character, however, showing different group numbers for its constituent basic stacks. The eight pitches sung during the repetitions of this guitar chord form two four-pitch constellations, each with a mixture of GROUP 1 and GROUP 2 qualities, as shown in figure.

MORE ABOUT PITCH CLASS SETS

At this point, we should note the correspondence of our interval quality groups with the classification of three–note set types standardized by Allen Forte. (See *The Structure of Atonal Music* or Rahn's *Basic Atonal Theory.*) The theoretical approach to sets categorizes only the possible combinations of completely *different* pitch classes, excluding stacks with octaves. Also, two sets with scale patterns inverted in relation to each other are considered the same **set type.** In this way, any set of three pitch classes can be placed in one of twelve possible types.

This is quite an abstraction, generalizing interval quality to a broad extent. In a distilled fashion, however, since it echoes our grouping of interval qualities in stacks, a comparison of approaches is worthwhile. Figure 6.13 shows

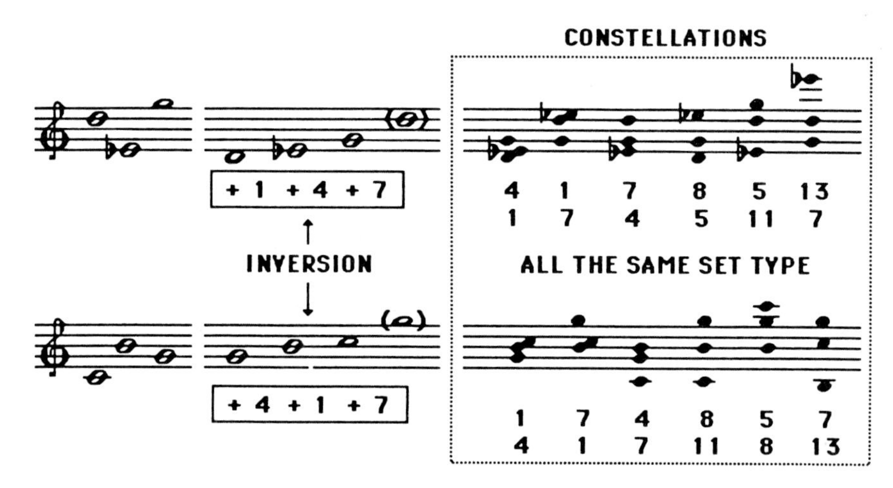

Figure 6.13 Variety of interval stacks in one set type

Height: / Set-type	2	3	4	5	6	7	8	9	10	11	13	14	15	16	17	18	19	20	21	22	
1	1 1									1 10	2 11	1 13								11 11	
2		1 2							1 9	2 9	3 10	3 11	2 13						10 11		
3			1 3					1 8		3 8	4 9		4 11	3 13				9 11			**GROUP 1**
4				1 4			1 7			4 7	5 8			5 11	4 13		8 11				
5					1 5	1 6				5 6	6 7				6 11	5 13					
6			2 2						2 8			4 10		2 14				10 10			
7				2 3				2 7	3 7			5 9	5 10		3 14		9 10				**GROUP 2**
8					2 4		2 6		4 6			6 8		6 10		4 14	8 10				
9						2 5			5 5			7 7			7 10		5 14				
10					3 3			3 6					6 9								
11						3 4	3 5	4 5					7 8	7 9	8 9						**GROUP 3**
12							4 4							8 8							

Figure 6.14 Basic interval stacks with no octave: set type, framework, interval quality group

a set of three pitches with its scale pattern followed by several actual constellations made from the three pitch classes. Then three different pitches making a set with an inverted scale pattern yield several more possible constellations.

In addition to being of the same set type, all of these interval stacks are in GROUP 1. The set types draw together large families of some rather different interval patterns. On the other hand, they do not acknowledge the similarity between many interval stacks which have the same framework. Basic interval stacks **4 7** and **3 8,** for example, both have the important 11 semitone framework and are both in our GROUP 1, but fall into different set types.

The chart given in figure 6.14 will summarize the comparison of modes of thinking by correlating each basic interval stack containing no octave with its set type as well as with the size of its framework. Now the interval quality groups are clearly visible blocks.

Useful by their generality for analysis of already composed music, set types are broad categorizations of interval relationships. Constellations and their interval stacks are not really categories but actual descriptions of interval patterns in pitch space. They provide a way of thinking about a pitch combination that suggests how to move on to other pitch combinations in a coherent fashion. Interval quality groups are just initial aural assessments to help start becoming familiar with the vast variety of constellations possible in pitch space.

TRANSFORMATIONS

A particular interval stack can not only be used repeatedly as the basis for a simple continuity of language, it can be subtly changed by strategically adding, removing, or respacing intervals. Thus, different interval stacks are formed, each sharing some qualities with the one that generated it. **Transformations** are operations demonstrating similarities between two constellations by showing how the interval stack of one could be derived from the other, the basic means of variation in a coherent compositional process. It is important to note that these transformations work with interval structures; specific pitches are necessary simply as markers locating the resulting interval stacks in pitch space. This implies the seemingly radical idea that intervals are more important for the composer to think about than pitches. Indeed, creative thinking about pitch primarily involves proportioning segments of space—**intervals.**

Here, then, are ways to make subtle changes in an interval stack, ordered beginning with the transformations of least impact on the sound quality of the stack:

Open—To expand an interval by an octave, adding 12 semitones

Fuse—To join two adjacent intervals to make a larger interval, the sum of their sizes

Delete—To remove an interval, shortening a stack's height

Subdivide—By inserting a pitch, to divide an interval into two smaller intervals whose sum will equal the original interval

Propagate—To append or insert an interval of a size already present in a stack, making another basic stack identical to one in the original

Invert—To reverse the entire registral order of intervals

In figure 6.15 the same starting stack is treated in three different ways, each time with two stages of transformation. Note that to open an interval or invert a stack does not change the number of elements; to fuse or delete removes one element; to propagate or subdivide adds one element.

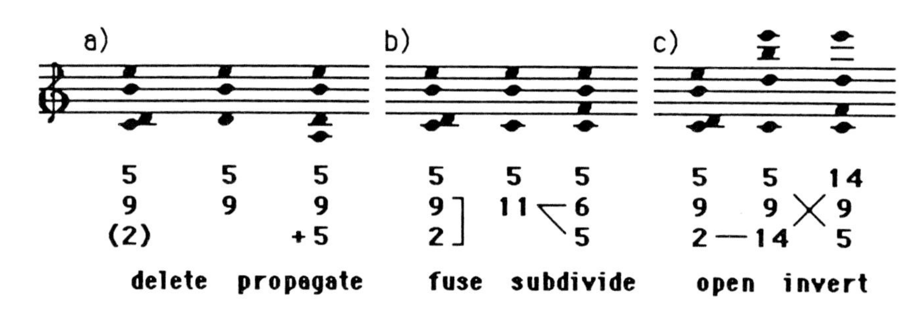

Figure 6.15 Examples of simple transformations of an interval stack

SIMILARITY

While generating many closely related interval stacks, transforming operations bring out interval differences in a rich diversity of qualities. Composers instinctively think this way, starting with some choice of pattern, then varying it, exploring its transformational potential. The beauty is in the paradox of a process that both relates and differentiates. Imagine a group of constellations, all of which are relatively simple transformations of one basic stack. (Overindulging in metaphor, we might call this a galaxy!) Or a basic stack could generate a long chain of related but diverse constellations transformed one to another.

On the other hand, a more remote interval association is indicated when the derivation of one stack from another can be achieved only by a long string of transformations. In this way, how different two constellations are in interval quality can be assessed by how many transforming operations are necessary to change one into the other.

ALTERATIONS Other operations are also possible which would have a greater impact, significantly changing interval quality. They produce interval stacks of noticeably different character. As with transformations, they are defined in order progressing toward the most sweeping alteration possible without losing all resemblance to the original interval stack:

Redistribute—To fuse two intervals and then subdivide the resulting interval into two smaller intervals different than the intervals originally fused

Stretch or **shrink**—To alter one interval size by other than an octave, leaving others unchanged

Expand or **compress**—To alter all intervals by adding, subtracting, multiplying or dividing by some constant number, preserving only the possible symmetry of the original stack

In figure 6.16 the stack of a three–pitch constellation is successively altered in all five different ways, resulting in five distinctly different constellations.

compress stretch redistribute shrink expand

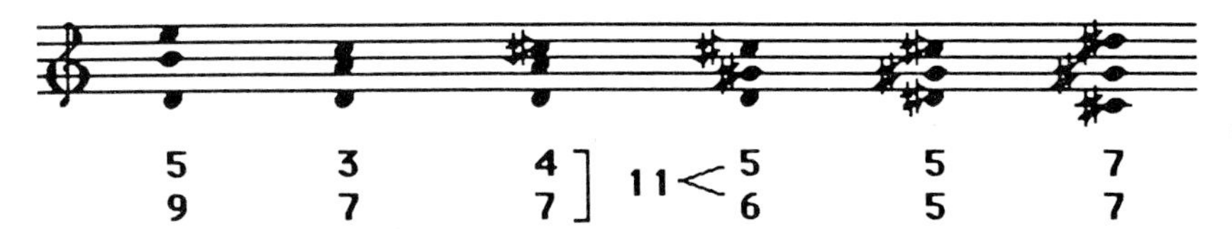

Figure 6.16 Operations significantly altering quality of an interval stack

When used in actual musical contexts, constellations may be surrounded in time by their transformed relatives. For an example of this, figure 6.17 examines the four guitar chords that precede the one analyzed in figure 6.11. More remote interval connections could be used as well to form a transformational stream of basic connections in a coherent interval scheme.

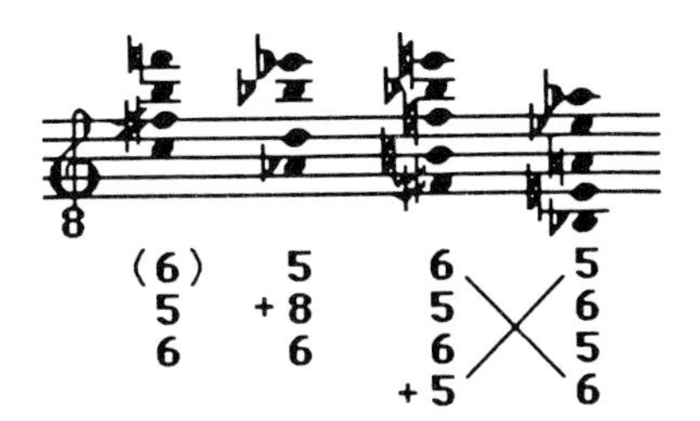

Figure 6.17 Close interval association in guitar chords, line 5 of excerpt 8

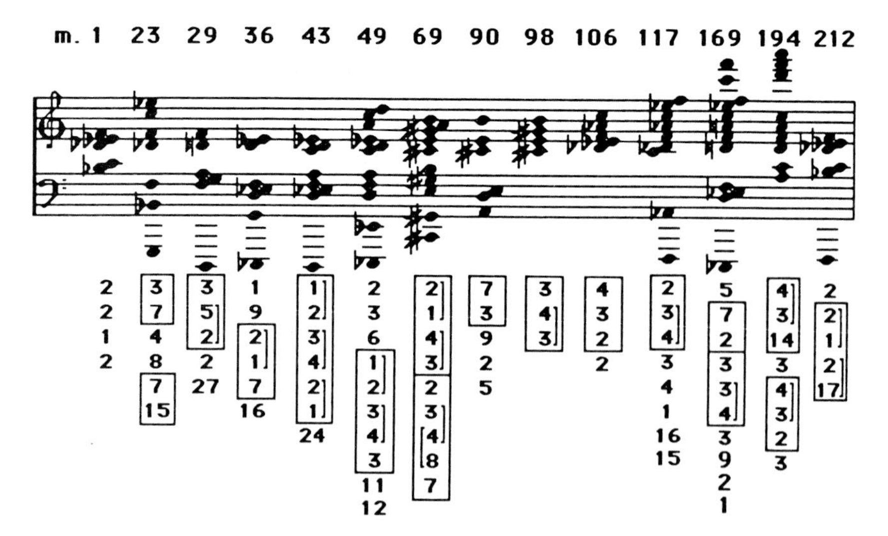

Figure 6.18 Broad constellations of *Harmonium's* second movement

The pitch scheme for the second movement of John Adam's *Harmonium* is a procession of constellations, some rather large, each articulated in time so elaborately that its presence can be prolonged for many measures. Their interval stacks are all drawn from **triads** and **scale clusters,** making a high degree of intervallic similarity and coherence. Figure 6.18 shows their pitch contents and many manifestations of one triadic pattern, the basic interval stack, **7 3.**

A very large source stack is also possible, thinking of a process of filtering or carving out instead of amplifying and filling out. To see this process at work, we will consider more closely a segment of *Harmonium,* measures 169 to 193. This passage is intricately orchestrated with segments of a large constellation (actually more detailed than shown previously) articulated by different sound colors as distinct smaller constellations.

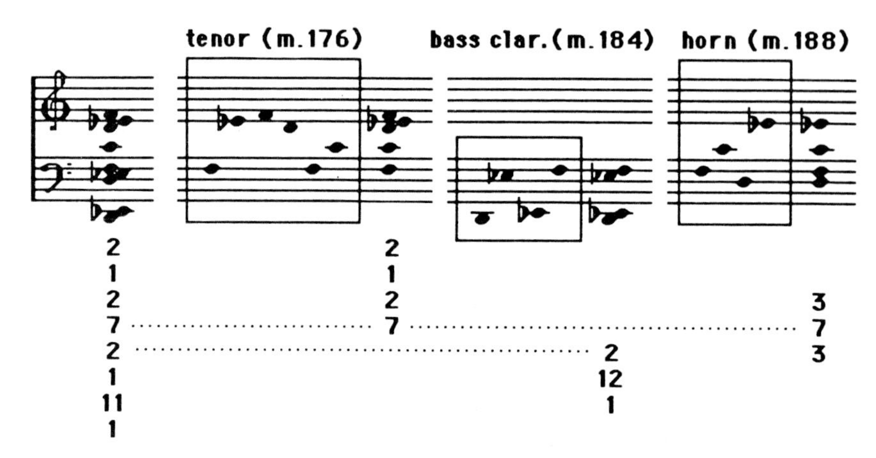

Figure 6.19 Smaller constellations articulated in m. 169–193 of *Harmonium*

TRANSPOSITION AND PITCH CONNECTION

Linking constellations not just by interval similarities but through their actual pitch content provides another kind of connection. Factors making certain transpositional levels of two stacks produce a more connected succession of constellations are:

Common tone—Specific pitch shared by two constellations

Semitone displacement—A pitch in a constellation only one semitone away from a pitch in the previous constellation

Figure 6.20 compares five different relationships of transpositional level between the same two interval stacks; they range from remote or no pitch connection, through connections only by semitone displacement, to a close pitch connection involving two common tones and a semitone displacement.

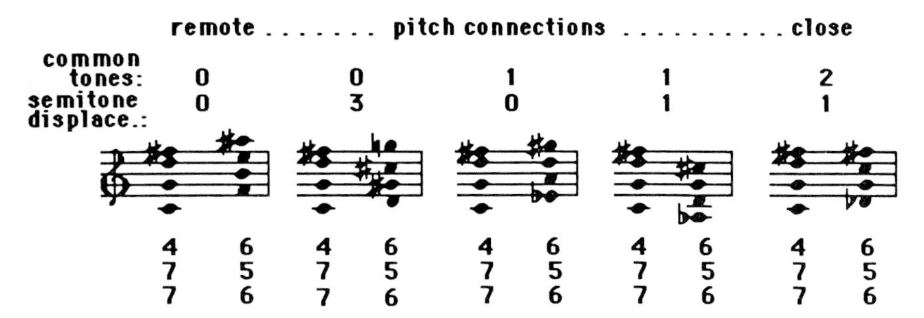

Figure 6.20 Degrees of connection between pitch levels of interval stacks

One traditional way to take advantage of pitch connections and make a strongly cohesive group of constellations is to have one pitch common to all. That "super" common tone can be sustained while the other pitches change around it (called a "pedal point" from the tradition of doing this with one of the pedals of a pipe organ); or it could be reiterated in some prominent way to highlight its connecting role. Even without either textural emphasis, the effect will be a strong feeling of connection, possibly even a stationary feeling that movement has been frozen. The pitch scheme from the beginning of the second movement of *Harmonium* shows many common tones between constellations, creating a steady, slow-moving quality that balances the very animated quality of their rich rhythmic textures.

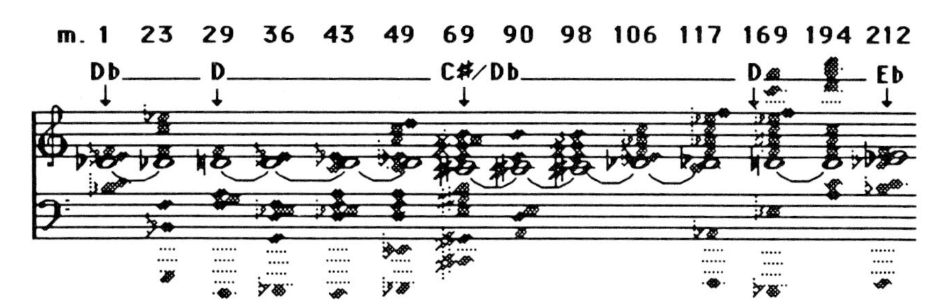

Figure 6.21 Pervasive common-tone pitch connections in *Harmonium*

SUCCESSIONS OF CONSTELLATIONS

Pitch connections can complement or contradict interval associations from one constellation to another. A succession of constellations, each on some pitch level, is like a stream; its flow or sense of progression is a kind of momentum. Close interval associations or pitch connections make low momentum, a gentle flow without strong sense of progression. More remote interval associations or pitch connections make higher momentum, more forceful flow or sense of change. **Pitch momentum** in a stream of constellations, then, is the degree of interval and pitch change. It can be assessed by identifying the extent of interval transformation (which contributes momentum) and the degree of pitch connection (which retards momentum) in each succession from one constellation to the next.

Mixtures of these qualities can promote a satisfying sense of balance, as when there is close interval association with little pitch connection, or remote interval association but thoroughly close pitch connections. Many processes can be designed to explore such possibilities, and figure 6.22 shows some examples. In it, the first series of chords alternates between various transformations of two basic interval stacks, with consistent pitch connection by common tone and semitone displacement. The second stream of sonorities utilizes a different process, a variety of transformations all from one source stack, **8 6,** with no common tones from one to the next, only semitone pitch connections.

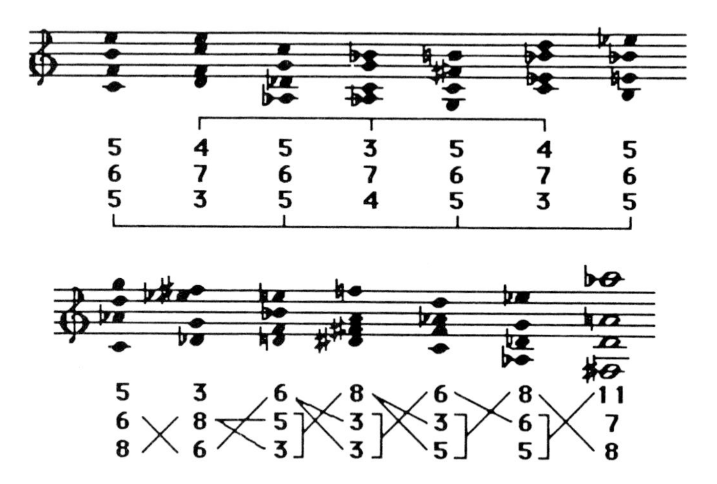

Figure 6.22 Sample processes for constructing transformational streams

Such transformational processes can make coherent streams of constellations. With the concept of pitch progress to guide the flow of those streams, the infinite, colorful possibilities of chromatic pitch space can be inventively explored.

TIME ORDERING PITCHES

Constellations, then, are a way of thinking about order and patterns in pitch space. When a succession of constellations transpires, pitch space is opened or unfolded, sculpted, shaped and reshaped in time. Some simple ways of unfolding pitch spaces in time are basic schemes for planning the registers of textures in a piece.

A space can be opened suddenly just by presenting a constellation as a chord (the pitches of a constellation sounded together in time). The whole pitch space that may be utilized by other constellations to follow might well be larger than the opening chord, however. Then a more gradual opening can be built, leading to high and low points within the succession. Those high and low points might arrive simultaneously or each at their own special moments, marking "corners" in the unfolding shape of pitch space. The same considerations apply to closing a pitch space in a sudden or gradual way.

Not all successful schemes for opening and closing pitch spaces are such distinct progressions of ceiling and floor outward and inward. In fact, most

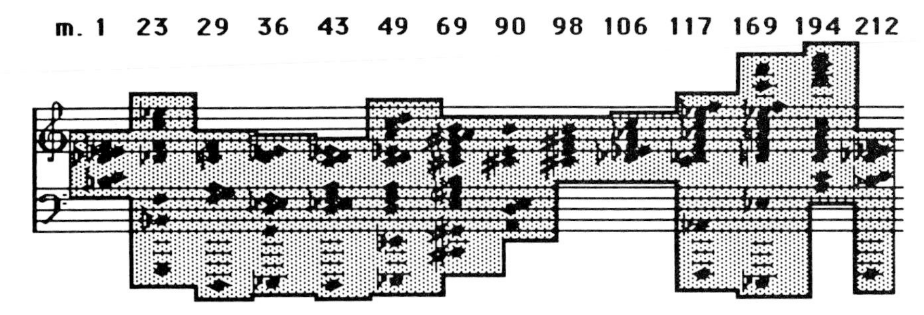

Figure 6.23 Unfolding of pitch spaces in the second movement of *Harmonium*

actual successions of constellations make a rather jagged progress toward a goal, making frequent small expansions and contractions of pitch space (figure 6.23). Such detours allow elaborately contoured shapes to form while still being controlled by the overall trends of an underlying scheme. The bays and inlets of coastlines bounding a peninsula are shaped just this way, small interesting variants in an overall shape. Although the view of a coast may look quite different depending on your vantage point—jagged or restlessly convoluted when viewed from its sandy shore, a broad smooth curve viewed from an airplane or satellite photo—the seemingly contradictory shapes are intimately related. It is, after all, the net effect of many small possibly jagged changes that create the larger trends.

The first stage, then, of planning the unfolding of pitch space in time is choosing a broad scheme to open and close the space and when to reach high and low points at the boundaries of the space to be used. The second stage is considering how smooth or jagged will be the lines made by the tops and bottoms of each chunk of pitch space in succession, the constellations.

As a succession of constellations is designed, aspects and relationship of internal pitch and internal structure then become important. How strong the interval continuity, how many close pitch connections from one constellation to the next add to the choice of whether the top or bottom of the space will pull in or bulge out.

Finally, when a succession of constellations is established, there is still one more stage of decision making about shape. The individual pitches of each constellation can be ordered in time, presented one-by-one in a line instead of as a chord sounding simultaneously. Although the results can resemble chord arpeggios, countless other patterns are possible. At this stage, however, the many possible procedures for ordering do result in patterns of a few basic types:

Ramp—Pitches of a constellation presented in a straight ascending or descending order

Wave—An alternation of ascending and descending ramps, through a constellation then turning to go back through it again, or through one constellation then turning to go through the next

Spiral—Compound ramps and waves—just as in the general unfolding of pitch spaces, ramps and waves can take small detours while maintaining the progress of their general shapes

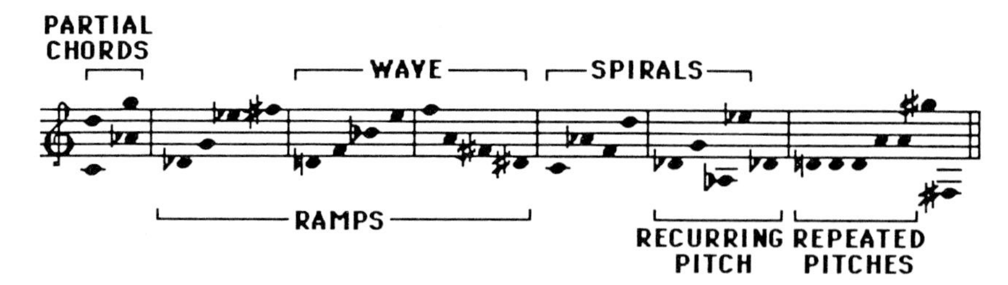

Figure 6.24 Prototype time-orderings of constellations

Recurring pitch—Presented more than once in the ordering of a constellation's pitches, tones begin to take on a role as focal points within the space

Repeated pitch—Actually more a function of rhythm, immediately repeated pitches affect the pitch shape of a line even more emphatically than just sustaining it longer than others

Using the stream of constellations in figure 6.22 as a source of pitches, figure 6.24 gives brief examples of these processes.

When these procedures are mixed together, a line with intricate and dramatically varied shape can be made. One other possibility, drawing out the interval **residue** of a line by selectively sustaining some of its pitches to sound together with subsequent pitches, is mainly a contrapuntal technique and will be discussed in chapter 8, **MUSICAL ARCHITECTURE.**

SERIAL ORDERING

The process of ordering pitches in time from a succession of constellations can be formalized. Serial processes with rows are now a traditional means of organizing pitch space by establishing and continually reusing a particular way of ordering pitches. The most common kind of row is a series of intervals which will present in some order all twelve possible pitch classes. If a certain tonal quality is desired and patterns can be made which achieve it, those patterns can be used again and again. This is true for the selection of intervals to construct constellations and the pitch connections between them as well as for the ordering of their pitches in time, making what is called a **pitch series.**

To demonstrate fixed serial patterns, let's consider in constellation terms a now very common technique, the **twelve-tone row.** We will start with a succession of four three-note constellations (fig. 6.25).

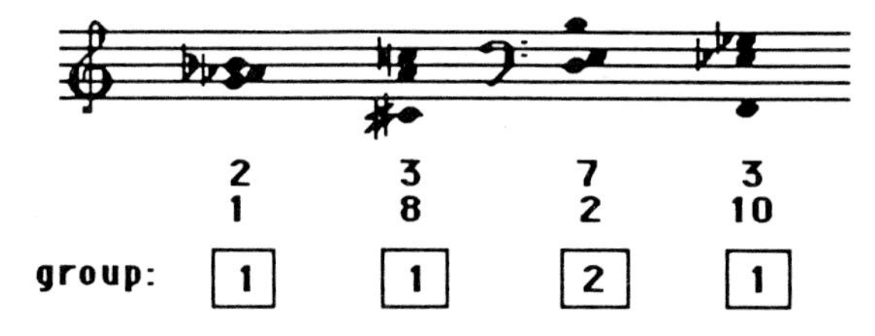

Figure 6.25 Constellations to begin building a tone row

Notice that none of these constellations has an octave as any of its three intervals. Also, there are no common tones from one to the next or, for that matter, between any two of the constellations. This all means that each of the twelve semitone divisions of octaves is represented. And since there are only twelve notes, no **pitch class** (as these semitone divisions of every octave are called) is represented more than once.

Next, let's order these twelve pitches in a way just as stated by the piano near the end of Austin's *Sinfonia Concertante* (fig. 6.26), **excerpt 15.** Now we

Figure 6.26 Twelve-tone row as played by piano at 53 of excerpt 15

have a unique and nonduplicating ordering of all twelve pitch classes, a particular way of expressing the chromatic scale. This linear pattern takes on a life of its own in a serial ordering of pitch space. It can become the pitch shape of melodies or contrapuntal lines.

Any row can be transformed in three simple ways. Each kind of transformation preserves the general pattern of intervals in the original row, but supplies a new succession of pitch classes to express those intervals. Before we learn those transformations, we need a way to identify a general interval pattern so that we can trace it through transformations of a row. Remember that a representative of a pitch class can be found in any octave. Then consider the octave arrangement of the *Sinfonia* row in figure 6.27.

Figure 6.27 Row arranged to show all ascending intervals

In this arrangement, all the intervals are the smallest possible **ascending interval** to get to some pitch of the next class. Now we can do the simplest transformation, **transposition,** quite easily. We can start on any pitch and just move up by the same **serial intervals** through all the other pitch classes. Starting on B-flat produces the pitch series found in the woodwinds (fig. 6.28).

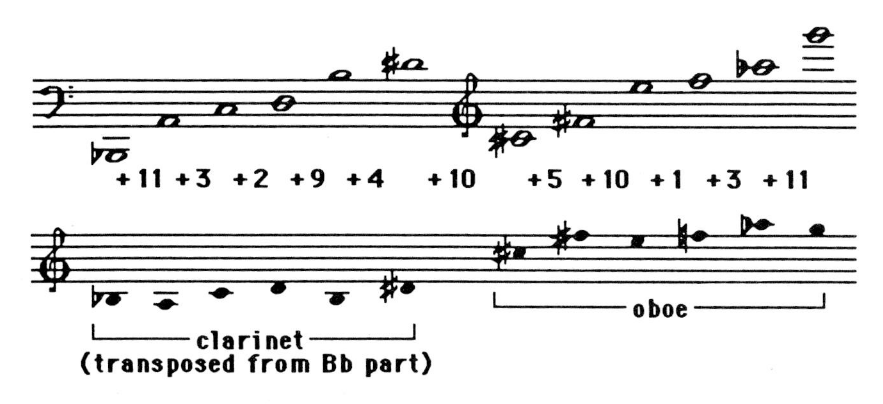

Figure 6.28 Transposition of row to clarinet/oboe level at 53 of excerpt 15

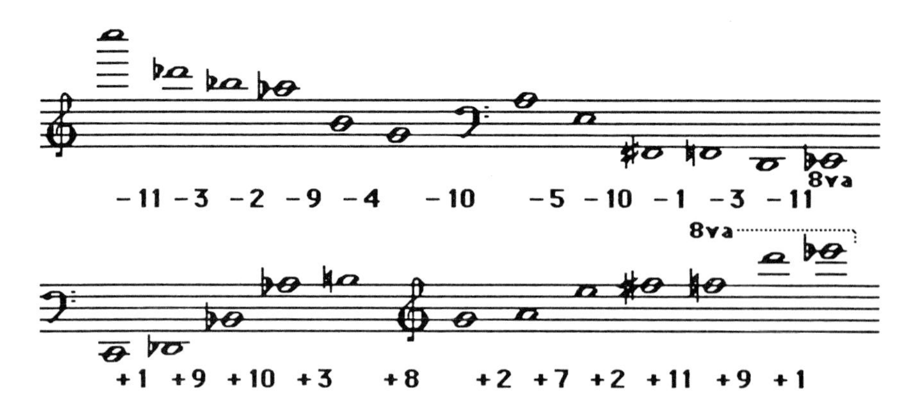

Figure 6.29 Inversion of row, showing equivalent ascending intervals

Note that the clarinet is a B-flat **transposing instrument.** That means that its first note appears in the score as a C but will actually sound as a B-flat. In fact, the pitch specified in any instrument's transposition name is precisely that—the pitch that will sound when the player reads a C.

Making an **inversion** of a row is also quite simple, turning each successive interval in the opposite direction. If we do this with the ascending ordered form in figure 6.28, we get a succession of pitches going down (figure 6.29). If that ordering of pitch classes is put into our standard form with all ascending intervals, the interval sizes are the complements of the original ascending interval sizes. (The sizes of the original ascending serial interval and the **ascending equivalent** of the inverted interval always add up to twelve.) Now we can quickly make an inverted form of the row starting on any pitch by moving through the series of complementary ascending intervals. Starting on the pitch C, we'll do just that but with a reminder that the resulting pitches can be freely placed into any octave to make more interesting shapes.

One more kind of transformation can be applied to any original, transposed, or inverted form—the time order of pitches reversed, making what is called a **retrograde.** Showing the retrograde of an inverse form of the *Sinfonia* row will explain the continuation of the piano at S4. The last two pitches of its initial thirteen-note group were a low F (the last pitch of a row form shown in figure 6.26) and an unexplained extra pitch, E. Now we can explain the E's presence as well as its shared role with the F to link row forms carrying into the next note group in the piano (fig. 6.30). So the low F near the end of the initial piano note-group plays a double function as the last pitch of one row form and the first pitch of the next form used. This is a common technique for choosing row forms and their transposition levels to link one to the next in a coherent way.

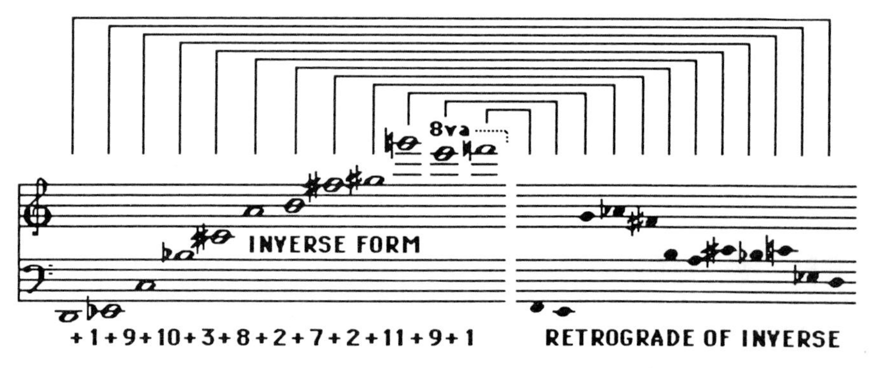

Figure 6.30 Retrograde of inverse form and its piano setting after 54

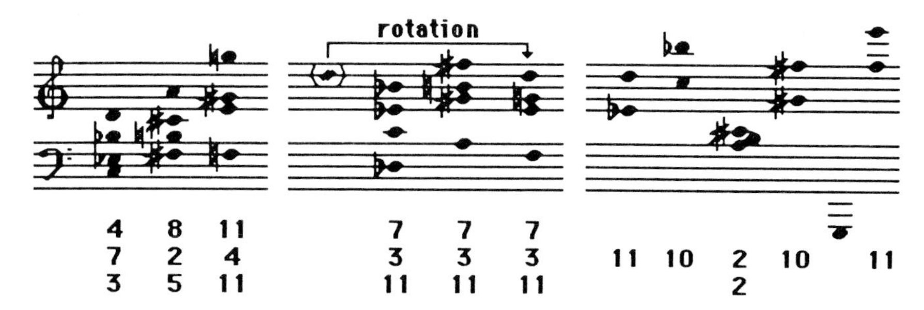

Figure 6.31 Segmenting and rotating the same row in a variety of ways

A row can be used to make chords as well as lines simply by collecting up a few successive pitches to sound together. Collecting adjacent pitches of the row into a chord can form many different successive constellations, depending on how the collecting process is segmented. Using the inverse form starting on D shown in figure 6.30, several very different chord groupings with different interval stacks can be made, showing some of the many possibilities. With the rotation of one pitch, simply transfering it from one end of the row to the other, the middle example of figure 6.31 produced a startling result: three four-pitch constellations with identical interval stacks. Each of these sample ways to segment the row produced results quite unlike the others and unlike the quality of patterns as used in *Sinfonia Concertante.* One row, transformed and segmented in so many possible ways, is a highly fertile source for making patterns in pitch space.

These are the bare essentials, the basic tools for generating time-ordered patterns in pitch space by a formalized serial process. The universe of possible pitch patterns to explore in this manner is virtually infinite, and so are the variations one can devise in a personal technique. For example, a row need not use all twelve pitch classes, nor need it avoid duplicating pitch classes. Stravinsky used in canon a simple five-tone row for *In Memoriam Dylan Thomas* (1954), and two entirely different rows for a very late work, the elegant and sonorous *Requiem Canticles* (1965–66). Anything is possible with such a versatile, inventive tool as a series.

Rows and, for that matter, constellations are modes of thinking about arrangements in pitch space, ways to explore a vast universe of possibilities. Stravinsky is an excellent model, having conducted his explorations with discipline, crafty intelligence and, above all, a keen "ear" for sonority. The result in each of his pieces was a vivid and unique coherence of patterns in pitch space. And that is, after all, the goal of every composer.

INVENTION 14 Trying any strategically or randomly chosen pattern of pitches, make up a six-note scale different than the whole-tone scale. Play the pattern, listen to it carefully and repeatedly to identify which pitch if any sounds like a focus or center of its interval environment. Then rearrange the pitches into an ascending one octave catalog, putting that focal pitch on the bottom. Identify the scale pattern of the result.

Write out all eleven other transpositions of the scale (or six-note set if you prefer to think of it in those terms). Find the transposition which has the fewest pitch classes in common with the original. These two will make a pair of scales with the same scale pattern but contrasting pitch contents.

Many uses are now possible for this pair of scales. Here is one: spin out a melodic line from one scale, accompanying it with simple chords of two or three pitches each from the other scale. When this arrangement tires, switch scales between melody and chords.

INVENTION 14 VARIATION Use the same six-note scale as before or design a new one, perhaps a five-note set. Make a melodic line, using all its pitches just once rather than repeatedly as before. When all the original pitches have been used, the last will become a linking pitch to a transposition of the scale or set. Any transposition containing this pitch can be chosen. If there is more than one possibility for that, think about how many pitch classes each one has with the previous scale. You may choose transpositions with the most contrasting pitch content or the most similar content.

Make a melodic ordering of pitches from this next scale, then repeat the process, taking the last pitch used as a link into the next scale level.

INVENTION 15 Choose two different basic interval stacks for constructing three-pitch constellations. Make a succession of chords which alternates between the two interval stacks and has no common tones.

INVENTION 16 Make a succession of four-pitch constellations, each of which is a different transformation of the same basic interval stack. Choose pitch levels for the constellations to make some common tone connections from one constellation to the next.

INVENTION 17 Make a succession of five-pitch constellations with highly varied interval qualities by altering each to make the next. Try to use as many semitone displacements as possible. (This may come out sounding a bit like Chopin, especially if you start with an interval stack emphasizing GROUP 3!)

INVENTION 18 Build a four-pitch constellation you like the sound of and write it at the end of a staff line. Identify its interval stack and think of two different transformations of it. Write those transformed stacks at the beginning and middle of the line, finding pitch levels for each that will produce common tones with the original constellation at the end of the line.

Design alterations from the first stack and transformations from the middle stack. Find pitch levels for constellations with these stacks, in the early stages seeking close pitch associations by common tones, then later avoiding common tones and instead emphasizing semitone connections.

INVENTION 19 Make a twelve-tone row in the way described in the previous discussion. Then make an inverse form of the row whose first pitch is the same as the last pitch of the original. Then make a transposition of the original whose first pitch is the same as the last pitch of the inversion just made. Experiment with choosing octaves for each pitch to shape a line. Don't be afraid to use very large intervals. Plan to play it on the piano instead of singing it.

Now search for a pitch here and there to remove from the stream and place into a supporting line. Think of the intervals it will make with the pitches following if it is sustained in an octave below the main line.

OTHER READINGS

Books:

Cowell, Henry. *New Musical Resources.* New York: Something Else Press, 1969.

Forte, Allen. *The Structure of Atonal Music.* New Haven, Conn.: Yale University Press, 1973.

Hansen, Howard. *Harmonic Materials of Modern Music: Resources of the Tempered Scale.* New York: Appleton-Century-Crofts, 1960.

Hindemith, Paul. *The Craft of Musical Composition.* Arthur Mendel, trans. New York: Schott, (1942) 1970.

Messaien, Olivier. *Techniques of My Musical Language.* Paris: Alphonse Leduc, 1944.

Partch, Harry. *Genesis of a New Music.* Madison, Wisc.: Univ. of Wisconsin Press, 1949.

Perle, George. *Serial Composition and Atonality.* Berkeley, Calif.: Univ. of California Press, 1962.

Rahn, John. *Basic Atonal Theory.* New York: Longman Inc., 1980.

Articles:

Berger, Arthur. "Problems of Pitch Organization in Stravinsky's Music." *Perspectives of New Music 2,* no. 1 (1963): 11–42.

Chrisman, Richard. "Describing Structural Aspects of Pitch-Sets Using Successive Interval Arrays." *Journal of Music Theory* 21, no. 1 (1977): 1–23.

Kresky, Jeffrey. "A Path Through Density." *Perspectives of New Music 23,* no. 1 (1984): 318–33.

CHAPTER 7
SOUND COLOR

Color is a quality often ascribed to music. It seems to exist in the very nature of musical sounds. We know intuitively that color is important in music; the absence of color is, in reality, the absence of sound itself.

Is color ever not important in music? One would think never. But to better understand the significance of our world of musical color, we should think of situations where color seems a relatively unimportant compositional consideration.

Is color unimportant when the piece is composed for an unspecified musical medium? Here, the composer doesn't indicate the sound-making means, furnishing only the durations and dynamic levels of the pitches to be performed; or the composer provides a scheme for improvisation by any group of players or singers. With the absence of compositional choice of color, the composer actually causes the importance of color in a piece of music to be enhanced. Bach's *Art of the Fugue,* an open, unspecified score, and Cage's *Variations III,* cited in the opening chapter for its seeming abrogation of color choice, are, nevertheless, "colorful" in performance. One can't reasonably argue that the absence of specific color choice negates the importance of color in these pieces. Indeed, the open choice for the performer can actually lead to quite inventive use of color, the value of the performance and even the piece often judged, in great part, by that very factor.

Is color unimportant when the work is for a solo instrument, a single sound source, or voice alone? Only if we mistakenly assert that there is no range of color change within that instrument, sound source, or voice. A colorless instrument or voice is a physical contradiction. Even the electronically generated sine tone with its single, fundamental harmonic, the simplest and "purest" of sounds, has a dark, almost foreboding lowest range; a neutral, familiar test-tone-like mid-range; and a bright, even piercing high range. We can't dismiss such perceptions.

Is color unimportant when the work is for a group of the same instruments or a group of instruments of the same family? Here, the fascination a composer might have with a particular musical color is certainly of prime importance. The composer composes for, say, a choir of cellos, precisely because of the cello's broad range of colors, as well as the rich combination of sound colors many cellos together can produce. And, of course, the string quartet's attraction as a "family" ensemble is its potential for both blend and distinction of similar instrumental colors—the two violins, the viola, and the cello.

Is color unimportant when the composer wishes to put a particular part of the composition into "colorless" relief? Here, the absence of or flatness of color in the course of a piece actually causes the listener to develop a heightened awareness of color contrast, when it eventually occurs. Color, by its informed and thoughtful use, is form-giving.

Is color unimportant when the piece is integral to a sound installation and meant to be a part of the special acoustical environment? Here, the composer's sensitivity to sound color is vital, if, for example, the piece is to succeed in blending natural sounds with carefully designed musical sounds.

Color in music, then, is important. Our notions of what it really means are, however, often unclear, hard to articulate and in turn hard for the less experienced composer to make part of the modeling process. We stated at the outset that color is the nature of music's sounds. How do we come to this conclusion when so much of what we study in music separates out the pitch and rhythmic domain from color? We study orchestration, the musician's traditional discipline for learning about musical color, separately from harmony and counterpoint. But the presumption, in this case, that timbre is everything about a sound except pitch and loudness is contradicted by the fact that modifying pitch and loudness changes the characteristics of the sound, its timbre.

The nature of a sound is its timbre, its color. A sound is identified by its color, as it unfolds in time. **Frequency** and **amplitude**—pitch and loudness—are both functions of time. Color, then, is a multifaceted phenomenon of music. Color is the spectral envelope of a sound, not only its timbre but the evolution of its pitch, loudness and timbral characteristics in time.

COLOR AND TRADITION

Music's established, traditional colors are, of course, readily identified and categorized. Orchestration textbooks, with their detailed itemizations of instrument ranges and characteristic use in orchestral scores, are indispensible to the composer in first learning the basic possibilities of instruments in combination.

Before continuing with our discussion, however, we must clarify our use of such well-known musical terms as instrumentation and orchestration, explaining, as well, our adoption of the newer musical term, coloration. **Instrumentation** is the musical medium(s) chosen to create particular kinds of sound color and color combinations, including all mediums of musical expression: vocal, instrumental, electroacoustic, intermedia, and/or any combination of musical means designated by the composer. **Orchestration** refers, as it has traditionally, to both the instrumentation and coloration of the medium of the modern symphony orchestra, chamber orchestra, or other comparable grouping of primarily traditional orchestral instruments. **Coloration** is the modeling of sound color in a piece of music.

Interestingly, while the traditional musical terms—*orchestra, instrument,* and *score*—have been carried over into the terminology of the computer music medium to describe the functional relationships between the sound colors (instruments), their combination (orchestra) and continuity (score), the term *orchestration* hasn't seemed appropriate, even metaphorically. Instead, a word like *design* is substituted. Apparently, when computer music practitioners fashion sound colors as part of their compositional modeling process, they feel they are undertaking something more fundamental than the realization of an orchestration: they design a total coloration for the piece.

Coloration, then, is a complex, dynamic phenomenon, where the composer models specific colors in succession and combination. This chapter will focus on elucidating coloration as a powerful, form-giving part of the composer's modeling process.

THE COMPOSER AND COLOR

With all that has been stressed so far about the importance of color in music, the anomaly is that the composer, most commonly, does not always choose the overall array of colors a particular piece will have—as an artist might experiment with the mixing of different colors, the most appropriate becoming integral to the composition of a painting. Instead, the composer is given the task, invited or commissioned to compose for a particular instrumentation, say a piece for clarinet, cello, and piano—three distinctive instrumental colors, each having its own rich timbral spectrum of color variety. True, composers experiment with speculative, unusual color combinations, but, by and large, such color experiments usually reveal even more the strength of well-known color combinations. The symphony orchestra, for example, except for enlargement of the wind, brass, and percussion sections, has remained relatively unchanged in instrumentation for two centuries. This is both because of its acceptance by our culture as a rich resource of instrumental color combinations and the traditional repertory that continues to be important. Composers, intuitively and through experimentation, learn that certain color successions and/or combinations in the orchestral medium work well, others not. Does it follow that composers, who become expert in their knowledge and use of tested color combinations, will necessarily create model, artful scores? No, that depends on the individual composer, of course; but there are other critical factors that impel us to explore musical color itself, its perception in music and how we as composers can become more creative in its use.

THE DYNAMISM OF SOUND COLOR

As listeners, we know that a performer playing all the proper pitches in tune and in proper rhythm never impresses beyond nominal skill until control over the color nuances of the instrument and the music yield the beauty of what we term **interpretation** in performance. Similarly, the composer, appreciating and invoking the potency of music's color realms, can imbue a piece with a real, interpretive quality, properly performed and presented. The color of a musical sound is dynamic, changing in time. That's why continuous, relatively unchanging sound from a machine, for instance, unless it is overbearingly loud, is quickly relegated to the background of our aural consciousness. It is of no interest because it lacks change, even subtle change in coloration. An apparent contradiction to this exists, however, in performance practice of the traditional classical music of our culture: the closer to a consistent, seemingly nonchanging color a performer can achieve throughout the range of an instrument, the more expert that performer is considered. What is really happening is that, as listeners (including the performer, as well) we experience the aural illusion that the instrument is being controlled consistently throughout its range, when dynamic changes in color are actually taking place continuously. What, then, does the composer gain from developing a fine sense of musical color and its use in the modeling process, if it seems contrary to what we seemingly want to experience or even contrary to traditional performance practice?

Careful use of color can bring dynamism to the form the composer's piece is taking. The piece can be given a particular hue that evokes an essential character in its continuity: the color can, in fact, become the prime focus of the piece. Sharply contrasting or subtly similar colors can be explored to give the piece vivid piquancy or slowly evolved shadings. Color can be used to extend a line, to sustain a texture, to create a sudden contrast, to realize an expectation, or to mark an important arrival point. A vivid, colorful impression of a piece's form can thus be achieved.

It is significant to note that electroacoustic and computer music systems can produce continuous, uninterrupted, virtually unchanging sound—never having to pause to take in another lungful of air or draw the bow in the opposite direction or strike the keys over and over. Color and the dynamism of controlled, subtle change can, more than ever before, become prime compositional challenges in this medium.

The advent and spread of the use of such systems has heightened awareness of the importance of understanding color not only among practitioners of computer and electroacoustic music but among composers universally. This heightened sense and growing knowledge of the nature of sound and the potential for new musical explorations has, interestingly, caused composers and performers to listen anew to traditional acoustical instruments. A new array of instrumental colors have been explored, evoked rarely in instrumental scores before the last half of the twentieth century. Indeed, such explorations and use of these "extrainstrumental," nonidiomatic colors have given rise to an era of "textural" pieces, as they are often referred to, where change in textural color detail is paramount in the continuity of the piece. Not only are new instrumental colors being explored, but there is a new understanding and appreciation of the color potential of the most natural musical instrument, the human voice. The voice—speaking, singing, or simply sounding—is one of the most complex vibratory phenomena, its parameters of pitch, amplitude, and formant in constant, complex interaction. Analysis of the pitches in a single, spoken word, for instance, reveals as much as an octave pitch fluctuation, especially if the word is expressively inflected. Automated, computer-synthesized voices, without careful design, sound unreal, artificial, precisely because they lack this dynamic process of color change that is natural to the human voice.

Our highly developed musical systems of tuning, dividing each octave into twelve equidistant pitches, and our durational gradations in metered notation seem crude compared to the potential of continuously variable color systems that are being devised. Indeed, computer music practitioners are concentrating on such color systems with more and more impressive results.

HEARING COLOR

Composers intuitively grasp how they hear color in music but find that gift difficult to explain deductively. This faculty to "hear color" is sometimes referred to as synaesthetic: a sensory impression from an impression of another sense. In this case the aural impression being experienced is described by a familiar visual impression. This **synaesthetic** process is, of course, common to all human beings and understood with ease. Among composers it is a heightened and carefully cultivated technique.

Not being able to taste, touch, smell, or see a sound, we quite naturally attribute qualities to it that are modeled and assimilated in our sensory experience: the visual, spatial, tangible, or even "taste-ible" of our everyday world. "I want this sound to be dark and distant, but dry." Or even, "That was a deliciously rich sonority!" Sounds are dark, bright, light, thick, thin, distant, close, shaded, masked, brilliant, somber, wet, dry, or transparent, all words understood in the world of vision and space. As music theorist and phenomenologist Thomas Clifton (1983) explains in his important book, *Music as Heard: A Study in Applied Phenomenology,* musical color's perception is synaesthetic. ". . . it is a movement of the body, not a product of deductive thinking." He explains that the sense organs are not functionally independent of one another, as we tend to think of them. They are, instead, part of a "centralizing self" which is constantly synthesizing all discrete perceptions we experience. "There are no empirically 'dark' or 'bright' tones, but there is an indivisible self for whom the experience of dark or bright tones constitutes a meaning." In other words, the "lines of communication" among the senses are always open, and the senses are always comparing and exchanging messages (Clifton 1983, 66). Such synaesthetic experience is exemplified in our perception, for example, when we see the juiciness of an orange without having to taste it or the coarseness of sandpaper without having to feel it. Our perceptive sense of color in music is synaesthetic as well: the experience of music is "seen" as more than strictly an acoustical phenomenon. It stimulates our visual sense as well. It is our integrated system of comprehending the world. And when that world specifically includes a piece of music, its creation and perception is auditory, visual and even tactile. Synaesthetic perception is experienced, and, in the composer's case, that suggests a kind of synaesthetic modeling. Clifton suggests that:

> . . . the search for new sonorities throughout musical history was motivated by the awareness of the special meaning they bring to a composition: a meaning which establishes not only its uniqueness but a prepredicative immediacy. Most importantly, these nameless sonorities convey the self into the presence of the unknown, an experience both disturbing and lonely. (1983, 68)

In a sense, musical sonorities remained "nameless" until the seventeenth century, when composers like Monteverdi began to specify the instruments they preferred for performances of their music. It is significant, too, that the development of the modern concept of composing as an artform concurred with this new awareness of the importance of color and sonority. Assigning specific instruments to specific musical roles caused instrumental coloration to be an important factor in the texture and, in the largest sense, the architecture of the composition.

At this point we should stress that synaesthetic processes having to do with sound nominally involve only the **degree of luminosity** in colors, ranging from, say, brilliant to dark or from transparent to opaque. With some unusual exceptions, we never seem to carry this association further to the primary colors and their derivatives. There is no consistent method for producing a musical sound that could be called a red sound or a green sound or a yellow sound, though fascinating theoretical and aesthetic forays have been made in this mysterious realm. Include in a score the instruction, "dark," for a clarinetist, and the composer can expect an experienced clarinetist to muffle the higher harmonic partials in the tone; substitute, say, "green," and the same clarinetist will probably be puzzled by the instruction, asking the conductor or composer what such a word means in terms of the performance.

As a caveat, we stress further that to carry synaesthesia to its extreme, where it is, from time to time, claimed that there is a direct correlation of specific visual colors—red, green, yellow and all their derivative colors—with specific pitches, keys, instruments, scales, melodies, or harmonies, is interesting to consider and quite regularly put forward; but its theories only seem to apply to individual synaesthetic experiences of composers (Scriabin, Messiaen, MacDowell, Gretry, Busoni), poets, theorists, and philosophers (Rimbaud, Aristotle, Ptolemy), who have experimented with and written about such concepts. The seductive idea, artistically, that sound is color made audible, and color is sound made visible, is certainly not a well-supported physical or psychoacoustical theory. Such a belief remains a composer's or painter's creative fantasy, special to a way of working with and inventing musical material. The fact is that any visual color can be associated with any sound, and agreement as well as disagreement about the appropriateness of a particular association will immediately ensue.

Even when sound is used as the electronic excitant for the generation of video or projected color imagery on a screen, any composed relationships between sound and sight can be arbitrarily chosen and are, at best, artistically fortuitous: a loud sound can generate green or yellow or red, depending only on the aesthetic choice of the artist involved; or high sounds can generate yellow, low sounds purple. Any color/sound relation is entirely dependent on the choice of the creator, interpreted freely by the beholder/listener, and is not the result of any known principles relating discrete colors to discrete sound phenomena.

Particular relationships between sound and color can be forged, though, in music combined with a visual medium. Chapter 3, **MEDIUMS AND IDIOMS** touches upon recent uses of modern technology which explore this fascinating realm of possible aesthetic links between sound and color in new intermedia genres.

COLOR AND PITCH

Here is a simple experiment to try:

1. Imagine a very low pitch.
2. Now, imagine a very high pitch.
3. Sing your highest pitch.
4. Play the lowest note on the piano.
5. Play the highest note on the piano.

Unless your eyes skipped ahead to this sentence, you have probably followed instructions 1 and 2, while you may not, yet, have actually vocalized or played a piano in the last four instructions. For those who have now completed all six, you're commended, and you're ready for the point of our little exercise, to wit, to pose a question. How is it that you were able to imagine a very low pitch or a high one? The mind is not a vibrating acoustical medium like vocal cords or piano strings or the column of air in a trumpet. There were no actual sounding pitches heard by your ears. Yet, except for the exercise perhaps seeming trivial, you probably did not question the basis for the first two instructions. Indeed, your mind imagined—or, if you're still balking at following instructions, your mind is capable of imagining—those low and high pitches.

Ask a painter to imagine the color yellow. The painter may be puzzled, but, nevertheless, will be quite able to "see" yellow. Asked to explain how yellow is "seen" in the mind, the painter might describe the experience as a kind of tactile sensation, feeling yellow's warmth. This feeling for yellow is neither strictly visual nor tactile, but **kinesthetic**—a sensory experience derived from and mediated by the network of nerves in the muscles, tendons, and joints in our body stimulated by bodily movements and tensions. The painter experiences the bodily sensation of yellow. Clifton puts it another way:

> The blue of the sky is not just the blue caused by certain vibrations of wavicles. It is a restful blue, because my body has adopted, as a mode of motor behavior, an attitude of restfulness. (1983, 70)

In the same way, we are able to imagine a very low pitch or a very high pitch. We experience them kinesthetically.

Another way of understanding how it is that you imagined the pitches of the first two instructions lies in the final four. In instruction 3, you probably relaxed your vocal cords and sang a sound that was relatively much richer in harmonics than your highest pitch, sung in instruction 4. Similarly, the lowest note on the piano was rich, vibrant, and long-lived, while the highest was thin, dry, and short-lived. We know how to differentiate the pitches in these extremes precisely because of their extreme differences in color. Persons with a very high degree of pitch discrimination—so-called "absolute pitch"—can, of course, recognize and name specific pitches, because they can match those pitches they are hearing with pitches they have, in effect, "memorized" from their first musical experiences. And, in great part, that "pitch memory" is based on musical color discrimination. For example, the lowest pitch on the piano, an A, is much harder to designate in the pitch-class A than the A four octaves higher. Persons with "perfect pitch"—another misnomer—do, indeed, recognize the lowest pitch as an A, but they get their pitch cue more from the overtone at the octave that the string is generating than from the fundamental pitch, oscillating at the barely perceptible rate of 27.5 cycles per second. They get their pitch cue from a musical color phenomenon: the sounding waveform complex. Pitch, rather than being identified apart from musical color—timbre—is identifiable because it is integral to timbre. Pitch, then, is an attribute of and ascribed by its timbre.

What does this have to do with composing? If a composer is neither intuitively gifted nor empirically experienced with pitch as an attribute of musical color, the composer will, for instance, not appreciate how "muddy," how "pitchless," even how "dissonant" a major triad sounds in the lowest reaches of combined bass instruments or the piano. In traditional scoring, such sensitivity is critical, where musical color, represented in the instrumental timbres, is principally the **carrier** of pitch. In pieces where musical color, as such, is the most important aspect of the form, such sensitivity to the pitch spacing of a timbral event stream is equally critical.

What about all the many pitches in between these outer extremes of our exercise? Do we discriminate color differences within, say, not seven octaves but the more usual three or four octave range of wind, brass and string instruments or the two or three octave range of the voice? Orchestration textbooks and treatises discuss **registers,** divisions of the full range of instruments or voices into two, three, or four areas of different sound production quality. Often, these registers will encompass about an octave. In each register the performer can be expected, nominally, to produce a relatively consistent sound color, trying always to move from register to register with as little color change as possible. Registers are defined, most commonly, in wind instruments and the voice and are given names like "chalameau" (the lowest octave of the clarinet range), "throat tone," "chest tone," or simply high, middle, or low. String instruments, rather than registers, have the differing physical nature of their lowest to highest strings and the various fingering positions on those strings as distinct sound color regions. Registrations for organ compositions are created by the composer or the organist, assigning "stops" for various ranks of pipes, many modeled on orchestral instruments. The interesting difference, however, between the organ "oboe stop" and the real oboe sound is that the organ stop is not capable of imitating the oboe's dynamic change in sound color throughout its range. (It is interesting here to note that, over the last several hundred years, as instrumental colors have become accepted and well established in their use by composers and performers, keyboard imitations of such instruments have inevitably been developed. The pipe organ, the Hammond electric organ, and, today, the plethora of digital synthesizers are all the result of this cultural compulsion to put all instrumental colors "at our fingertips" for one-person music making on a grand scale, a one-person orchestra!)

Not only are there differences between different registers or octaves or strings of instruments or voices but between adjacent notes of the same chromatic scale! Using any vowel sound—a, e, i, o, or u—sing an ascending chromatic scale from your lowest pitch to as high as you can sing, comfortably, not changing the vowel sound. Difficult, isn't it? And amazing, because of the great difference in color between every adjacent pitch! And with certain vowel sounds it is impossible to sing much more than an octave. Such clearly audible changes in color can be demonstrated on all instruments, creating, for the composer, a large array of potential sound color material to consider.

Of course, depending on the nature of the piece, the composer directs our focus of perception to this or that feature in creating the modeling process for the form of the piece. If continuity is focused largely on pitch progression, the composer intuitively and wisely uses musical color to make clear the importance of pitch, for instance, assigning the string colors uniformly to important pitch material. What we have intended to stress in this section on color and pitch is that they have a mutuality of importance to which the composer should always be sensitive.

COLOR THROUGH TIME

Color changes not only as pitch changes but also as time passes. Each musical tone an instrument or voice produces is, in itself, a stream of constantly changing relationships of pitch, loudness, timbre, and expressive nuance—or as acousticians prefer, **frequency, amplitude, harmonic spectrum** and **formant.** The attack, prolongation, and release of a musical tone, are termed the **onset, steady-state** and **decay** of the **spectral envelope.** In our earlier color/pitch exercise, each time you sang or played a pitch, you created a musical tone with a spectral envelope, constantly changing its timbral content every moment. In spite of this change, you probably accepted it as natural and continued to focus on its pitch identity. In composer/researcher Robert Erickson's important book, *Sound Structure in Music* (1975), he refers to sounds as **"timbral objects,"** made distinct not only because they are "recognizable" but because they are "multi-dimensional wholes, individual and various: it is that they exist in time, exhibit changes during their time course," still retaining their particular identity. The fact that sounds are temporarily dynamic creates a dilemma for acousticians. Do we select out the nominally sustained (steady-state) portion of a sound for analysis, modeling our findings on formant studies of the human voice, as composer-theorist Wayne Slawson demonstrates in his important treatise *Sound Color* (1985)? Or do we decide a sound's properties and nature in the overall sonic context of its musical existence, as Robert Cogan demonstrates in his graphically vivid "spectrum photos" of whole sections of compositions, illustrated in his *New Images of Musical Sound* (1984)? Or do we intuitively ascribe abstract aesthetic traits to the sound, categorizing it formally, much as we would families of related instruments, as Pierre Schaeffer's *Traite des Objets Musicaux* (1968)?

Because of rapid technological advances, compelling theories of sound color have begun to emerge. Detailed analysis is now possible of not only a single sound's spectral characteristics but the analysis, both in graphic display and mathematical formulation of whole pieces of combined instrumental and vocal sound spectra, such as in Cogan's "phonological theory of tone color." Slawson's theory, on the other hand, extends to an elaborate, personal system of composition with sound color, ordering the properties of sound colors in series and formalizing their combination. He bases his theory and its practice on his observation that the dimensions of sound color are continuous, physically measurable quantities functioning as filter resonance frequencies. Experimentation with such theories is important, for these are now beginning to provide impressive new information for the composer to incorporate in modeling sound color in a piece.

COLOR AND TEXTURE

When we study a fine painting, we appreciate the composition of its colors, seen in the brushstroke texture of the surface on the painted canvas. (A Van Gogh painting examined closely would reveal a vivid, brushed texture of colors.) The colors have their distinctive essence and hue, textural depth and detail, all of these qualities dynamically interacting. The mutuality of color and texture in painting is well understood: color can define the textures in a painting, while the texture of the painting can, in turn, articulate its colors.

As the degrees of luminosity of colors can heighten our sense of spatial relation in a painting, so can the degree of luminosity a composer gives different strands in the texture of the composition. A bright trumpet passage can suddenly pierce and illuminate the quietly sustained continuum of slowly evolving string sonorities. Charles Ives uses this contrast with vivid dramatic effect in *The Unanswered Question* (1906).

Does this corollary between the colors and textures of painting and music extend to, say, a black-on-white line drawing? One clue to the answer is in the word *line,* used both in graphic art and composing. In a pencil drawing our perception is focused on the interlacing framework of lines and the contrasting shades of black on white. In a very real sense, though, our visual acuity for color and texture is actually heightened by their absence. We imagine that we see the green of the drawing of a tree's thick foliage, because of the lines and subtle shadings of the leaves—individually and in clusters, every perception distilled and synthesized. In music, this could be the formalized continuity of color and texture created by the composer deciding to score lines solely for a particular instrument or family of instruments. In such a seemingly spartan combination of sound colors, our sense of color and texture is, like our perception of the drawing, heightened by the absence of many and varied colors; our ear focuses on the shadings of color in the contrasting instrumental registers and in the interweaving fabric of lines and sonorities. A work such as Karlheinz Stockhausen's *Kontrapunkte* (1953) typifies this approach.

Color-and-pitch, color-through-time, color-and-texture are mutually interacting qualities of **sonorities** combined. Composers, however intuitively sensitive to this relation, may not fully appreciate its scope and power in modeling the sound colors of a piece. Typically, the less experienced composer simply assigns this or that instrument to this or that role in the progress of the piece. A more effective modeling process integrates the invention of material with its coloration, modeling a sound color image for the piece.

COLORATION: THE SOUND COLOR IMAGE

Coloration is the modeling of sound color from the smallest to largest detail of form to create a **sound color image** for the piece. The sound color image reflects the quality, combination, mutuality, and merging of the confluent sonorities in a composition. For coloration to be integral to the modeling process, the composer establishes degrees of variability for the colors, chosen through spatial modeling and tested through temporal modeling. These conditions can be relatively stable or in continual flux, tending toward one or another degree of "luminosity," establishing a kind of revolving prism of coloration, refracting and dispersing the sound color image of the piece. Listed are variables of coloration possible for integration in the modeling process. Each variable has its range of possibilities, applicable to every aspect of sound color image in a composition.

Variables of Coloration

heightened color sense—heightened pitch sense
object—carrier
heightened loudness—heightened softness
diffusion—concentration
integration, fusion, modulation—separation, conjunction, alternation

As in modeling rhythmic qualities, the composer can model the coloration in a piece by creating a **coloration curve** through the course of the piece. In studying the variables above and the coloration potential, one should feel free to design the curve using any combination of variable and/or constant conditions that work best in the modeling process conceived for the piece.

Heightened color or pitch sense—When, in the progress of a piece, the composer models the pitch space to be essentially undifferentiated, the composer correspondingly heightens the importance of color in the texture. For example, in the opening measures of Gyorgy Ligeti's orchestral composition, *Atmospheres* (1960), the extremely soft, massive chords sustained by all the instruments of the orchestra present, all at once, a pitch constellation with all twelve pitch-classes in almost all the possible registers of color in the full orchestra. By including all pitches in many registers by many families of instruments, any focus on this or that pitch as more important than others is lessened significantly. Included in the preface to the published score are Ligeti's "remarks concerning rehearsal," stressing the crucial importance of performing properly the nuances of the sound color image he envisions for the piece:

> All entrances are to be played imperceptibly and *dolcissimo.* The winds especially must always enter unobtrusively. The differences between "sul tasto"—"ordinario"—"sul ponticello" in the strings are to be maintained with exaggerated exactness. Not a single instrument is to play without mute in the "con sordino" places for strings (this applies especially to the contrabasses!), since, because of the total divisi, every instrument is heard and a single unmuted one will stand out readily.

Ligeti has caused us to focus on the richness of color and great mass of the orchestral sonority in his sound color image of a sonic atmosphere.

Equally as compelling as Ligeti's use of all pitches to heighten our color sense is Alban Berg's "invention on one note," also scored for full orchestra, occurring at the climax of the murder scene in act 3 of his opera, *Wozzeck* (1925). Here, the instruments of the orchestra enter one after another, almost imperceptibly, always on the same pitch, B3, in a common unison, culminating on a brutal, *ffff* hammerstroke chord. In his book, *New Images of Musical Sound* (1984), Robert Cogan displays a composite spectral photo of this stunning moment, vividly conveying the heightened sense of dramatically changing orchestral color spectra achieved by Berg. (Photo on p. 94, discussion on p. 92–96.)

As striking as these two examples of heightened color sense are, they do not—cannot—completely neutralize our sense of pitch. By the same token, sound color can never be completely neutralized in a piece. When the composer models the material for a piece so that our primary perceptual focus is on the pitch space and its evolving pitch constellations, our sense of color can, nevertheless, be subtly focused. In Milton Babbitt's *Sheer Pluck* (1984), a composition for solo guitar composed for the concert guitarist, David Starobin, the composer presents a carefully conceived, serial development of pitch constellations within a carefully designed sound color spectrum. The guitarist is asked to pluck the strings in three different ways: 1) *ordinario,* where the nail and flesh pluck the string slightly behind the sound-hole; 2) *pizzicato,* a muffled sound created by resting the palm of the right hand near the bridge while plucking the string with the flesh of the thumb; and 3) *sul ponticello,* where the nail and flesh pluck the strings near the bridge. Through the piece, these colors alternate with one another, sometimes through several note sequences, sometimes every note or two. Babbitt is very sensitive to the color registrations and differences in color between loud and soft notes. The piece ends delicately on the only string sounding a harmonic in the whole piece, this after a flurry of tremolos and angular pitch and rhythm combinations.

In contrast, it would seem that, with no discernible pitch base, no heightened sense of pitch can accrue. But, where pitch is absent, **color registration** itself provides its own functionality. There is, in fact, a vast, unlimited realm of nonpitched sound colors available to model in the coloration of a piece. **Nonpitched** refers to those instruments and sounds that have complex sound spectra not centered on one fundamental frequency, especially including most kinds of percussion instruments. In Edgard Varese's *Ionisation* (1929–31), vivid use of nonpitched percussion instruments to intensify our sense of color builds through the first five minutes of this six and one-half minute piece, climaxing just before the first entry of the three pitched instruments, the piano, bells, and "glockenspiel, a clavier," their pitch world finally asserting itself, but dying away through the final minute. Varese effectively uses color and pitch in striking relief.

In yet another way, Varese, in calling for the slow, mechanical, whining glissando of both high and low sirens, washes the pitch space of all centered pitches in *Ionisation.* Even so, our pitch sense is never completely "cleansed" in the piece. Sustained, centered pitches being absent, we focus our perception on sound colors, their spectra, in turn, yielding ranges of **color registrations,** broader than pitch constellations but modeled nonetheless.

This heightened consciousness of the close relationship between the worlds of color and pitch is of pronounced significance in the world of computer music, where digital instruments can be designed specifically for color and/or pitch intensification. Composer James Dashow designs such computer music instruments in his computer music scores actually to perform waveform "spectra as chords." In his computer music composition, *In Winter Shine* (1983), our graphic event representation of the piece appearing in **excerpt 6,** the sonorities are at the same time rich in color and functional in the relatedness of common tones in their chord-like pitch constellations. Dashow explains his concept for such spectral organization, as follows:

> The basic concept is using pitches to generate these inharmonic spectra, in the same sense that one would conceive of pitches as being accompanied by chords. Each spectrum is considered to be a chord and is treated as a chordal structure. With certain of these chords I

> can prolong these pitches, because they are literally (physically) present to a varying degree in these chord spectra. At the same time I give the pitches a range of harmonizations. This would be comparable to a melody tone that you hear in any voice and a piano composition is harmonized by a series of chords that form different relationships to the held pitch. (1985, 37)

Thus, in modeling the coloration of a piece, the composer can enhance the effect of the composition by heightening—or lessening—our sense of color's relative importance at any one moment in the piece. In doing so, the composer's attitude about the materials invented for the piece play an important role. Will the material, for instance, be "carried" by a particular instrumental color, or will each particular sound color be "objectified" in the continuity of the piece?

Object or **carrier**—With the widespread availability of electroacoustic music systems beginning with the tape recorder in the late forties and, in the decades since then, the practical performance of continuously sounding instruments, sound color exploration naturally has become more systematized and, in turn, objectified. In actuality, the magnetic particles of a tape, in fixed recorded relation, became manipulatable objects. Even the name of a particular genre of tape music celebrated this compositional approach: *musique concrete* or objectified music, referring, as composer Pierre Schaeffer systematized, to the materials of such compositions as *objets sonore,* **sound objects.** Indeed, the art of deftly cutting, splicing, mixing, and ordering taped sounds in such works created primarily from the late forties through the sixties involved the composer with actual, physical lengths of tape—of sound objects a composer could actually touch, hold and handle. Interestingly, however, many such works simply substituted a recorded sound source for an instrument, making a recorded vocal sound, for instance, the carrier of a pitch sequence, modeled of course, on traditional scoring techniques in instrumental music. Schaeffer's own *Symphonie Pour un Homme Seul* (1950) typifies this approach: using a sound object as the carrier of musical lines and thematic material. In contrast, works such as Jean-Claude Risset's masterful *Sud* (1986) or Paul Lansky's brilliantly executed *Idle Chatter* (1985), both composed with digital processing and mixing of prerecorded natural and vocal sounds, the modeling of the coloration of the sound objects is original and compelling. In describing his piece, Risset states:

> *Sud* was . . . realized in 1985 at GRM (Groupe de Recherces Musicales) . . . the birthplace of 'musique concrete,' pioneered by Pierre Schaeffer around 1948 . . . *Sud* includes sounds synthesized by computer in Marseilles, but it comprises mostly recorded sounds subsequently processed by computer, in particular, sea and insect sounds recorded near Marseille. . . .The piece actually resorts to few germinal sounds recorded of the sea, insects, birds, wood and metal chimes, as well as brief 'gestures' played on the piano or synthesizer by computer: these were then transformed and multiplied using several operations: filtering, modulating, reverberating, spatializing, mixing, and hybridizings. Cezanne wanted to 'unite feminine curves and hilly shoulders': similarly, cross-synthesis permits to hybridize, for instance, metal and bird sounds. I have specially used it to impart to one sound the dynamic character of another one—for instance, to give the flux of seawaves to different sounds. Also, a

> major-minor pitch scale (G–B–E–F♯–G♯), first exposed by synthetic sounds, will gradually color various natural sounds—it will gradually become colored synthetic sounds, and become a harmonic grid, excited by birds or waves similarly to an aeolian harp. (Notes by the composer for the piece from 1986 ICMC program)

At the same time that Pierre Schaeffer was codifying his concept of *objet sonore,* John Cage was composing his important *Sonatas and Interludes* (1946–48) for his invention, the "prepared piano," developed by Cage a decade earlier to serve as a kind of keyboard orchestra of percussive sound objects. To prepare a piano, Cage experimented with objects inserted in and attached to the piano string at precisely measured points to create a particularly distinctive, often nonpitched, percussive sound. After deciding on a particular gamut of such "colored" strings, he modeled the piece according to a predetermined keyboard coloration scheme. He thought of the sounding strings not as a hierarchy of pitches but as a gamut of sounds. He extended this approach to other mediums as well.

In his *String Quartet in Four Parts* (1949–50), Cage refers, ironically it would seem, to this quartet as a work for "unprepared" string instruments. Cage, nevertheless, was intent on extending his carefully developed concept of sound objects in the prepared piano to the string quartet genre as well. In the same fashion as his prescribed preparations for piano, he lists, in performance instructions for his quartet, the complete gamut of fifty-eight distinctive sound colors he chose to be played through the piece: fourteen for each of the violins, another fourteen for the viola, and sixteen for the cello. Cage makes clear his conception of these sounds as objects by bracketing and thus segregating the four pitch-oriented patterns. Remarking on his concept for the work, Cage states:

> The composition, a melodic line without accompaniment, employs single tones, intervals, triads and aggregates requiring one or more of the instruments for their production. These constitute a gamut of sounds. The strings are played without vibration, and those to be used for the production of tones are specified. (From notes by Lejaren Hiller from "The Avant Garde String Quartet in the USA," VOX SVBX 5306, 1973)

Cage applies his gamut-of-sounds-as-objects principle most strictly in the third movement, which he names with a metaphor, "Nearly Stationary," shown in **excerpt 9.** Here, Cage models the coloration of the piece as a careful selection, ordering and distribution of a gamut of thirty-three sounds chosen from the fifty-eight available. These thirty-three are combined into twenty-four uniquely different sonorities, sounded alone as a quiescent, vibratoless stream of sound objects. Cage's sound color image provides a useful example, and study of the movement reveals important concepts for devising a coloration plan for a piece. Cage lists his gamut of fifty-eight sounds for the work, as shown in figure 7.1. The thirty-three sounds he chose for the third movement are shown in figure 7.2 in twenty-four unique combinations indicated by letters A through X. The resulting sonorities range from single-tone sounds (H, J, M, S, T) to double-, triple-, quadruple- and one septuple-tone sound (I), where all but one instrument sound two tones at once. All possible combinations of the different string instruments are employed but one: the viola

PLAY WITHOUT VIBRATO AND WITH ONLY MINIMUM WEIGHT ON THE BOW.

ACCIDENTALS AFFECT ONLY THOSE NOTES THEY DIRECTLY PRECEDE.

THE RHYTHMIC STRUCTURE OF THIS WORK IS $2\frac{1}{2} \cdot 1\frac{1}{2}$, $2 \cdot 3$, $6 \cdot 5$, $\frac{1}{2} \cdot 1\frac{1}{2}$. THE DISPOSITION OF THE TONES WITH RESPECT TO THE STRINGS IS AS FOLLOWS:

Figure 7.1 Cage's gamut of sounds for *String Quartet in Four Parts*

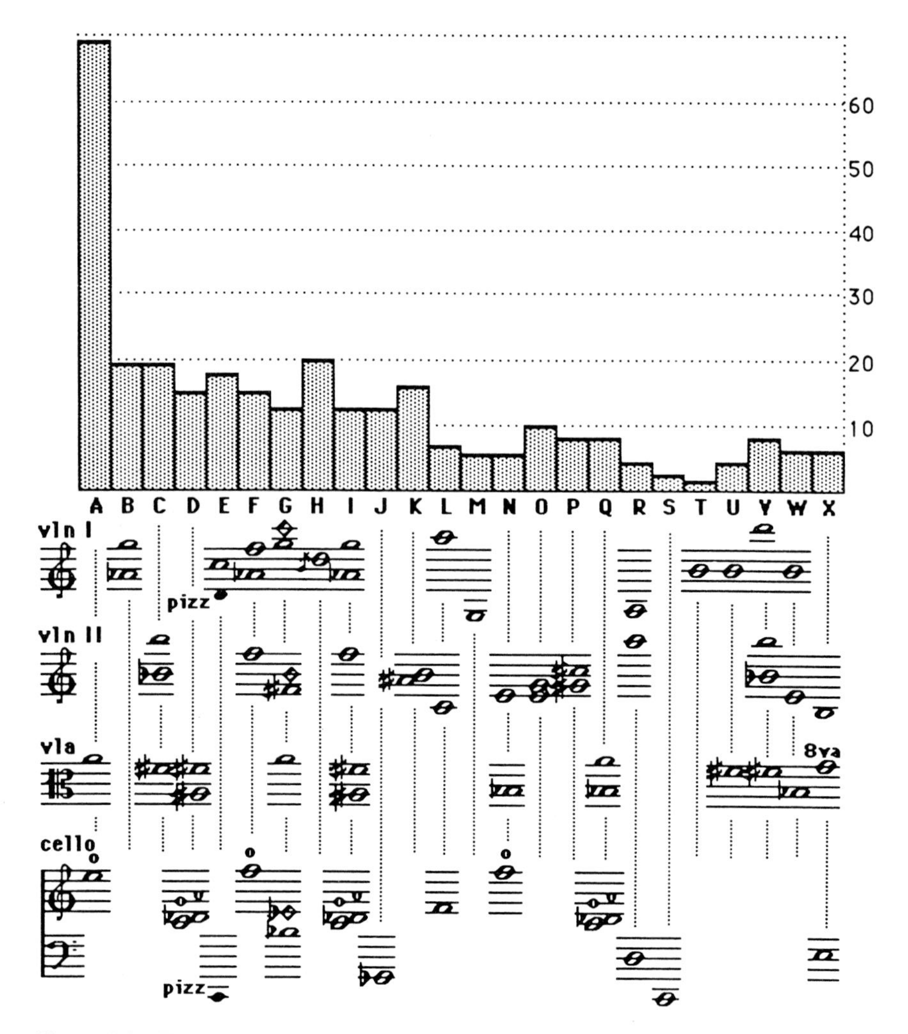

Figure 7.2 Frequency graph for all sound colors in *Nearly Stationary*

never sounds alone. In contrast, the range of sound colors that make up these sonorities is quite narrow, limited to *non vibrato* bowed tones, both single and doublestop; bowed-plus-plucked doublestops; single plucked tones; single and doublestop harmonics; doublestop *col legno;* and specially tuned natural harmonics.

In Figure 7.2, a graph depicts the frequency of recurrence through the movement of the gamut of twenty-four sound colors. The total number of iterations of all sounds is 303, the highest being 69, the least 1. The average number of iterations per sonority is 13, the mean number is 15. The graph clearly shows the hierarchical trend from the sonorities with the most iterations to sonorities with fewer and fewer, as the piece progresses. By the 143d measure of this 242 measure piece—three-fifths the length—the last of the twenty-four sonorities, X, is heard. It is important to note here that two of the sonorities, C and D, are significantly exact portions of two larger sonorities, respectively V and I. If we then consider C and D to be subsonorities of V and I, we are left with not twenty-four but twenty-two primary sonorities in Cage's "gamut of sounds" for this movement. Twenty-two is the sum of the numbers, which Cage refers to in his instruction page as "the rhythmic structure of the work." Another clue to Cage's coloration process in "Nearly Stationary" lies in the fact that he has described this movement metaphorically as "winter being expressed as a canon . . . a melodic line without accompaniment." We will return to the intriguing puzzle of "Nearly Stationary" in chapter 8, **MUSICAL ARCHITECTURE,** when we study Cage's process for structure in this piece.

In Elliott Carter's *Double Concerto for Harpsichord and Piano with Two Chamber Orchestras* (1961), the beauty and clarity of his sound image for the work is focused in his masterful use of color as carrier of essential, form-giving material. In notes for the piece, he explains the procedure:

> My *Double Concerto* is an antiphonal work for two small orchestras, each led by one of the soloists. The harpsichord is associated with an ensemble of flute, horn, trumpet, trombone, viola, contra-bass and percussion (largely metallophones and lignophones) while the piano is joined by an ensemble of oboe, clarinet, bassoon, horn, violin, cello and percussion (largely membranophones). In addition to being isolated in space and timbre, the antiphonal groups are partially separated musically by the fact that each emphasizes its own repertory of melodic and harmonic intervals, the harpsichord ensemble: minor seconds, minor thirds, perfect fourths, augmented fourths, minor sixths, minor sevenths and minor ninths; the piano ensemble: major seconds, major thirds, perfect fifths, major sixths, major sevenths and major ninths. Each of these intervals is associated, for the most part, with a certain metronomic speed with the result that the speeds and their interrelationships are also different for the two groups. . . .The motion of the work is from comparative unity with slight character differences to greater and greater diversity of material and character and return to unity. The form is that of confrontations of diversified action-patterns and a presentation of their mutual interactions, conflicts and resolutions, their growth and decay over various stretches of time. (Musical Quarterly, Vol. 48, no. 1, 1962, 97–98)

In *Double Concerto* we find a clear instance of Carter's coloration procedure at work. In the introduction, the instrumental colors of the two orchestras are carriers of identifying intervals—the piano's ensemble gesture answered in kind by the harpsichord's ensemble. Pitch constellations serve to identify the role of the instrumental colors and vice versa. One could go further, incidentally, to say that the two differentiated color groups are, in the larger sense, complex sound objects themselves. Carter, through the piece, ranges widely between all the conditions of coloration: integrating, fusing, modulating, separating, joining, and alternating the colors in a diverse sound color image for the piece.

The creation of a **sound color image** for a composition is a dynamic concept: it is temporal in the flow and confluence of sonorities in the event streams; it is spatial in its expression of textural dimensions in the work. The coloration procedures cited from various pieces thus far, and to follow, are meant to exemplify special instances, where the coloration is particularly vivid. It is actually more often the case that the sound color image of a work will show a broad, varied approach, not concentrating on one coloration to the exclusion of many others. The **variables of coloration,** more often, range both over the surface of the event streams of a piece and through the depths of the texture, from whole portions of the piece to the millisecond by millisecond transformation of one sound. Thus, as we proceed with further discussion of remaining variables of coloration, bear in mind that portions of scores cited here should also be studied thoroughly in the whole, from the largest to smallest details of form.

Heightened Loudness/Softness—We know from our training as musicians and, deductively, from scientific evidence, that the nature of a sound changes significantly as it becomes louder or softer. Even the traditional term for indicating the degrees of loudness in parts and scores—dynamics—is, itself, a metaphor for change. Composers have for centuries used this fundamental acoustical phenomenon to bring liveliness, drama, and subtle expressiveness to their music. Traditionally, the most striking use, for instance, is in the dynamic marking *fp*—*forte piano*—where, after the initial attack of a note is executed with a strong, loud accent, the tone suddenly quietens, dramatically changing the color of the sound, literally a breathtaking moment when used strategically in a piece. Or the drama of a long, gradual *crescendo,* as a full orchestra builds over several minutes from a small rustle of sound to a powerful, full sound. Our descriptions for these musical events are metaphors for what is happening acoustically: the louder a sound is, the more complex the relation of its partials, the more transformed with modulating distortion. These changes in sound not only affect amplitude but cause complex changes in sound color. In a *crescendo* we hear the pitch remaining constant as the sound changes its character, becoming increasingly brighter, fuller. Scientific studies have revealed that, in fact, we get our cues for **loudness** not only from the strength of the sound (its loudness measured in decibels, its impact measured by the membrane of the eardrum) but from the relative distortion of its composite partials—its color—and the amount of resonance or reverberation it possesses. The **softness** of sounds are described as muffled, subdued, subtone, dark, clearly indicating our sense that these tones are muted in effect, their audible partials fewer and freer of amplitude distortion.

Composer Morton Feldman's music is notable for the sustained softness of his sound color image in much of his work. Typically, no dynamic markings appear in his scores, other than admonishments that, "The attack of each sound should never be accented, and the dynamics throughout are to be kept very low." (*Out of Last Pieces,* for orchestra [1958]); or, "All sounds should be played with a minimum of attack. . . .Dynamics are very low." (*For Franz Kline,* for soprano and chamber group [1962].) With sustained softness and gently undulating sonorities, Feldman amplifies our sound color consciousness. With softness the overall hue, he highlights and shades the sonorities by carefully separating, alternating, and integrating their registers. In his orchestral works, particularly, he systematizes color registration with symbols for high, low, and middle registers—bright, dark, and half-tone colors. We learn in **excerpt 4,** the first of four *Last Pieces* (1959) for piano, that the pitch constellations are contrasted not only by their different interval stacks but by their variable octave displacements.

Feldman has, it would seem, made painting itself a metaphor for his music. It is well-known that through the early years of his career he associated closely with New York abstract expressionist painters, particularly Philip Guston, Wilem de Kooning, Franz Kline and Mark Rothko—seven works of Feldman are dedicated to painters. Feldman's music is often in what he termed "racecourse" notation, where durations and synchronization are relatively free. This free relation of sonorities, along with the absence of dramatic, forceful musical events, focuses our perception on the intermingled sounds, objectifying them into the sonic expression of the abstract painting he so much appreciated and understood.

Heightened loudness in the coloration of a piece can, of course, immediately focus our attention to the color of the sound. Sustained, excessive loudness, however, can have a dulling effect on our ability to perceive and appreciate sound color. This is apparently not the case with heightened, sustained softness, where our acuities for color, pitch, and texture are highly sensitized. Feldman was keenly aware of this phenomenon. Equally aware but radically different in disposition is composer/visual artist/performer Glenn Branca, whose music is unyielding in loudness. His *Symphony no. 2: The Peak of the Sacred* (1982) for ten electric guitars fiercely assaults our ears. John Rockwell, music critic of the New York Times, describes Branca and his music:

> Branca, who received no formal musical training, has been influenced by Varese and the *bruitisme* of the futurists, percussion composers of the 1930s, and the 'no-wave' instrumental art-rock of New York in the late 1970s. His music, deafeningly amplified, employs rapidly strummed electric guitars, percussion, and brass; the more recent 'symphonies' call for 'mallet guitars,' designed and constructed by Branca himself, which are essentially amplified dulcimers. Even though the harmonies are primordial and the rhythms plodding, the cumulative effect of his music, augmented by mystical subtitles and the bohemian raffishness of the performers, can be powerful. In 1982 at the New Music America Festival in Chicago, John Cage provoked a controversy by calling Branca's music, in its forceful insistence, 'fascist.' (New Groves Dictionary of American Music, 1984, Vol. 1, 285)

Indeed, immersing an audience in amplified, continuous "hyperloudness" has become, in the final decades of the twentieth century, a mass-cultural phenomenon. Audiences at rock concerts expect and want to experience the almost ecstatic state of being completely engulfed in very loud, amplified sound. The high risk of damage to the ears in such dangerous sound environments—not to mention the resulting desensitization to subtleties of sound—is well-known and scientifically documented.

Loudness, produced without electronic amplification, can be extreme as well, though with conventional, acoustical instruments harder to sustain over long periods of time. Sensitivity to color differences between instruments fades as they play louder and in extremely high or low registers. For instance, a loud, high sound on a clarinet is hard to distinguish from the same pitch played loudly by an oboe. These same sound colors, played softly, are readily distinguished.

Still, loudness of sound, like a splash of red or yellow in a painting, can brighten and articulate. Composers sense this intuitively, using loudness to energize their music with vivid contrast. The loud, resounding, repeated hammerstroke chords, a convention of the endings of hundreds of symphonic and piano works of the eighteenth and nineteenth centuries, attests to the proven importance of loudness in closing a piece, in expending its final energy with explosions of sound.

Joseph Schwantner's *And the Mountains Rising Nowhere,* composed in 1977 for the Eastman Wind Ensemble, has instrumental forces of indisputably powerful loudness potential: sixteen wind and thirteen brass instruments, piano, contrabass, and six percussionists playing no less than forty-nine separate percussion instruments. In **excerpt 13,** at one of several high points in the piece, this potential asserts itself dramatically. At measure 37, a *fortissimo* hammerstroke by the full ensemble rings brightly as four metal idiophones resound their bright resonance through the first seconds. Trombones on their lowest B rise and fall in loudness, as the rolling thunder of the timpanum, bass drum and tom gradually increase their heavy presence. At the fifth second of the sixteen-second, meterless measure, the ominous rolling is joined, darkly, by a dense but subdued constellation of twelve brass closely clustered, their ensemble attack masked and decorated by a quick flurry of piano and bell tree sounds. This occurs as the low percussion grows to *fortissimo,* in turn released by nine insistently accelerating percussion thrusts, all building to a *sforzando* jab over the sixteen-second stream of events. The accumulating energy builds momentum, faster and faster, released in a second flurry of metals and drums, these in turn hurling the full ensemble upward and upward through measure 40, where a sudden two second silence clears our ears.

These and other splashes of color, heightened by loudness, are put in subtle relief in several other sections of the piece—by softly sustained flute colors or by unexpected, soft whistling and vocal sounds, a "surprise" coloration after an assertive fanfare-like opening by the brass and percussion. With skillful use of heightened loudness and softness in relief, Schwantner imbues his score with rich and varied coloration.

Diffusion/Concentration—With full instrumentation, a contemporary symphony orchestra presents the composer with a richly diverse array of as many as twenty-two different instrumental colors, these plus the great number of percussion instruments available. Add to these colors the organ, vocal soloists and choruses, and taped or live electroacoustic sounds; multiply the winds and brasses by two, three, or four in number, the violins by twenty-four, the violas by twelve, the cellos by ten, and the contrabasses by eight; and, finally, multiply all the individual sound color sources by the great range of different color registers in the instruments and voices and the special instrumental color techniques that have become part of the composer's sound color pallette—the modern symphony orchestra has, by any measurement, a vast potential of diffusion of different sound colors, as well as large and various concentrations of the same sound colors.

Of course, coloration procedures in orchestral literature—evolved over the last two hundred years in hundreds of classic works composed for the orchestra—provide composers with sound color images, cited, discussed and analyzed in the many orchestration texts of the nineteenth and twentieth centuries, modeled anew in orchestral compositions that continue to enrich the repertoire today. This impressive potential for both color **diffusion** and **concentration** in the orchestra is, naturally, conditioned not only by tradition but by acoustical and perceptual considerations. Just as artists do not normally choose to paint all possible colors everywhere on their canvas, composers do not normally use all possible sound colors at all times in an orchestral work—diffusion of color in extreme. Likewise, exclusive use of only one color in paintings or pieces is unusual—concentration of color in extreme. As in heightened loudness and softness, the diffusion and concentration of sound colors is carefully planned and balanced in modeling the coloration of a piece, particularly an orchestral work.

Composer Jacob Druckman artfully modeled the sound color image for his episodic orchestral work, *Windows* (1972). In this twenty-one minute composition, constantly shifting textures, often with highly diffuse coloration, are skillfully balanced by intense sound color concentrations. Toward the end of the work, a growing diffusion of sound colors, more and more cathartic, climaxes in an intense, full orchestra *fortissimo* concentration of biting wind trills, high string tremolos, punctuated by flashing interjections from the brass. Just before this denouement of the piece we find excellent examples of diffuse and concentrated sound colors juxtaposed, seen in **excerpt 14.**

At first glance, this two-page segment of the score seems extremely diffuse, indeed, with instruments and their musics scattered everywhere! Closer study reveals, however, that nine highlighted and concentrated sound colors are variously juxtaposed with four, less active, "after-images," as Druckman terms them. The foreground colors are, not unexpectedly, the louder and larger instrumental sections of the orchestra, contrasted with the background softness of the solo harp, the small electric organ and the flutes. Some instruments alternate between foreground and background, as in the oboes, bass clarinet and piano. The piano, whose eight-pitch stack of thirds sounds *mezzo forte* with the hammerstroke *fortissimo* of the orchestra two measures before 30, resonates as a fading shadow of that sound through this two-measure "window" of softly lyric thirds played by the oboes as a single, delicate third is plucked in harmonics on the harp. This sudden shift from brightly colored foreground textures to the subdued, gentler background occurs here and again in the four measures before 31. The second instance, however, carries this coloration further with its own, interior juxtaposition of color: the darkly ominous, Stravinsky-like murmurings of the low-register flutes and bass clarinet contrasted and followed immediately by the rich brilliance of the Debussy-like dissonances of the horns combined with the strings in singing, ornamental octaves. Druckman describes this sound color imagery:

> The *Windows* of the title are windows inward. They are points of light which appear as thick orchestral textures part, allowing us to hear, fleetingly, moments out of time—memories, shadows of ghosts. The imagery is as though, having looked at an unpeopled wall of windows, one looks away and senses the after-image of a face. (From album notes)

The modern orchestra, as we have observed and as Druckman demonstrates, has great potential for diffusion of coloration. Of course, it seems rhetorical to state that ensembles smaller than the orchestra have, accordingly, fewer sound colors—potentially less diffusion—in smaller concentrations, typically only one instrument or voice of a kind. Yet, the color combinations of such small, mixed ensembles can be expanded by the composer to color the range of each instrument from subtle, microtonal pitch colorations to complex, almost "noisy" distortions of color such as "multiphonics," that can now be produced and precisely controlled on wind and brass instruments. In fact, composers and performers have, since the early sixties, explored and experimented with an ever-widening array of available sound colors, produced and controlled in acoustic instruments, voices, as well as electroacoustic instrument systems. Such explorations with acoustic instruments began to be formalized in the sixties and seventies with the publication of several books devoted to the detailed explication of special techniques involved in producing and controlling, for instance, a variety of multiple sounds—**multiphonics**—and microtonal pitch control on conventional wind and brass instruments. These special performance techniques—sometimes referred to as "extended instrumental resources" and "extended vocal techniques"—have been tested and employed by composers in designing the coloration of their compositions, especially for soloists and small ensembles (see chapter 3, **MEDIUMS AND IDIOMS**).

Developments in electroacoustic music composition through the second half of the twentieth century have profoundly affected composers' attitudes about the sound color potential of traditional acoustical instruments and voices (see again **MEDIUMS AND IDIOMS**). Without doubt, the development of "extended instrumental resources" and "extended vocal techniques" has come about, for one thing, because composers and performers specializing in contemporary music have found themselves increasingly sensitive to the need for modeling the **integration** of acoustical and electroacoustical sound colors. Paradoxically, composers and performers, who in the sixties and the seventies were intent on modeling the distortion and modulation of electronic sound colors to achieve similar sound colors on acoustical instruments and the voice, now are equally intent in the final decades of the twentieth century on modeling the complex expressive qualities of acoustical instrumental sound colors on digital synthesizers and computer music systems! There has, indeed, been a crossing back and forth between acoustical and electronically produced sound colors.

Composers of music for acoustical instruments, voices, and taped and/or live electroacoustic sounds have been, from the beginning of experimentation with this fascinating "crossing" of sound colors, acutely aware of the potential for achieving both beautifully integrated coloration and/or disturbingly clashing sound colors between the acoustic and electroacoustic sounds. Composer Morton Subotnick, both an expert clarinetist and a leading practitioner of electroacoustic music, integrates diffuse acoustic and electronically produced sound colors in his composition, *Parallel Lines* (1979), for solo piccolo, "ghost electronics," and a nine-member mixed instrumental ensemble.

In *Parallel Lines,* the sound color of the piccolo soloist is heard alternately with and without the variable "ghost electronics." Concerted with the soloist are two woodwind, two brass and three string instruments, as well as two percussionists performing two wood and two metal idiophones, four membranophones, chimes, sizzle cymbal, and large tam-tam. The ten performers are playing at various points in the piece from an array of twenty-three different sound colors, each of their different sound spectra greatly widened by a combination of electronics, multiphonics, and various coloration effects of the acoustic instruments. Where the coloration in Druckman's orchestral work was most diffuse in its simultaneous combination of many concentrated sound colors, Subotnick's chamber work exhibits diffusion by the great number of successive coloration changes composed for the instruments and electronics through the course of the piece.

What Subotnick refers to as "ghost electronics" is a digital control system, activated by a sensitivity to the pitch and loudness changes of the piccolo in live performance. The system is programmed to modulate and shift the frequency to produce a "parallel line" of sound color; it is, in turn, programmed to produce series of different signal frequencies at controlled, repeated rates, modulating the sustained piccolo sound.

During the middle, "visceral" section of *Parallel Lines* (**excerpt 12**), the piccolo insistently asserts its butterfly-like dartings-about with the electronically modulated "flutter-like sound" in a constantly fluctuating events stream of sound color effects. The ensemble, at the same time, reacts noisily to the piccolo's excited flutterings, an instrumental chorus "crying out" with animal or insect-like sounds. They make a virtual rain forest of natural sounds painted by Subotnick as an electroacoustic soundscape. The three-page excerpt is a catalog of sound color effects, heightened by contrasts of exaggerated loudness and softness. All of these elements are integrated in his sound color image.

In author Thomas Clark's *Peninsula* (1984), for piano and tape (**excerpt 7**), resynthesized timbres from digital recordings of five acoustical sound sources—guitar, saxophone, marimba, piano, and whispering voices—form the ensemble of taped sounds. Piano sonorities resonate as repeated tones, arpeggios and two-pitch constellations in waves of sound, sustained in the accumulating "wetness" of strings vibrating by means of damper and sustaining pedals. In relief, three event streams are not pedaled or sustained, the "dryness" of their sudden color change delineated by the starkness of two-pitch sonorities. In the score, the tape part appears in one-second increments, indicating only the density of sounds heard to guide the pianist's pacing. In figure 7.3, however, the individual sound colors are graphically plotted, showing their diffusion and concentrations.

The percussive, synthetic timbres gradually become more dense and insistent. The pianist's acoustical colors are integrated into this trajectory, a drive toward repeatedly accented four-pitch constellations, the goal of this first section of the piece.

Separation and Integration—In *Parallel Lines,* Subotnick blends acoustic with electronic sound colors through the fusion and modulation of the piccolo with an electronically produced signal; at the same time he models that electroacoustic distortion of timbre with acoustical distortion of the sound colors of the diverse wind, brass, string, and percussion instruments, achieving an overall sound color integration. Clark, too, achieves integration of piano and tape sound colors by complementing the intermittent, dry, damped, nonresonating piano sounds with dry, percussion-like synthetic sounds; while, in contrast, the wet, nondamped resonant piano colors provide a reverberant "acoustical environment" for the taped electroacoustic sounds, achieving, in alternation, both separation and integration of events.

In titling, his *Sinfonia Concertante: A Mozartean Episode* (1986), for chamber orchestra and taped computer music narrative, author Larry Austin not only invoked the formal premise of a classic, eighteenth century instrumental form but gave an important clue about the sound color image he envisioned for the piece. In notes for the piece, he explains:

> *Sinfonia Concertante* is modeled on the dramatic essence of its classic namesake: the interplay of the chamber orchestra and the computer music narrative; of sweet consonance and angry dissonance; of innocence and duplicity; of pleasure and sorrow. Dualities intrigue me, precisely because they are never completely reconciled, just as extreme polarities in the fortunes of life are never completely understood.

In **excerpt 15,** the separation of five small instrumental ensembles and the taped computer music narrative are grouped visually in the score. Except for the trumpet/timpani/bass group, the various ensembles derive their instrumentation for the soloists indicated in four of Mozart's own *sinfonie concertanti.* Through the piece, Austin alternates, separates and fuses these ensemble carriers, at times in concentrated conjunction, at times in the diffusion of the traditional orchestral tutti.

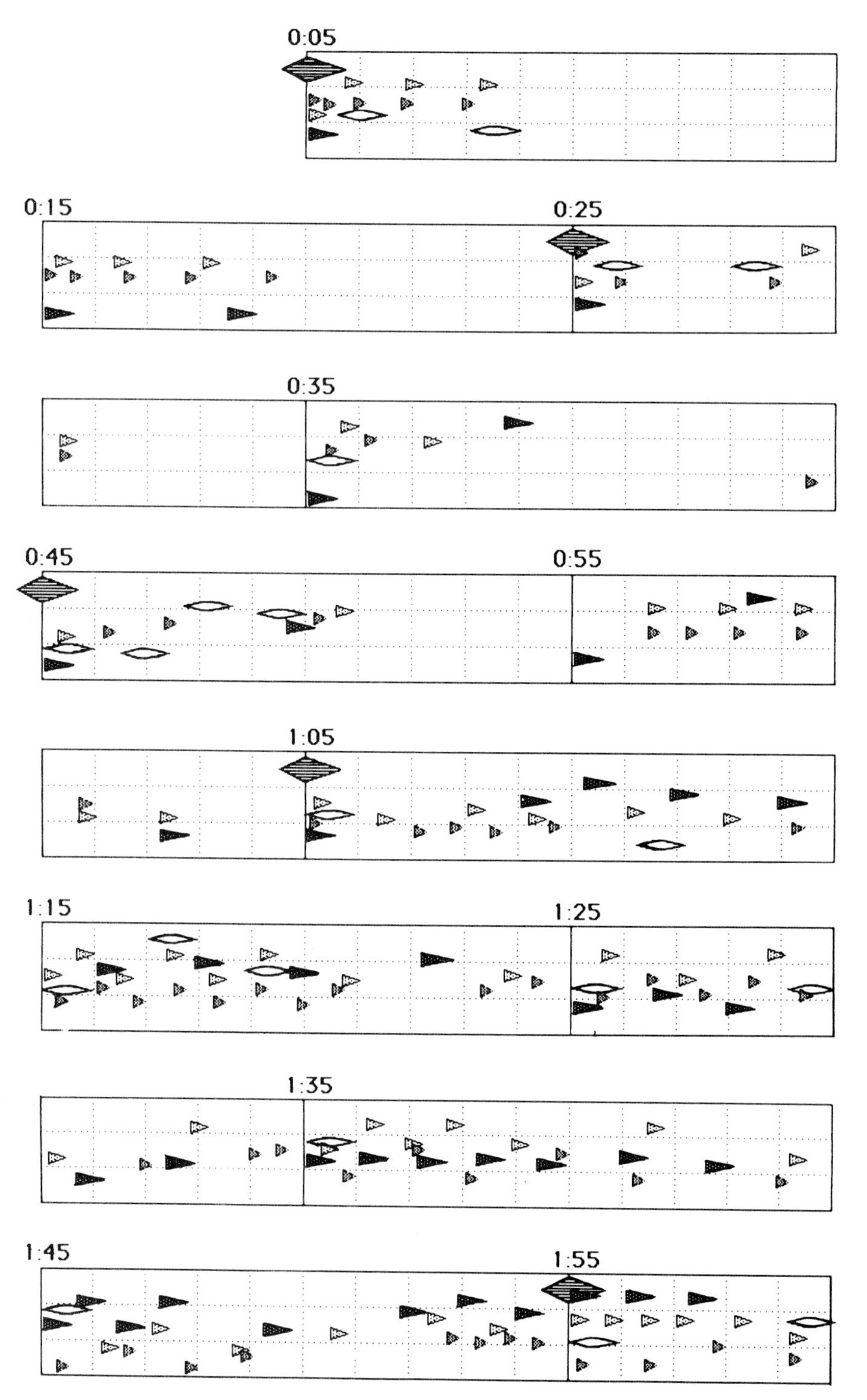

Figure 7.3 Color distinctions in the synthetic sounds of *Peninsula*

The taped narrative of excerpted Mozart letters is heard prominently through the course of the piece in **conjunction** and **alternation** with the various orchestral groupings. At the same time, taped computer music—pitched, talking-singing timbres and events derived from the voice of the recorded narrator—serves as a unique sound color itself, sometimes voice-like, sometimes instrument-like, sometimes a fusion of both sound colors. These computer-generated timbres were created utilizing voice analysis/synthesis techniques developed by composer Paul Lansky. Lansky's program provided the composer with analysis data of discrete, 1/100th second "frames" of the loudness, pitch and timbral characteristics of the digitally recorded voice. Further, Austin could change those same characteristics to alter, delete, or reiterate any or all of the frames. Through repeated experimentation with the threshold for voiced and unvoiced sounds of the voice, Austin modeled his resynthesis on what he terms a "fusion of vocal/instrumental sound color."

Excerpt 15 reveals a montage of diffuse sound colors, musics, narration, and the conflicting sentiments of the text. The taped "vocal-instrumental" timbre combines its resounding, pulsating, low-frequency sonorities every seven seconds with the *pizzicato* bass, harp, and timpani; as the rich sweetness of the violin/piano duo dies away at R–1, the oboe—accompanied by the clarinet, horn, and bassoon—rises to its shrillest register at R–5; while, in the distance—*lontano*—the flute and harp harmonics are heard as a gentle background coloration. In strident contrast, the muted but *forte* trumpet along with the strings and piano rudely interject their disjunct gestures at every seven-second hammerstroke. Not notated in the score is another sound color in the montage: the "playing" of three Mozart fragments by the synthetic vocal-instrumental timbres. At S–2 the textural strands thin, the winds fading away as the strings, entering one by one, sustain a light wash of high harmonics, undulating in the background to S–5. There, the gathering flurries of woodwind and piano colors build to a *forte*. The orchestra suddenly falls silent, revealing the synthetic timbre to intone Mozart's farewell to his father. A final, Mozart-like orchestral tutti ends the piece.

John Adams' sound color image for *Harmonium* (1981), for mixed chorus and large orchestra, was clearly modeled from the affections of the poems he chose to set. Their moods are expressed through the expansive, exaggerated time-scale of harmonic rhythm in each of the three movements. Two of the poems—seventeenth century English poet John Donne's "Negative Love" and nineteenth century American poet Emily Dickinson's "Wild Nights"—concern the irony and ecstasy of human love, both set in brilliant, pulsating sound colors in the first and last movements. The middle movement, separated from the first but followed without pause by the third, is a setting of a second Dickinson poem of quite different poetic imagery:

Because I could not stop for Death,
He kindly stopped for me;
The carriage held but just ourselves
And Immortality.
We slowly drove, he knew no haste,
And I had put away
My labor, and my leisure too,
For his civility.
We passed the school where children played
At wrestling in a ring;
We passed the fields of gazing grain,
We passed the setting sun.

We paused before a house that seemed
A swelling of the ground;
The roof was scarcely visible,
The cornice but a mound.
Since then 'tis centuries; but each
Feels shorter than the day
I first surmised the horses' heads
Were toward eternity.

Adams explains that he "took advantage of the unhurried cinematographic unfolding of imagery . . . to once again utilize the expressive power of changes of key . . . placing the speaker—in a slowly moving carriage while the sights and sounds of her life gradually pass her by—creating an irresistible opportunity for a slow, disembodied rhythmic continuum." (CD notes) The darkness of the unknown is pervasive through the poem. The "eternity" of death blends with fleeting memories of childhood. Adams' choral/orchestral coloration of his setting mirrors these images with dark, muted colors set off at crucial moments in the piece with reverberantly bright sound colors.

In this eight-minute movement (ten minutes in the recording), Adams limits the number of elaborated pitch constellations to six, the first lasting 53 seconds, the second 72, the third 61, the fourth 100, the fifth 76, the last 110. With the ensemble sonorities changing pitch content at such slow rates and over long stretches of musical time, our receptivity to instrumental/vocal sound colors is much keener. In fact, Adams' coloration plan is central to our sense of change and flow of the event streams in the continuity of the piece. As Adams, himself, expresses, "form . . . was born out of the ongoing harmonic and rhythmic flow of the continuum . . . an aspect of the music's texture."

Listen carefully more than once to the second movement of *Harmonium,* considering the following description of coloration in the fourth and fifth sections, beginning immediately as the second stanza of text is finished.

Clarinets, muted horns and violas softly enter as the chorus ends the third section with a newly changed, darkly-colored constellation, joined quietly by the low, dark drone of celli and basses and, a few moments later, by bassoon. This dark background is set off by the entrance of the lighter colors of flutes, their slurred ostinato line outlined by plucked tones of the harp. Then muted violins and more flutes enter in delayed imitation, echoing and distancing the first *ostinato* line. The muted horns leave the texture shortly after, the wind and string colors remaining to accompany the gentle entrance of sopranos, "no vibrato" in child-like vocal quality. Our ears focus on their foreground color. The sustained colors of clarinets and bassoons continue until the clarinets are replaced by open horn colors, while, just as subtly, a new pitch color—G—makes its entrance in the bass drone and a horn. This new pitch is heard both as an added tone in the now ambivalent pitch constellation and a new, less muted color. Complementing the darkness of the low strings drone, violins and clarinets enter with lighter, middle-register colors, first in unison, then dividing to sustain a third.

The voices, too, have enriched their colors, adding tenor voices in octaves with the sopranos, joined then by the basses, in unison with bassoon on a two-tone, chant-like counterpoint to the tenors and sopranos. The coloration is changing, with light against dark as the texture gradually thickens, then thins slightly as some colors leave before the next newly changed harmony. Here, all at once, both brighter and darker colors blend.

The new sonority is softly sustained during the first moments of this section by a blend of high but muted violins and a low drone of *divisi* basses coupled with the tuba in its lowest range. All frame a sonorous chord of thirds, sung by the sopranos and altos on the closed vowel, "*oo,*" a covered vocal sound, slightly muted. The harp, continuing its *ostinato* line from the previous section, is joined in unison by the brighter "celesta tone" of the synthesizer and an echoing piano. The tenors resume their child-like chant, now the focus of textual and melodic continuity. Changing their sustained vowel sound to an insistent, iterative rhythmic *ostinato,* the sopranos and altos, soon strengthened by the basses, *crescendo* toward a *forte* climax.

During this buildup, instrumental colors enter intermittently, adding to the dark/bright mixture. High violins and muted celli "sing" the tenor's line in rhythmic augmentation, dividing into an ensemble sonority and smearing their colors with a sudden *glissando.* Then trumpets and trombones, their colors fresh from not being heard for over two minutes, enter the texture quietly but dramatically swell with the timpanum into the foreground during a climactic denouement. Quickly, the full ensemble and this whole section of the movement die away.

INVENTION 20

Study percussion instruments and their color potentials by listening to all of Mizelle's *Soundscape* (**excerpt 11**) and by consulting percussion books and performers. Make a catalog of interesting instruments grouped as in *Soundscape* by their material—skin, wood, earth, metal, glass. Choose three from each group and assign them to three players' parts on a score so that each player will then have one instrument from each group. The score can use five-line staves with each line of the staff representing a material group in each part.

Freely explore combinations of these colorful sounds, all very soft and mostly sustained or with simple pulse-like repetitions. Don't think about rhythm, but focus on melding and contrasting the sound qualities. Make chains of color as Cage did with strings in **excerpt 9.**

INVENTION 20 VARIATION

Study brass instruments as you did percussion, especially their most colorful effects: the many kinds of mutes they can employ; their capability for dynamic shapings of sustained sounds; and flutter tongue.

For a brass quintet (two trumpets, French horn, trombone, tuba) or a trio of only those instruments using the widest variety of mutes (trumpets and trombones), invent color chains which gradually modulate from one kind of sound to another, a metamorphosis of color. Still limit rhythms to sustained notes and simple pulse-like repetitions. For pitches, start with mid-range clusters of pitches very close together, then plan a registral trajectory that several times in different ways spreads out and reconverges to the original clusters.

INVENTION 5 VARIATION
(See page 55)

Continue exploring your personal electroacoustic medium. From other natural sources, develop other collections of transformed, extended sounds. Each will be a family of colors, like the instrumental families of an orchestra.

Plan a form for presenting these colors which moves from a high diffusion of all your colors in rapid succession to concentrating on one family of colors exclusively. Then model a reverse trajectory to follow, gradually adding back in color families until they are all present at the same time for a wild *finale.*

INVENTION 21

Obtain a score of Morton Feldman's *In Search of an Orchestration* (1967) for symphony orchestra, published by Universal Editions. Study the score carefully.

In some form of symbolic representation, all orchestra scores are a visual representation of the composer's sound color image for a piece. We can see the color of the sonorities, lines, and textures as they unfold, page by page. This is true of Feldman's piece, in spite of the irony in the title Feldman chose and the unorthodox appearance of the score. In fact, once you have assimilated Feldman's "Directions for Performance" and have practiced "reading" the score, the continuity of the event streams and their registered coloration is readily followed. You should be able to ***hear*** the piece in your mind's ear.

Now model a sound color image for an orchestra piece of your own, creating a method of detailing its continuity of coloration variables. You can adopt a variation of Feldman's matrix score approach or devise another, such as a color-coded bar graph or an x/y-axis graph plotting color and texture through time. You should go beyond this stage to score several passages of the piece, drawing on pitch constellations and event stream patterns you have learned to develop in other inventions.

OTHER READINGS

Books:

Arnheim, Rudolf. *Visual Thinking.* Berkeley, Calif.: University of California Press, 1969.
Clifton, Thomas. *Music as Heard: A Study in Applied Phenomenology.* New Haven, Conn.: Yale University Press, 1983.
Cogan, Robert. *New Images of Musical Sound.* Cambridge, Mass.: Harvard University Press, 1984.
Cogan, R., and P. Escot. *Sonic Design: The Nature of Sound and Music.* Englewood Cliffs, NJ: Prentice-Hall, 1976.
Erickson, Robert. *Sound Structure in Music.* Berkeley, Calif.: University of California Press, 1975.
Roads, Curtis. *Composers and the Computer.* Los Altos, Calif.: William Kaufmann, Inc., 1985.
Roederer, Juan G. *Introduction to the Physics and Psychophysics of Music,* 2nd ed. New York: Springer-Verlag, 1975.
Schaeffer, Pierre. *Traite des Objets Musicaux.* Paris: Editions du Seuill, 1966.
Schafer, R. Murray. *The Tuning of the World: Toward a Theory of Soundscape Design.* Philadelphia: University of Pennsylvania Press, 1980.
Slawson, Wayne. *Sound Color.* Berkeley, Calif.: University of California Press, 1985.

CHAPTER 8 MUSICAL ARCHITECTURE

How all the musical elements and the patterns made with them go together, fit and support and cross and connect with each other, is what we will call the **architecture** of a musical composition. As with real architecture, the ingredients involved are space (pitch space and "time space"), materials, shape, and structure. The architect asks what a building will be used for, what terrain has been selected, and how big it will need to be. This is the beginning of the architect's modeling process, comparable to what was described for composers in chapter 2, **FORM MODELING.** Already aware by training of what materials are available and their properties—brick, steel, glass, and wood—the architect goes into drawing floor plans, elevations, deciding where walls and ceilings will be, making large rooms, closets, hallways, and doorways. The materials selected, their strengths, and how they will connect to realize these plans must all be considered.

Before examining the grandest overall aspects of coherent structure, we must first extend our study of the individual elements of rhythm, pitch, and color. We must discover what their own indigenous patterns might have in common to use in connecting them.

SPANS

We normally think of an interval as a distance in pitch space, the difference in location of two "points" in that pitch space. Likewise, we have now studied time spans—the duration of time from one event or time point to another. Applied to sound color and to loudness, the concept of a span can be thought of similarly as the degree of difference between two sounds.

All of these kinds of intervals can be matched or otherwise linked to give rhythm to a pitch pattern, to color a rhythm, or to select constellations for fitting together instrumental colors. Let's start with perhaps the most obvious possibility: a direct matching link of long time spans with larger pitch intervals. Joan Tower's *Wings* (**excerpt 2**) provides a clear example in figure 8.1.

But now, working with the same link of pitch interval size to time span size, let's try something different than a direct match. How about the opposite: smaller pitch intervals generating longer durations, larger intervals more rapid as in figure 8.2?

Another possibility is to treat one particular pitch interval in a special way rhythmically. All of the 3-semitone intervals shown in figure 8.3 are given conforming rhythms of all equal note values.

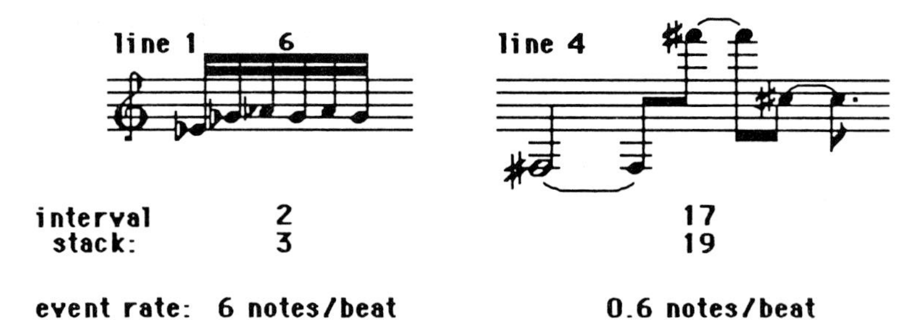

Figure 8.1 Direct link of interval size and time span in excerpt 2

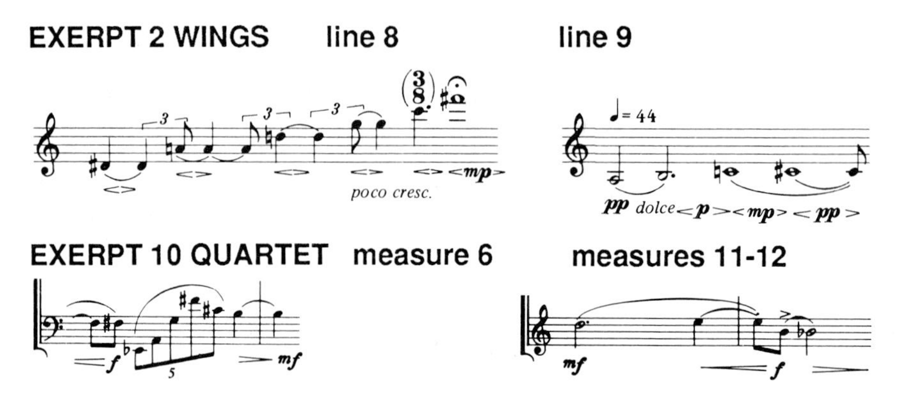

Figure 8.2 Reverse link of interval size with duration

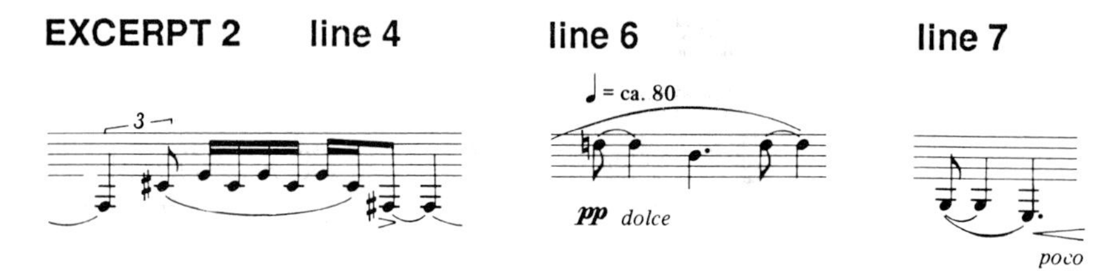

Figure 8.3 Consistent rhythmic treatment of an interval size in *Wings*

Links of this sort between pitch and time can be reversed, of course. Established time intervals can be used to determine the nature of constellations. The links can be large-scale, too. Imagine a stream of events alternating bursts of rapid activity with sounds "stretched" in time. For a general approach to pitch selection, this might suggest the use of small chromatic scale segments for the bursts, taller constellations for the stretched-out sonorities. But a selection of pitches with interval sizes quite the opposite could be used to contradict and balance out rhythmic extremes. Each excerpt in figure 8.4 shows a rapid passage followed by a much slower passage; in **excerpt 1** rapid notes are given smaller intervals and slower notes larger intervals, but in **excerpt 15** a reverse assignment is evident.

Having by no means begun to cover all the possibilities of linking time and pitch intervals, we will go on, adding color to our consideration. The simplest distinction of color "intervals" is to think of any significant color difference as a large span and no overt color difference as a very small color span

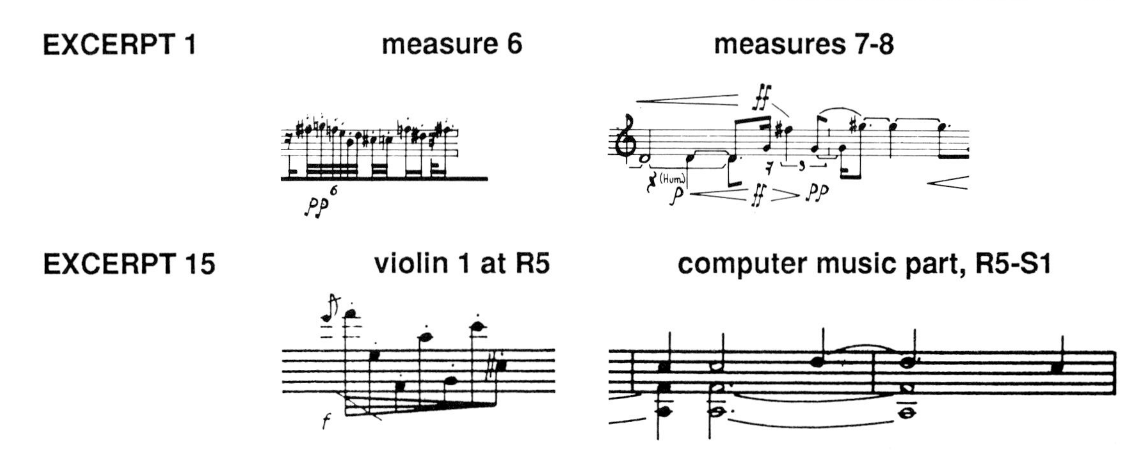

Figure 8.4 Direct and reversed links of durations and intervals

(allowing for the minute color differences in an instrument's various pitch registers, for example). Thinking in this way, a line of pitch intervals or time intervals or both could suggest when to change color, as when a different instrument might take over a line. Later, in the discussion of texture, this possibility will be considered further.

Associating instrumental colors with particular rhythmic qualities or pitch interval sizes is also possible. In figure 8.5, color differences between instruments are vividly reinforced by interval differences.

The selection of colors for voicing chords can be determined according to pitch intervals. Figure 8.6 is a constellation voiced orchestrally using a distinction of smaller intervals for wind instruments, larger for strings.

Figure 8.5 Interval sizes linked to color contrasts in excerpt 14, *Windows*

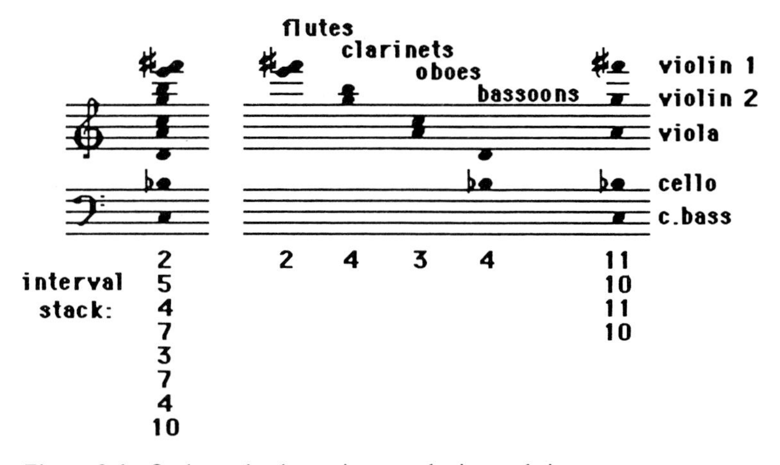

Figure 8.6 Orchestral color assignment by interval size

STRESS POINTS Each domain of structure, time, pitch, or color works on a concept of differences—intervals, as we have just seen. Likewise, each domain can have patterns with points of focus—special attention that will be paid to a moment, a pitch, or a certain color in its surroundings. These features can be linked or coordinated as intervals can.

In the time domain, we have already considered how a sound event stands out by agogic stress, by being longer than surrounding events. It is a simple matter of relative quantity. So is a dynamic accent or a textural accent, a moment of activity in more parts of the texture than surrounding events. In the pitch domain, we know that besides the traditional tonal focus of a pitch in a familiar diatonic scale, there is also an acoustic sense of root in some intervals that gives more weight to one of the participating pitches. These root qualities can build up into a strong pitch focus even in a so-called "atonal" pitch environment. Notes which are turning points in a line or otherwise placed at the fringe of an active pitch space are also given some sense of pitch focus by their isolation.

Now we can consider some examples of stress points from these distinct domains and how they may correspond or contradict each other in strategic ways. In figure 8.7 the highest pitch, the pitch center F-sharp, is also the longest, highlighting its eventual ascent to G.

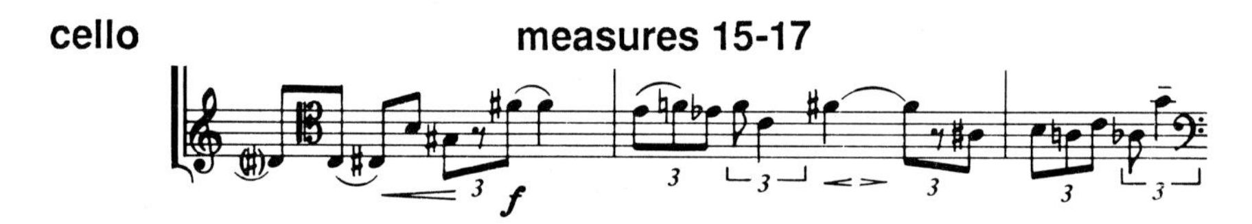

Figure 8.7 Corresponding pitch focus and agogic stress in excerpt 10

The pattern of stress points in one domain can take over from another domain or compete with it as the principal shaping of a stream of events. In figure 8.8 the focal pitch A-flat establishes a conforming rhythm in the voice, but contour stresses on a higher A-flat in the flute generate a more complex rhythm departing from the regularity of the vocal A-flats.

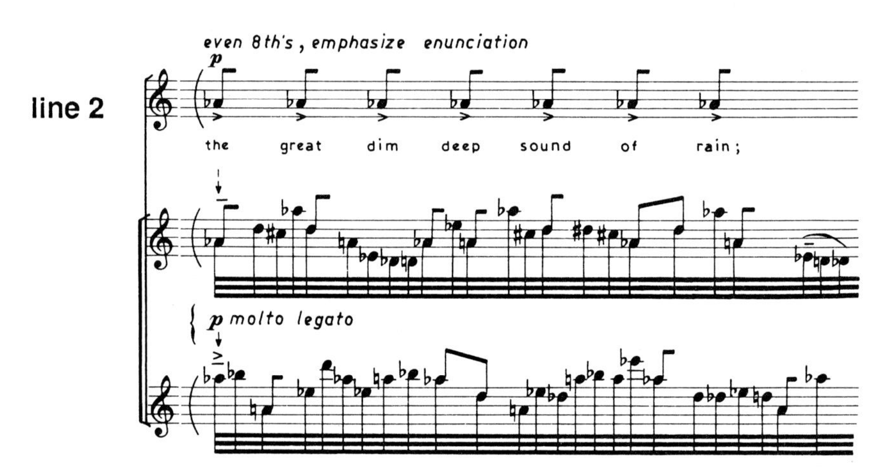

Figure 8.8 Pitch focus and rhythmic stresses in conflict, excerpt 8

The stress points in these distinct domains each make their own strata of time divisions. The pattern of durations from one focal pitch to the next, the pattern of time intervals of agogic stress, of color changes—all these patterns interact. When they correspond in time, there is a special sense of focus or resolution. When the stress points of rhythm, pitch, and color change do not correspond, tension is built up. Returning to our architectural analogy, the stresses (mostly gravity) on a building's parts are ideally distributed as well as possible but nonetheless are greater at certain points where strong supporting beams connect. Sturdy structure requires that the locations of these joints and means of connection be carefully planned.

ARCHITECTURAL SOURCES

Not only can one domain of structure guide design in other domains, but in fact, the planning of an architecture must start someplace. Patterns in one domain must first be devised in order to invoke span and stress point connections, suggesting how other domains of structure might be designed. Nonmusical images can be an initial stimulus, providing model patterns or properties of spacing and proportion that can be converted into starting ideas for a musical architecture. The process involves some way of **mapping** information from spatial or numerical patterns onto the elements of a rhythmic stream or the constellations of a pitch space design.

Mathematician Benoit Mandelbrot pioneered the study of complex natural patterns with multiple dimensions—the fascinating shapes of coastlines, tree branching forms, mountain ranges. His discovery, mathematical functions called **fractals,** explain such natural patterns and can simulate them with computers. Such creative work has stimulated composers' interest in the richness of patterns in the world outside music.

Peninsula (**excerpt 7**) is but one example of the vast possibilities of mapping procedures. It bases its architectural plan on the shapes of coastlines around a particular peninsula (the Leelanau peninsula in northern lower Michigan, itself a peninsula). Tracing these complex shapes onto graph paper, special points such as harbors were located, their positions yielding numerical coordinates. Figure 8.9 is a simplified version of the plot made this way.

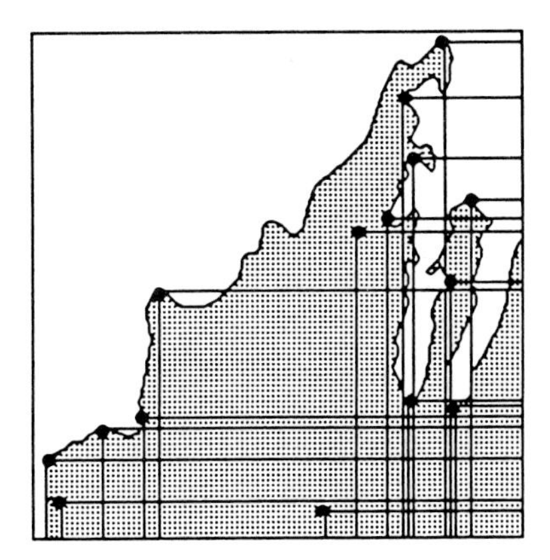

Figure 8.9 Map of Leelanau Peninsula with points of interest plotted

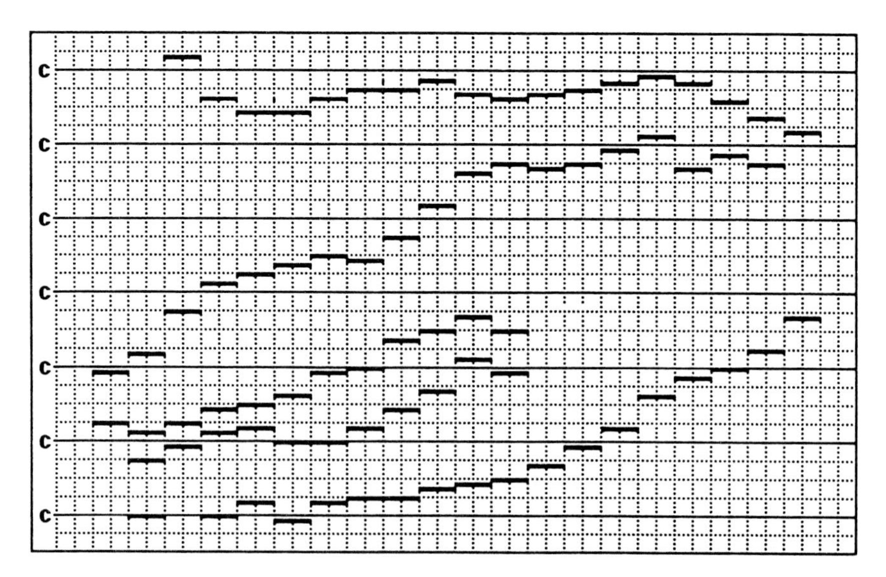

Figure 8.10 Peninsula map rotated on its side, placed on a pitch grid

Number coordinates for each point were used to determine the broad time proportion of a musical section and the density of events within it. The spatial network of points was interpreted as if in a pitch space, suggesting certain interval stacks, their time order and even contrapuntal strings of pitches (figure 8.10). Sorting, testing (aurally at a piano), selecting, and modifying some of these established basic constellation successions with which to generate the right number of notes prescribed for a section.

Not all the architecture was specifically prescribed by this process, however. A great deal was improvised by the composer, intuitively combining rhythm and pitch patterns into streams of events. Once collections of rhythmic patterns and pitch constellations are in mind, possible connections between them can leap easily into the imagination. Such a spontaneous process of architectural connection can even be set in operation by the composer simply providing patterns in one domain of structure and asking performers to imaginatively supply the rest of the architecture. If the specified ingredients are sufficiently vivid, performers can understand the intended architecture and finish building it.

Windows by Jacob Druckman (**excerpt 14**) frequently uses improvisation as a way of generating dense textures of animated activity in groups of instruments. At mark 30, boxes enclose collections of both rhythms and pitches to be combined by the players in their own individual ways. (Chapter 4, **DRAWING MUSIC** also considers this common scoring device.) The resulting streams of activity will be dense and complex, yet spontaneously energetic.

Morton Feldman extends further the scope of improvisation in many of his pieces. The score of *Last Pieces* (**excerpt 4**) is typical of his deeper approach to improvised architecture, providing in the score a long, slow succession of elegant, colorful piano sonorities but indicating nothing more specific about their timing. ("Durations are free.") Each sonority with its pitch spacing and interval qualities is part of an architectural framework, each intuitively suggesting a temporal response by the pianist, who determines the "right" moment for it to be succeeded by the next. A subtle and unique, broad rhythm is thus built.

Improvisation, then, is both impelled and controlled by the expression of a partial architecture which it works to complete.

SHAPE

Let us now consider the most basic kind of unit in musical architecture, a single line. After considering the combined properties of individual lines, we can understand better their roles as basic elements in thicker textures.

It is in a single line that we can most easily illustrate and explore the concept of shape. Since a line exists not only in pitch space but in time and in sound color, its shape is a composite of many characteristics, including but much more than the direction and size of pitch intervals. We will consider how each of the characteristics and their interaction contribute to relative degrees of a single quality, **angularity.** This quality is what the composer thinks of and wishes to control when planning and building the shape of a line's architecture.

Imagine a line drawn on an ordinary two-dimensional graph. What shape is the line? A straight line? A curve? A wave of zigzag pattern? A random squiggle? Trigonometry explains curves in terms of angles, changes of direction in a line. A straight line by definition makes no changes of direction, maintaining a consistent slope. The curve is a line continuously changing direction.

Angularity, then, is just a way to think about how changeably the elements of a line behave. Figure 8.11 illustrates several possible levels of angularity. The very least would be in a line with regular, comforming durations, pitch steadily rising and falling by the same size intervals, and no color or loudness change, as in example ***a.*** Even gradual changes in any or all of the elements produce smoothly curving patterns with what we might still consider a low angularity, as in example ***b.*** It is only when changes in the pattern elements of a line become unpredictable—changes in the changes—that angular qualities in a line are strong, as in example ***c.***

Figure 8.11 Lines with minimal to strong angularity

With angularity as a gauge, the composer can combine rhythm, pitch, color and loudness patterns to create lines of varied character. Combining lines, then, within the same time frame forms **counterpoint,** the most essential kind of texture, a weaving together of distinct lines. Successively in time, lines of various character and angularity make much of the contrast and variety needed for the continuity of a well-modeled form.

COUNTERPOINT

As was just stated, putting together lines of distinct character within the same time frame is one of the most important of all compositional techniques. Counterpoint is a venerated and traditionally central skill in a composer's craft, described in detail by many musical scholars throughout history. Studying the counterpoint of music in any historical period, going back even as far as to the fourteenth century, is an excellent way to understand how musical style comes about by looking into the composer's architectural logic. Such historical style analysis is strongly recommended for the composition student. A few of the basic principles of all contrapuntal approaches need to be mentioned and defined as tools for exploration.

Rhythmic Alignment. Is the extent to which the beginnings of time intervals in two or more streams of events are simultaneous, synchronous in time. With the almost universal notational convention for vertical alignment of notes starting at the same time, rhythmic alignment is readily apparent to the eye in a score. The discussion in chapter 5, **TIME STREAMS,** pointed out that nonmatching rhythms contribute to the distinction of lines combined contrapuntally, resisting a feeling of blend. They also create a composite stream of time intervals more complex than any of the individual components. This has a direct impact on pitch, making a richer or more extensive stream of pitch intervals formed between lines. For example, in figure 8.12 the combination of lines, when rhythmically aligned, makes a simple stream of contrapuntal pitch intervals. But when the alignment is dismantled, many new intervals are created by pitches overlapping in time.

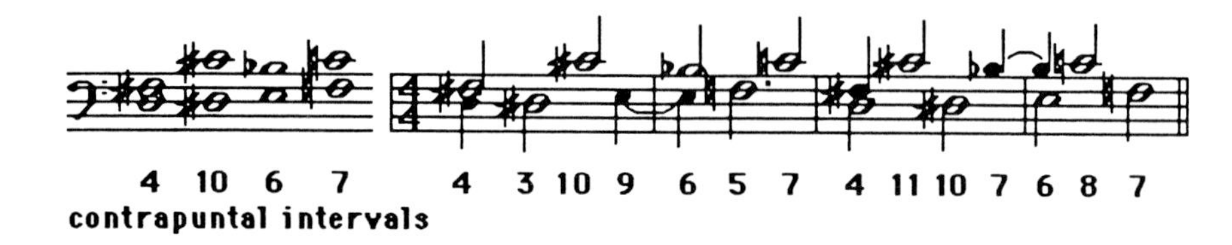

Figure 8.12 Effects of rhythmic alignment on contrapuntal intervals

In such a rich stream of pitch intervals between lines, however, those whose pitches do fall into alignment, beginning at the same moment, are marked by **contrapuntal accent.** They tend to stand out and form in the ear a set of **principal intervals** dominating the contrapuntal quality. A single principal interval used consistently and exclusively at points of alignment or contrapuntal accent will establish a strongly focused or unified pitch fabric. More variety of interval sizes contrapuntally accented by appearing at points of alignment will make a more diverse or loose fabric. This, coupled with the kind of principal intervals chosen, acoustically simple or complex, and the mixture or variety of intervals used in the individual lines, establishes the basic character of a counterpoint's pitch fabric.

In figure 8.13, note that the cello sounds above the violin even though it appears below in the score. Contrapuntal intervals expanding from one semitone out to six semitones are set with diverging rhythms. When the contrapuntal interval snaps back to the tighter two semitones, the temporal alignment of contrapuntal accent, as well as loudness accent, marks and reinforces this contrapuntal change of course.

violin 1 and cello measures 11-12

Figure 8.13 Contrapuntal alignment and intervals in excerpt 10

Counterpoint is a complex phenomenon, embodying so many of the important features of musical structure. To review, here is a list of factors to consider when designing counterpoint:

- Rhythmic conformity/elasticity of individual lines;
- Rhythmic alignment;
- Complexity of composite rhythm;
- Variety of pitch intervals in individual lines;
- Quality and prevalence of principal contrapuntal intervals.

TEXTURE

Other factors affect the nature of a contrapuntal combination of lines: how far apart in the pitch space the lines are situated; how different and how varied the colors that present them; loudness balance or dynamic distinction of foreground, supporting or background line; even spatial proximity, how close together or separated in physical space are the origins of the lines' sounds. These same considerations apply to other components of a texture as well as to lines.

Musical **texture** is a broader concept that includes counterpoint; it is the combination of distinct events within a time frame. To analyze the texture of a real fabric, a weaving of fibers into cloth, we want to know not only about the kind of thread and of what colors but also how tight the weave and whether the colors group into stripes or larger patterns such as plaid.

The factors that distinguish musical events, making distinct parts of a texture, are similar. Any domain of musical structure—time, pitch, space, color, loudness—can provide distinguishing elements. Each can also contribute to a sense of depth in a texture; foreground/background distinction of parts.

In the time domain, parts of a texture can be distinguished by **event rate.** More rapid events may stand out as foreground, but if conforming, very regular, and lacking variety of durations in their rapidity, may form a busy background for some other more elastic rhythm. So **rhythmic elasticity** can play a role, with more varied or elastic parts of a texture standing out as prominent foreground events. And even with streams of events relatively similar in rate and elasticity, a lack of **rhythmic alignment** can keep separate the parts without making foreground/background distinctions.

In the pitch domain, spacing or distribution of sounds is important in marking separate parts. This is a broader concern than that of lines and contrapuntal pitch intervals already discussed. Separation of sounds in pitch space can isolate a stream of events as a foreground part; distributing aligned or matching sounds over a wide register of pitch space can create a diffuse textural background. The role of color in distinguishing streams of events was already discussed in chapter 7, **SOUND COLOR.** Foreground/background distinctions made by color differences are much the same as with pitch spacing. A stream of sounds would be an **isolated color** if unlike the colors of surrounding sounds. A **distributed color** configuration combines different but generally similar colors, often making a good supporting or "middle-ground" part. (Imagine in a painting or photograph the rich mixing of oranges and pinks in a sunset sky, standing out from the deeper and duller azure background, yet being a surrounding for the focus on the bright red ball of the sun itself.)

In measures 42 through 46 of **excerpt 13,** we hear timpani as the principal outstanding element of the texture not only because of its active rhythm but because it is an isolated color. In contrast, the woodwinds starting in measure 45 accomplish a subordinate textural role with distributed color.

Color usually plays an important role in creating and clarifying texture. There are at least three basic functional ways color can be used in scoring a texture: we will call them **color highlighting, color chains,** and **color refraction.**

Consider mark 115 of Subotnick's *Parallel Lines* in **excerpt 12.** In this example, the principal line is presented with a relatively uniform color by the solo piccolo. At this important moment, when the oboe and clarinet are also entering with a new dynamic supporting material, the first four notes are specially articulated by the piccolo. The harp reinforces these notes, duplicating their pitches and to a certain extent their distinctly enunciated articulation while adding the variety of the harp color. Percussion instruments are often used for this kind of **color highlighting** both in *Parallel Lines* and in much other instrumental ensemble music.

Now let's consider a single line of a texture that is recolored, one instrument taking over for another in relay fashion. The technique, extensively developed in the music of early twentieth century composer Anton Webern, is often referred to in German as *Klangfarbenmelodie.*

Measures 38 and 39 of **excerpt 13** show a rapidly rising line carried through five octaves of pitch space by a chain of colors starting with bassoons and quickly moving through trombones, oboes, trumpets, clarinets, and flutes to piccolo. The piano cements the chain by reinforcing the entire ascent.

All of **excerpt 10,** from the third movement of Cage's *String Quartet in Four Parts,* is essentially a **color chain** elaborately building a single architectural line. This twenty-two measure section is the first of eleven such color chains in the movement. The colors in it are examined in detail in chapter 7, **SOUND COLOR.** Figure 8.14 shows how the stream of constellations might have looked before this color chain process was applied.

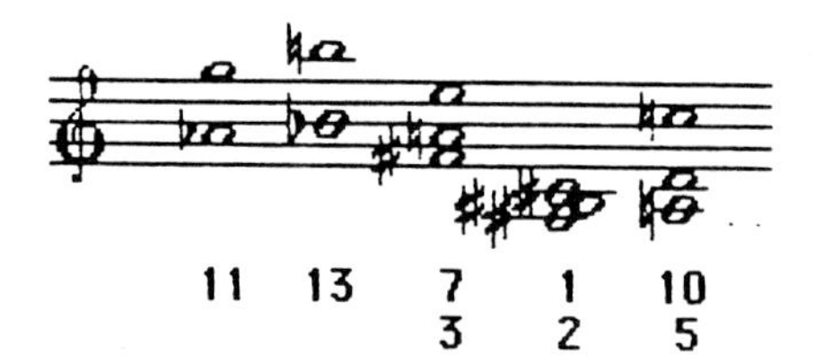

Figure 8.14 Simple stream of constellations for a color chain in excerpt 9

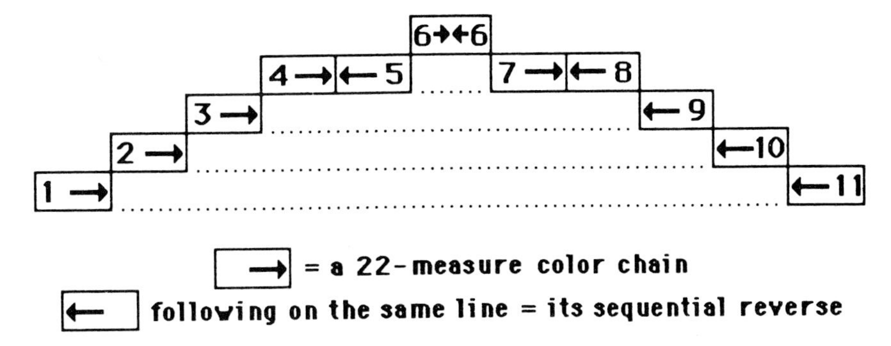

Figure 8.15 Form of the color chain palindrome in *Nearly Stationary*

Cage describes this movement simply as a "canon." In the traditionally accepted sense, a **canon** involves contrapuntal imitation of a line by other lines removed by a time delay and possibly some pitch interval from the original. Cage challenges the listener to "solve" the puzzle of what must be some color chain canon. Studying **excerpt 9,** we find no apparent canonic process at work. What is found upon studying the entire movement is a larger architectural process at work. Cage means by "canon" its broader, more fundamental meaning as a strictly applied principle of symmetrical organization. Except for the middle color chain of the movement, number 6, every other color chain appears in the first half of the movement and then again in the second half with its sequence of colors exactly reversed in time order (called a **retrograde**). The sixth color chain does this to itself, as it were, with its first eleven measures reversed in order to make the other eleven measures of another twenty-two measure section.

Such a process of matching a pattern with its retrograde to make a form symmetrical around its middle or, in other words, the same overall sequence forward or backward, is called a **palindrome.** (Letter palindromes are fun, such as the sentence, "*NAME NO ONE MAN.*") Cage uses the color chain palindrome as an architectural principle to build the entire movement.

Finally, there is the possibility of a mass of contrapuntal activity; more than one line of distinct character sounding at the same time. Assigning different instruments to different "voices," clearly differentiating them as separate although simultaneous, is the simplest and most common kind of **color refraction.** In **excerpt 14,** just before mark 31 a "window" opens to reveal a gently moving trio of two flutes and bass clarinet. The bass clarinet line definitely belongs to this group, but it is separated from the other parts not only in register and, after the entrance, in rhythmic alignment but also in its rich, resonant contrasting color.

Even a single architectural unit can reveal an elaborate inner structure of distinct patterns if contrasting colors are used to distinguish them. Thus an especially delicate kind of counterpoint can be refracted out of a single line. In **excerpt 8,** consider the similarity of the 32d-note lines in the flute and guitar in line 2. (Remember to read the guitar pitches down an octave from where they are shown.) They are essentially the same pitch line, refracted into two by the contrasting flute and guitar colors, set in relief by rhythmic divergence.

CONTRAST

Having considered all these ways that the parts of a texture can be distinguished, we will now consider textures as entities and how they can be distinguished from one another.

As with pitch constellations, each textural design is a unique combination and relationship of parts. And as with constellations, textures can be sharply contrasted to each other or they can be similar as they are related by subtle transformations.

Definite contrast is the easiest to understand. Thinking of the various factors already listed that distinguish textural parts—event rate, elasticity, and alignment; registral isolation, and size of prominent intervals; color distribution; loudness differential—we can make textural contrast by rearranging several distinguishing differences to create new parts.

To work fluently with texture, though, it is necessary to be able also to make smaller changes, creating new but similar textures. A simple transformation of texture might involve changing just one key factor, such as reassigning colors to otherwise fixed parts defined by the same rhythmic and dynamic distinctions. For example, in **excerpt 13,** the same basic texture of ascending 32nd-notes described above as a color chain in measures 38–39 and used again in measure 41 is rescored imaginatively in measure 44 for horns and trumpets, with a strikingly fresh result.

This is a basic procedure for **variation** techniques: to change textural factors one by one while keeping other factors and parts consistent. In the traditional theme and variations form, usually the harmonic framework and larger time frame of a theme are kept constant while rhythmic rates, registral spacing, color assignment, and loudness balance of parts are each chosen successively to produce the texture of new variations.

Yet subtler transformations of texture can be brought about by increasing or decreasing only the **density** of time, pitch, and/or color factors without reconfiguring their distinctions of basic textural parts. Density is a quantitative notion. In physical science it is the ratio of a mass to its volume or, in other words, an assessment of how filled up the space is. Increasing the event rate of one or more parts will fill up a given time space more. Bringing parts into closer proximity of register will increase the ratio of interval patterns to pitch space by shrinking the space. Adding the color of another instrument "doubling" or duplicating the activity of a part already present will enrich color density of a texture. And, of course, a *crescendo* is, in a way, the simplest of density increases.

The possibilities for building textures, transforming, and contrasting them are so numerous that these processes can be made fundamental to modeling form. Instead of relying on themes to lead and shape the progress of a piece, a sketch of changing textures (as described in chapter 4, **DRAWING MUSIC**) can be a plan to guide the composition of specific rhythmic and pitch materials.

AUTOMATED COMPOSITION

As processes of structuring pitch patterns can be formalized by serial techniques, so architectural designs can also be "automated." Combinations of rhythmic data, pitch selection, loudness behavior, and color assignment for streams of sound events can be determined by formal processes. If a process can be precisely explained step-by-step as an **algorithm** and the kinds of patterns it takes as models and is meant to produce can be architecturally analyzed and described, then the process can be programmed. This may mean simply that the composer learns a disciplined method of achieving certain results working with musical materials. Or it may involve the aid of a computer programmed to carry out numerically the selecting and transforming processes of a compositional method.

Model patterns are needed, since one must "teach" the computer program what kinds of patterns are desired. Models may come from the composer's experience and intuition, or could be derived from nonmusical sources such as mapping processes or fractals already described. Mathematical pattern models are also of great interest, such as the **Fibonacci** series, in which each term is the sum of the previous two terms, for example, 1 2 3 5 8 13 21 34 55 and so on.

To make choices, a computer program first generates options either by an exhaustive account of all possibilities or by a random function. Then it uses the criteria put into it to evaluate the options posed. In this way, randomly generated possibilities are sifted, introducing coherence by the consistency of choices made.

Many composers have used computers to make patterns by such numerical processes. Since computed results are already in a digital code, it is convenient to have a computer generate actual sounds for the patterns designed. In this way, the composer can listen to the results and get immediate aural feedback from which to revise the architectural models.

Two important issues are raised by automated composing, bearing critically on the aesthetic value of its products. One is that the architectural models on which processes are based should be vivid, clear, and drawn from thoughtful experience with "manual" composing. The other is that an algorithm will tend to produce a volume of largely similar patterns; but effective architectural modeling must be flexible and evolve to create meaningful form. Thus the composer must have a workable concept, rather than turning on the machine to search for a concept; and the composer must diligently monitor and adapt the process to give it life.

Computer-assisted composition is a very young field, but already it has developed into a rigorous and well documented endeavor. Much has been written about its research into the creative nature of musical architecture. We leave it to our reader to explore this field through some of these other writings. In fact, the very concept of musical architecture has been pioneered largely by composers using computers. Thus, their writings exclusively constitute the list of other readings at the end of this chapter.

Those who are devoted to these values and to finding intelligent approaches—composers such as Lejaren Hiller, Gottfried Michael Koenig, Barry Truax, Otto Laske, Charles Ames, or Sever Tipei—have succeeded in creating elegant, fascinating music with the aid of computers.

COHERENCE AND FORM

We have begun to hint at the role which architecture, the interrelationship of patterns from the separate domains of structure, plays in the design of form. Now a deeper consideration of that role is in order.

Although the essence of form is continuous and connected change, some notion of separate, definable maneuvers is useful. A form of any scope could be said to consist of three phases: a presentation, an elaboration, and a conclusion of material. In the discussions of variations and of transforming textures, many ideas about elaboration have been explored. **Elaboration** is an infinity of possibilities for transforming and developing ideas, spinning a mazelike network of doors and corridors connecting events. A closer look at the openings and closings of a form must concentrate on the shaping role of architecture. Sensing the architecture of a musical event involves a great deal of perceptual information about diverse aspects of sound and time; we must consider how this information will be absorbed and with what likely response by the listener.

Information about a musical architecture is a clear impression of how patterns in the domains of structure relate to each other, a definite character associating, say, an oboe color with slow, elastic rhythm and wide intervals over a background of rapid, regular, soft, *staccato* notes close together in pitch, played by clarinet and flute. How do we get such a clear impression of architectural character? How, for that matter, do we get our first impression of a building?

There is a difference. We usually approach a building from outside, able to see the whole form before we enter one of its parts, a room. Listening to a musical composition, however, affords no such overview except by inference from a title. The whole form must be gradually put together by memory and imagination while moving through time. It is rather like entering a building by elevator from an underground garage, seeing each floor and its rooms only one at a time, noticing similarities and differences from room to room and floor to floor. Music is even less predictable, though, full of wonderfully surprising discoveries. We walk through a set of rooms forming together a rectangle and we make a prediction that the next floor will also be rectangular. When we get there we find it to be so but smaller, and we develop a hypothesis of a building narrowing as it ascends, and so on. Information about its architecture is gradually gathered and assimilated, forming the basis for predicting what might come next.

What this means for the **presentation** phase of a musical form is a need for these features of architecture:

- A fixed relationship of rhythm, pitch, color, and loudness patterns;
- A texture with vivid distinction of parts, whether by register, loudness, color, or rhythm, probably with more than one factor at work linked to strengthen each other in distinguishing parts;
- Single streams of events without significant transformation of their architecture, clearly delineated from other event streams that may present a different architecture; silence or pause is an effective delineator if the architectures are similar and might be confused if joined or overlapped.

Consider how James Dashow begins *In Winter Shine* (**excerpt 6**). Two streams of sound events are distinguished by register—one high, the other mid-range; by rhythm—one sustained, the other active; by loudness—one pulsing, the other uniform; and by different colors. Reinforcing distinctions between streams of sound create a vivid opening architecture.

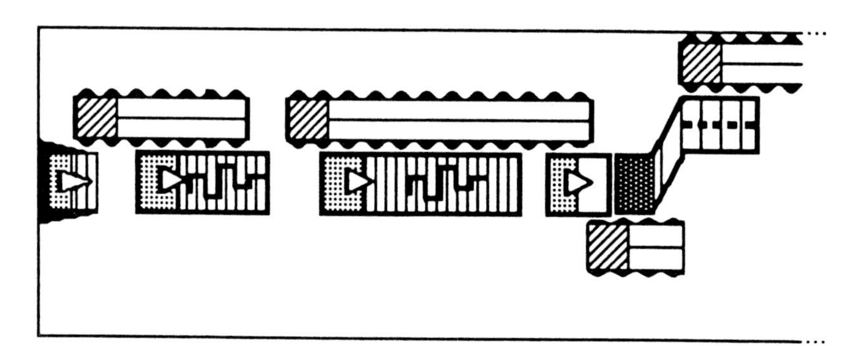

Figure 8.16 Architecture of opening material in excerpt 6

Pauses are like the short elevator ride to the next floor, a moment to reflect on what has just been experienced and what might be encountered next. Here, there is the balance between the certainty of information and the uncertainty of expectancy and wondering. Information science calls this uncertainty **entropy,** stemming from a lack of complete predictive information. (We don't carry a blueprint when we listen!) The balance between information and entropy is important—enough information to let us start to learn about the music, enough entropy to engender the excitement of discovery.

Entropy is also a good concept for understanding **conclusions.** To achieve what would normally be called a cadence—a convincing completion and satisfying closure of a musical form—information must build up to a certainty of outcome that outweighs remaining entropy.

Repetition of an event is one direct way to accomplish that, building a certainty that the final event when it occurs will be of like kind. But one uncertainty still remains: which reiteration will be the last? Marking the final event, then, entails some last-minute alteration of the idea's architecture:

- A wider or narrower texture;
- A sudden recoloring;
- Slowing, speeding up, increasing or decreasing the loudness;
- Extending the idea to add an accented sound;
- Inflecting rhythm or pitch patterns to bring them into greater alignment or consonance;
- Injecting a surprise, then returning to restate a conclusive idea.

As an example, consider how the end of Austin's *Sinfonia Concertante* (**excerpt 15**) employs rhythmic alignment, *crescendo,* and a final accented chord of suddenly wider register to cap off a dramatic piece. This example shows that ways to mark a final event could be applied even if no repetition immediately precedes. In this case, the architecture of the final event might be recognizable because of previous presentation and elaboration.

Conclusion, then, requires the certainty of two kinds of information: that an event is readily recognizable as an idea important enough to be the last; and that it is marked by some "last-minute" alteration to warn that it is, indeed, the last event. These principles apply not only to the end of a piece but to the conclusion of any stream of events.

As with a smaller stream of events, a piece can stop without conclusion. A process interrupted or abruptly terminated before reaching conclusion leaves the effect of a question mark. Many contemporary novels and films choose this rather existential approach. Instead of succumbing to a final certainty, entropy explodes, leaving us to wonder and reflect.

INVENTION 22 Construct a long string of pitches, using any of the processes described in chapter 6, **PITCH SPACE.** Then draw a melodic contour above another staff. Write pitches on the staff from the string, changing the octave of pitches as needed to follow roughly the contour drawn above. When the contoured pitch string is complete, write the size (in semitones) of each melodic interval below. Find out their average size as well as noticing the largest and smallest interval size used.

Now rhythmic values will be assigned to each pitch. Choose a medium duration such as a quarter note. It will be the assigned value for any melodic pitch approached by the average sized interval or an interval one semitone larger or smaller. For all pitches approached by other than these three interval sizes, other rhythmic values will be assigned.

For pitches approached by smaller intervals, assign a shorter duration. It could be any value shorter than the medium duration selected, or it could be consistently a value one-fourth or one-third the medium duration. For pitches approached by larger intervals, assign a longer duration, at least twice the value of the medium duration.

To consider possible meters for this string of notes, first identify the line's stress points. Agogic stresses (on the longer notes) will be readily apparent and will automatically be associated with contour stresses of the pitches approached by large intervals, since that architectural link was specified by the note-selecting process. Mark each one with a dash above the note. Also, find the other contour stresses of pitches at turning points in the register of the line and mark these with asterisks above those notes. Using the chosen medium note value as a pulse and counting unit, measure the time from each stress point to the next stress point of any sort. When this is an integer (a whole number), it can become the upper number of a meter signature for a measure starting with a stressed note and ending just before the next stress point. When the time span between stresses involves a fraction of the medium value, place the bar line after a pulse unit and let the stress point become a syncopation just before or sometime after the bar line. When stresses fall close together, choose which will get metric stress (by coming at the beginning of a new measure) and let the other syncopate.

Play the line on a piano or other instrument, observing how some stress points can be heightened by approaching them with crescendos. In longer stretches of notes between stress points, experiment with dynamically accenting an otherwise unstressed note to help maintain energy.

INVENTION 22 VARIATION

Reverse the association of intervals and durations by assigning pitches approached by smaller intervals the longer duration. Likewise, give the pitches approached by larger intervals the shorter, more rapid values.

In this architecture, agogic and contour stresses will no longer automatically correspond but will contradict instead. The result is a much more complex melodic structure and stress rhythm. Determining the placement of bar lines according to architectural stress points might be confusing or impossible.

An arbitrary meter could be chosen, letting the stress points "fall where they may." Try instead, though, translating the rhythmic values into time proportional notation. In this more neutral notation, dynamic shaping with *crescendo/diminuendo* marks and dynamic stress highlighting with accent marks become even more important to complete and clarify the architecture.

Try both this variation and the original procedure with other completely different pitch strings. Different modes of time ordering constellations will produce more or less angular lines with correspondingly more complex or simpler contour stress patterns.

INVENTION 23

Find a "natural" or nonmusical pattern of any sort that can be mapped onto a two-dimensional graph—a coastline or river on a map; a star plot; a photograph of the skyline of a city; a tide table; and so on. Any image with an identifiable set of points will work. The points (such as the corners of the buildings in the skyline) will have a measurable position in a rectangular two-dimensional space.

If the pattern is a visual image, trace these points onto graph paper with quarter-inch squares. Find the highest, lowest, left-most, and right-most points and draw a boundary rectangle one graph square out beyond these extremes. Now each point has coordinates, a pair of numbers expressing its distance from the left boundary of the graph and its height from the bottom boundary.

If the pattern is numerical, such pairs of numbers should be extracted and plotted on a graph just to visualize the pattern's shape.

Each pair of numbers can now be used to make choices for a rhythmic pattern. The first number can represent a duration, a number of pulses or small divisions of a pulse. The second number of the pair, then, can represent the number of notes to occur in that duration.

Next, determine the rhythmic "spacing" of those notes within that overall duration. They could all be exploded at the start of the time span as equal, small, rapid note values. To pursue a more elaborate architecture, though, more varied distributions might be devised.

Make a separate series of numbers from the first number of each pair. This will offer a model for the distribution of any number of notes within a specified duration, a model echoing on a small scale the larger proportions of time spans. Take as much of the model as needed to distribute a given sized group of notes within its total duration. Considerable approximation of proportions will be necessary to fit into a reasonable scale of small notational units of time. For this reason, the more flexible proportional time notation might be an appropriate choice.

Now design the rest of an architecture around this rhythmic scheme. Choose a single pitch in a particular register. It will sound at the beginning of each large durational unit, a marker or signal. Choose different constellations to surround that pitch following each of these signal points. Each constellation could contain at least one special interval to be used within each section of notes as the approach to the longest note of that section.

Devise a suitable medium for coloring the rhythm and pitch results. Piano will work for most outcomes; what other colorations might be used? Imagine a pointillistic setting in which each note is unlike the note immediately before it and immediately after it in color.

OTHER READINGS

Books:

Hiller, Lejaren. *Experimental Music.* New York: McGraw-Hill, 1959.

Koenig, Gottfried Michael. *Computer Composition.* Utrecht, The Netherlands: Institut voor Sonologie, 1969.

Mandelbrot, Benoit. *The Fractal Geometry of Nature.* San Francisco: Freeman and Co., 1982.

Winsor, Phil. *Computer-Assisted Composition: A Primer in Basic.* Princeton, NJ: Petrocelli Books, 1987.

Xenakis, Iannis. *Formalized Music.* Bloomington, Ind.: Indiana University Press, 1971.

Articles:

Ames, Charles. "Automated Composition in Retrospect: 1956–1986." *LEONARDO: Journal of the International Society for Science.* Oxford, 1987.

Austin, L., and E. De Lisa. "Modeling Processes of Musical Invention." *PROCEEDINGS of the 1987 International Computer Music Conference.* Champaign, Ill.: University of Illinois, 206–11.

Bolgnesi, Tommaso. "Automatic Composition: Experiments with Self-Similar Music." *Computer Music Journal* 7, no. 1 (1983):25–36.

Clark, Thomas. "Duality of Process and Drama in Larry Austin's SONATA CONCERTANTE." *Perspectives of New Music* 23, no. 1 (1984):112–125.

Englert, Giuseppe. "Automated Composition and Composed Automation." *Computer Music Journal* 5, no. 4 (1981):30–35.

Jones, Kevin. "Compositional Applications of Stochastic Processes." *Computer Music Journal* 5, no. 2 (1981):45–61.

Lorrain, Dennis. "A Panoply of Stochastic 'Cannons.'" *Computer Music Journal* 4 no.1 (1980):53–81.

CHAPTER 9
CONTEXTS FOR COMPOSING

In February, 1986, author Larry Austin and fellow composers David Behrman and Lois V Vierk were enjoying an early evening conversation in Behrman's loft in downtown New York before leaving for a late evening concert of new music at the Experimental Intermedia Foundation a few blocks away. Austin was describing his participation earlier that month in a composer's panel for the National Endowment for the Arts (NEA) in Washington, D.C. The panel was charged with recommending grants for music centers, institutions, and agencies around the United States who provided facilities and services for professional composers. In their final meeting, the five composer panelists were invited by then NEA Music Program Director Edward Birdwell to discuss and recommend refinements of existing guidelines for the program. At issue was the interpretation of the guideline for funding composer residencies at "centers for new music resources," where such composers have regular access to well-equipped, specialized facilities such as institutional computer music studios. Since the NEA cannot directly fund educational functions of such institutions and hence cannot fund student composers, only designated professional composers can benefit from such grants. Leading the discussion, Director Birdwell posed the central question to the panelists, "Tell me, just what is a professional composer?" It was suddenly quiet. After a few moments, the panelists began to respond, agreeing in essence that a professional composer is a person who receives fees and other forms of compensation through commissions for compositions. These might include royalty payments for professional performances of compositions; royalties from published and recorded works; and fees for consultation services, as well as lecturing, writing about and participating in performances of the composer's work. At this point Austin asked his New York composer friends how they might have defined a professional composer. Composer Vierk quickly responded, "A professional composer is a person who works from nine to five doing something else!"

THE PROFESSIONAL COMPOSER: THREE PROFILES

"Doing something else" does continue at times to occupy Vierk several days a week as a graphic arts designer, helping to sustain her in New York as a working professional composer. But, as her music becomes more widely recognized and performed, she more and more relies on her work as a composer to provide a reasonable economic base. Compiling a 1987 profile outlining her accomplishments as a composer points up the diverse activity she has set for herself, not unlike many emerging composers working in their profession today.

Lois V Vierk. Born in Chicago in 1951, her works have been performed throughout North America, Europe, and Japan, recently including New Music America Festivals in 1985 and 1986, The Kitchen, Roulette, Experimental Intermedia Foundation, Second International Alternative Arts Festival (Japan), National Public Radio, West German Radio, Concerts By Composers radio series, Dance Theater Workshop, and the 1987 Exploratorium 'Speaking of Music' series in San Francisco. Before moving to New York in 1984, Vierk spent two years in Japan studying *ryuteki,* dragon flute, with Sukeyasu Shiba, principal *ryuteki* player with the emperor's Gagaku Court Music Orchestra in Tokyo. Before that she had studied Gagaku for ten years with Suenobu Togi, formerly of the same ensemble, now at UCLA. Studies in composition include an MFA from Cal Arts (1978), working there with Mel Powell and Morton Subotnick, and summer study with Jacob Druckman at Tanglewood in 1978. Past positions include Assistant Music Director KPFK Los Angeles (1978–81), composer-in-residence at Crossroads School in Santa Monica, Instructor in Music at College of the Canyons, Valencia, California, and President and Cofounder of the Independent Composers Association in Los Angeles (1977–78). She has received several grants from the New York State Council for the Arts, enabling her to compose commissioned works for performers specializing in the performance of work by living composers, including violinist Malcolm Goldstein, accordionist Guy Klucevasek, and cellist Theodore Mook. In 1987 she collaborated with dancer Anita Feldman, composing a work for three tap dancers and percussion and completed a commissioned work for the Relache Ensemble of Philadelphia while in residence at Yellow Springs Institute. Her work has been described as "a dazzling display of pure creative energy" (*New West Magazine*), "genuinely exciting" (*New York Times*), and "riotous, upbeat and technically sophisticated" (*Los Angeles Herald Examiner*).

Vierk is like many other emerging composers in the midst of building careers, some like the career nurtured in New York since the sixties by David Behrman. As Lois Vierk observed, "David's decision in 1965 to pursue his composing career without relying on a regular academic position was possible then but seems more competitively difficult today." It was possible then, as it still is today, with the help and sponsorship of commissions, fellowships, subsidized residencies as a composer, and, most of all, a consistently determined effort by Behrman to perform his own work with like-minded, fellow composer-performers. His profile reveals these important traits.

David Behrman.—Born in Salzburg, Austria in 1937, Behrman is the son of the New York playwright S. N. Behrman and nephew of violinist Jasha Heifetz. Behrman studied with Wallingford Riegger in New York and at Harvard with Walter Piston, receiving a bachelor's degree. Awarded a Paine Traveling Fellowship, he studied in Europe with Karlheinz Stockhausen and Henri Pousseur. Returning to the United States, he received a master's degree in theory at Columbia. From 1965–70 he worked for Columbia Masterworks in New York, where he produced an important series of experimental music recordings, including the influential pattern music composition, Terry Riley's *In C.* Together with Robert Ashley, Alvin Lucier, and Gordon Mumma, Behrman founded the Sonic Arts Union in 1966, performing extensively in the United States and Europe from 1966 to 1976. From 1970 to 1976 he also toured as composer/performer with the Merce Cunningham Dance Company, composing several of the company's repertory pieces, including *Walkaround Time*

(1968), *Rebus* (1974), and *Pictures* (1984). He has been composer-in-residence at a number of schools, among them Mills College in Oakland, where he and Robert Ashley were codirectors of the Center for Contemporary Music (1975–80). In 1983 and 1984, as a consultant to Children's Television Workshop in New York, he composed music and designed sound software for children's educational games on home computers. In 1987 and 1988 he received extended composer-in-residence fellowships in Berlin and Tokyo.

Behrman performs his music widely in solo concerts in the United States, Europe and Japan. He also designs sound installations using video graphics displays, computer music hardware and sensors linking people to electronic music systems. New York Times critic John Rockwell writes: "No matter what electronics he uses, Behrman writes music that is prevailingly lyrical, even pastoral, and thus eloquently refutes the notion that electronic music must be futuristic and dehumanizing." (*New Groves Dictionary of American Music,* 1984, Vol. 1, 179)

Behrman's work as a professional composer has been sustained through over two decades by his specialized talent and inventiveness in the live performance of electroacoustic music. He has worked particularly in the eighties with computer music systems designed to be responsive and integral to human performance and in designing sound installations for museums. Vierk's work thrives on commissions, opportunities to collaborate with other artists, and fees from her participation in performances of her music.

In contrast to both Behrman and Vierk, composer Leslie Bassett's professional life, like the majority of art music composers in the United States today, has been sustained by his work as a composer and teacher in a university. His long and distinguished career centers in academic life.

Leslie Bassett. Born in 1923 in Hanford, California. At the University of Michigan in Ann Arbor he studied with Ross Lee Finney, followed later by composition lessons with Nadia Boulanger (1950–51), Roberto Gerhard (1960), and Mario Davidovsky (1964). Completing his doctorate in music composition at Michigan, he became a member of the composition faculty there in 1952, head of the composition faculty in 1970 and honored as Albert A. Stanley Professor in 1977. His works are well known and widely performed, bringing him awards, fellowships and honors, including the Rome Prize residency at the American Academy in Rome (1961–63), the Pulitzer Prize in 1966 for his *Variations for Orchestra,* two Guggenheim Fellowships in 1973 and 1980, the Naumberg Foundation recording award in 1974 for his *Sextet* for piano and strings, a Bicentennial commission from the Philadelphia Orchestra for his *Echoes From an Invisible World,* and election to membership to the American Academy and Institute of Arts and Letters in 1976. Of Bassett's music, Edith Borroff writes in the *New Groves Dictionary of American Music:*

> Bassett's music is carefully structured, its formal processes clear; conventional pitch materials are frequently deployed in an original manner. Even his writing for voices is instrumental in character, a quality he uses to advantage in the choral works, where voices and instruments are cohesively combined. (1986, vol. 1, 159)

Vierk, Behrman, and Bassett, in modeling their ongoing work as professional composers, are sustaining and fulfilling themselves through their music. Their music is highly regarded, in great part, because they have been singularly dedicated to the worth of their own music. Indeed, the first, last, and always most important champion of a professional composer's music is that composer. When dedication to and confidence in the worth of one's own music is strong and well supported, the next step is to establish and sustain its sponsorship and performance.

SPONSORSHIP

In the early decades of the twentieth century, it is well known that the great American composer Charles Ives was not only prolific in creating innovative music that would influence composers for generations to come but was very successful as the co-owner of a prosperous New York insurance company, Ives and Myrick. It is less well known and appreciated that Ives was a generous and consistent patron of other composers' music. Through his anonymous contributions, he subsidized composer Henry Cowell's New Music Society, New Music Quarterly, and New Music Quarterly Recordings, performing, publishing, and recording innovative American and European composers' music during the period from 1925 to 1958. Ives's patronage of Cowell's enterprises was so crucial that, when Ives died in 1954, the New Music Edition immediately experienced financial difficulties and was sold to music publisher Theodore Presser.

During that same period there was a correspondingly important increase in the number of universities, conservatories, and colleges in the United States which were appointing professional composers to their faculties, not only to teach general music courses but sponsoring them as composers-in-residence. The principle was being established that a composer can contribute significantly to the contemporary cultural acumen of an academic institution and that compositions created in this environment are important artistic achievements, ranking with the products of scientific and scholarly research. In the United States by the mid-twentieth century, academic institutions had become the chief sponsor of professional composers of art music. Thus, as the eighteenth and nineteenth century European tradition of individual, philanthropic patronage of living composers and their music faded in the twentieth century, institutional, governmental, and academic sponsorship increased dramatically in both Europe and North America.

Today, individual professional composers rarely enjoy complete, continual patronage to sustain them in their composing over long periods. Composer La Monte Young, a notable exception, enjoyed a ten-year (1975–85) "commission" from the exclusive patronage of the Dia Art Foundation in New York, where their support enabled him to establish a large, well equipped sound installation and performance and living space for research and presentation of his unique, extended duration compositions. Today, professional composers are most likely to be sustained by residencies and teaching responsibilities as music faculty in an academic setting, where, in the best situations, their work is nurtured, performed, appreciated and encouraged.

Composers chuckle knowingly when they hear the intellectually gifted and much honored American composer Milton Babbitt wryly refer to himself as a "part-time composer." Such ironic statements belie Babbitt's impressive list of influential works or the numerous composing awards he has received, such as his Pulitzer Prize Special Citation for "his life's work as a distinguished and seminal American Composer." Should Babbitt's long, distinguished career as a teacher of composition at Princeton University and later at Juilliard School of Music be characterized as the other part-time jobs he has held? Was his work as a professional composer somehow compromised by his academic responsibilities? Or—by his vigorous, ongoing dialogue with colleagues in philosophy, linguistics, mathematics and the physical sciences and his rigorous musical dialogue with his musical colleagues and students—was his music nurtured, his ways of thinking, talking, and writing about music stimulated, focused and strengthened? Babbitt would certainly agree that the latter is the case. The fact is that, today, the major sponsorship of American composers comes from academic institutions, where, for the most part, composers are thriving, actively composing, enjoying performances of their pieces, and interacting with stimulating performers and students.

Composing Fellowships, Grants, and Residencies. Institutional sponsorship enabling composers to devote extended periods of time exclusively to their work is universally well established. Such support exists in fellowships and special residencies awarded competitively to composers. It is interesting to note that the terms themselves—fellowship, grant, and residency—derive from their use in academic and scientific disciplines. "Fellowship" and "grant" normally refer to a sum of money allocated from funds dedicated to advanced work by an individual in some particular field of study. "Residency" refers to the formal period of time devoted to such study while in residence at an institution specializing in that field. Thus, we composers are no longer "commanded" as the appointed "court composer" to compose new works for our patron, the prince or king, but instead apply and compete to be awarded a fellowship or grant which will enable us to compose a new work. Or we apply to be provided with subsistence and a residency so that we can devote our full creative energies to composing for an extended period.

The professional profiles of three American composers were presented earlier to describe their background and accomplishments, citing various fellowships, grants, and residencies each had received. A quick glance reveals a sampling of such opportunities open to all applicant composers: Vierk—composer-in-residence in a California school and at Yellow Springs Institute in Pennsylvania, as well as several composing grants from the New York State Council for the Arts; Behrman—the Paine Traveling Fellowship from Harvard, an extended appointment as composer-in-residence at Mills College, and two overseas fellowships for extended residencies in Berlin and Tokyo; Bassett—the Rome Prize for a two-year residency at the American Academy in Rome and two year-long Guggenheim Fellowships.

Consulting reference works like *The New Groves Dictionary of American Music* (1986), one finds professional biographies of composers whose works have been selected for our **PORTFOLIO.** In total, their careers have included a wide range of institutional sponsorship.

It is certainly reassuring that these important opportunities for sponsorship exist for composers throughout the United States. It is equally important to realize that local, state, and regional sponsorship is available. For composers enrolled in or recently graduated from colleges, conservatories, and universities, there is also a great variety of special fellowships and grants available, including Fulbright and Woodrow Wilson Fellowships. Many schools also offer fellowships for study abroad, for example, the Paine Traveling Fellowship from Harvard or the George Ladd Fellowship from the University of California, Berkeley, for a two-year residency in Paris. Others provide grants for special composition projects or research.

Governmental arts agencies in all states and most major cities provide programs sponsoring composers, such as the New York State Council for the Arts grant programs for composers or the North Carolina Fine Arts Council periodic grant awards to composers from that state. These agencies are responsive to and encourage inquiries about such programs. If sponsorship programs do not yet exist in your city or state, as a citizen you may work to influence government officials to discuss and consider the worth of such programs and to work for their implementation.

It seems rhetorical to state that institutions sponsoring programs for composer fellowships, grants, and residencies are founded to encourage and aid as many composers, qualified under their guidelines, as their resources allow. In fact, such agencies need and welcome inquiries and applications to their programs. Without applicants, their programs would languish and eventually be withdrawn. After all, the programs were created and continue to exist to foster the composer's important contribution to society—the creation of significant works of art that reflect the values of our culture. Yet, for various reasons, composers sometimes turn away from the many opportunities available to them, perhaps discouraged by letters of rejection that are an inevitable part of one's first efforts in this pursuit. Several hundred professional composers throughout the United States apply for NEA Composer Fellowships each year, and allocated funds make it possible for an average of about 5 percent of the applicants to be awarded fellowships for grants ranging from $5,000 to $15,000. The professional composer must be steeled to persevere and follow the dictum: "Apply, and you might receive; do not apply, and you will definitely not receive."

Competitions, Prizes and Awards. Typically, application forms for fellowships, grants, and residencies ask the applicant composer to list prizes and awards previously received. It is reasonable for institutional sponsors to expect that composers who have confidence in the merit of their work will have entered their pieces in composition contests, winning some if judged the best entry. One measure of the quality of a composer's work exists in the number, competitive quality, prize amount, and historical distinction of the composition contests that composer has won. Winning one composition contest does not, of course, "a composer make," but it does establish the probability that future works by this composer will be equal to or better than that composition. Fair competition among one's peers establishes in our society a record of proven achievement of excellence. Besides such intangible benefits of winning there is, of course, the prize money, and for most composers the possibility of winning that money is quite enough motivation to enter.

The number and kinds of composition competitions in the United States and those open to Americans in Europe are truly amazing! They can be *ad hoc* contests occurring only once, offering a modest prize of, say, $100, allowing pieces in only one medium, perhaps charging an entry fee of $10, and limiting composer entrants to a narrow age group or particular locale. Or they can be international competitions like the Grawemeyer Award sponsored by the University of Louisville, occurring annually, offering an award of $150,000, allowing any type of composition to be entered, charging no entry fee, and open to all composers of any age or background from anywhere in the world! Or they can be long established, prestigious awards like the much coveted Pulitzer Prize, for which composers cannot directly apply and which offers a plaque and a prize of $1,000. Most prizes lie between these wide-ranging differences, are held annually, average about $1,000 for the first prize, are open to a variety of mediums, and are reasonably unrestricted for all composers.

Regular announcements of the hundreds of composition competitions appear in music periodicals and professional composer organization newsletters and publications. In addition, formal printed announcements of the contests are usually produced by the sponsors and mailed widely to universities, colleges, conservatories and composers' organizations. The American Music Center in New York City publishes and regularly updates a very useful booklet, *Opportunities for Composers,* containing a large, comprehensive listing of composition contests in the United States and Europe. Each listing cites the name of the competition, the address of the sponsor, the purpose, award amount, essential guidelines and restrictions, deadline for entry, and scheduled recurrence, if any. To obtain the booklet, write the American Music Center, 250 West 54th St., Suite 300, New York, NY 10019.

Commissions and Performances. The most direct and beneficial form of sponsorship of a composer's work comes in the form of commissions and performances. At the heart of a professional composer's career are the quality, frequency, and significance of the commissions for and performances of compositions. Composers soon understand that, beyond the personal gratification they understandably experience in having created a new work, a piece is not fully consummated until at least one other human being has listened intently and responded seriously to the full effect of the piece. For student composers, that person is often their composition teacher, who week by week hears the piece take form. For professional composers, the first "performance" might take place privately in the first "try-out" of the piece by performers who may have commissioned it. Of course, these preliminary stages all precede and anticipate the first public performance—what composers, performers and audiences celebrate as "The Premiere." All of this is not to declare that a composer's composition that is only performed privately is somehow incomplete. It is to say that, to be fully considered and valued as musical art by others, the piece should be heard in public performance.

Professional composers who also teach composition wisely counsel their students first to seek and find both performers and a performance venue for a piece they wish to compose. The teacher knows from experience that when good performers are identified and engaged from its beginning in the process of creating a piece, they respond positively and often commit themselves more fully to its performance once it is finished. When the student composer finds a performer to perform a piece the composer is proposing to write, that is, in effect, a commission. In such a case, the compensation is not a contracted fee but simply a promise to perform.

A composer that makes a piece without being commissioned is speculating on the chances of its being performed. When the piece is in its complete and hopefully compelling form, the composer may find a number of performers who express "interest" in performing it, but that "interest" may not readily translate into a firm performance commitment. With a commission for performance, the composer delivers the finished piece to the performer, and the performer "pays" for the piece with an enthusiastic performance. With a speculative piece, you "take your chances." With a commissioned piece, the composer has only the risk of a broken contract or a poor performance; contracts can be mended, and performances can be perfected.

The seemingly obvious exception to this logical cycle of commission/compose/perform is the case of a composer who always performs as well as composes pieces. Such is the case, as discussed in chapter 3, **MEDIUMS AND IDIOMS,** when a composer has created a personalized medium for compositions or is part of a special ensemble devoted to the performance of the music. But only the emphasis is different. Instead of the commission being the driving force for the full consummation of the piece, the performance opportunity and venue become all-important. This is particularly true, for example, in a "performerless" medium like electroacoustic music on tape. Composers working in this medium don't often have commissions to compose such works. Instead, they develop performance networks with other composers of electroacoustic tape music and with record companies and concert series devoted to the genre.

Professional composers are equally as concerned with gaining commissions to compose new pieces as they are with developing performance opportunities and venues for all the existing pieces in their portfolio. Often a commissioned work will include an agreement involving the commissioner's right to present the first performance in exchange for the composer's expectation that the performance will take place within a particular time. Composers should be careful to reach agreement about all aspects of first and subsequent performances of a commissioned piece. Guaranteeing the first public performance of a work as part of the commission agreement is crucial for the composer. We will discuss performance rights for composers in detail later in this chapter.

So the piece is commissioned, composed, rehearsed, and presented in its premiere public performance. Now on to the next piece, but at the same time composers want and certainly need performances of their pieces beyond the premiere. If the commissioned work is for a touring recitalist or chamber group, it was probably meant to be added to their concert repertory and will, if they are pleased with the piece, be performed many more times in many different venues over the next several years. That, certainly, is the ideal situation for the composer. If, as so often is the case, the piece was commissioned by, say, a symphony orchestra which has agreed only to present the first set of performances in a particular season, it is entirely the composer's responsibility (and the publisher's, if any) to seek and arrange subsequent performances of the piece. The sad fact is that many fine orchestral works languish unperformed for years after their first set of performances. How does a composer develop a "clientele" of performers and performance venues for both commissioned and speculative compositions? It begins first by fully exploring and nurturing the performance opportunities "in your own backyard."

For the student composer enrolled in a music school, the clientele is obvious: fellow music students, all of whom, like the composer, play an instrument and/or sing as members of small and large ensembles organized in a music curriculum. The composer approaches the best performers to be found and negotiates a commission for a performance. It's not that simple, of course, but opportunities are usually abundant and promising in a thriving musical environment like a music school.

Getting pieces played by official music school ensembles is another matter. In most schools an established protocol exists for periodic readings and selective performances of student compositions. If not, the student should ask his/her composition teacher to help in securing an ensemble performance. Also, there are usually well-established concert series devoted exclusively to the performance of new works by student composers. If not, the student should organize fellow composers to establish a cooperative performance venture. They can volunteer their own collective performance skills in return for the inclusion of their pieces on the concerts that result.

There are many variations to these approaches in musical school environments. It is important for student composers to be alert at all times to possible performance opportunities that could be developed with ingenuity, energy and an entrepreneurial spirit.

For that matter, student composers should not limit their search for commissions and performances to their music school. In the same community are churches and civic music organizations which, to the surprise of many young composers, enthusiastically welcome newly composed music when it is composed especially for their group. Student composers should explore and cultivate venues "in their own backyard."

Meanwhile, student composers should make sure that they are aware of, attend, and actively support concert series devoted to the performance of contemporary music in their area. Soon they may be submitting works for performance consideration to these same series, and it's never too soon to learn how that process works. The success of a student composer's brief career in a music school and in a local music community is a mirror of future success developing clientele as a professional composer.

COMPOSERS' ORGANIZATIONS: THREE PROFILES

Composer Robert X. Rodriguez likes to relate Dostoevsky's description of Hell as a great banquet where the guests are starving, unable to eat because they cannot bend their arms. At the same banquet in Heaven, the guests—also unable to bend their arms—have learned that they must feed one another in order to enjoy the feast. While most professional composers are neither starving nor, necessarily, feasting at some great banquet of performances and commissions, they have, nevertheless, learned the power and gratification of banding together for "the cause of new music," as Rodriguez puts it.

A Regional Organization. As a successful composer living, teaching, and actively composing in Texas today, Rodriguez fervently espouses the many benefits of supporting and participating in composers' organizations. As president of the Texas Composers Forum (TCF), he and his colleagues in the organization are enthusiastic advocates for the work of fellow Texas composers through services and sponsorship the TCF provides. Composers throughout Texas and beyond have benefited through the years from TCF's Meet-the-Composer (MTC) grant program, providing funds for personal appearances by composers at performances and other public events. The composer, compensated by a fee from the concert presenter matched by a grant from TCF, may conduct, perform, supervise rehearsals and talk to an audience.

Through TCF "showcase concerts," Texas music presenters regularly give programs of Texas composers' works, promoting audience and performer support for new music. Rodriguez explains in the TCF newsletter, *Composer News:*

> . . . With today's challenging new music we recognize that audiences and performers often need more than just a brief preconcert explanation from the composer. Like a new microwave oven, new music often needs a kind of 'owner's manual' in order to be more 'user-friendly' to the audiences and performers who, we hope, will derive lasting meaning and enjoyment from it. That's why we've begun our state-wide series of educational Composer Forums, in which composers can perform and discuss their works at greater length and answer questions about the wonderful and mysterious process of turning a blank page into music.

TCF is a relatively new regional composers' organization. Known first as Meet-the-Composer/Texas, it was founded in 1980 by a coalition of Texas composers, including Jerry Hunt, Karl Korte, and Larry Austin. With vital initial funding by and affiliation with the well-established Meet-the-Composer/New York, the organization began its first modest grant program to foster performances of the music of Texas composers. Gradually, as their Texas colleagues and music presenters learned of this new venture, the applications for matching funds for concerts of new music increased every year until, in 1987, thirty-nine different Texas presenting institutions were awarded grants for matching fund commissions and appearances by over one hundred composers from Texas and "the rest of the USA." In 1985, Meet-the-Composer/Texas was renamed the Texas Composers Forum in recognition of the fact that the organization's scope and services had expanded to include educational and presenter activities.

To sustain its services, TCF relies on annual grants from the Services to Composers program of the National Endowment for the Arts, the Texas Commission on the Arts, the City of Dallas Arts Program, as well as matching grants from Meet-the-Composer/New York, foundations and corporations, and income from benefit concerts instigated by composers. There are no membership dues; instead, composers and supporters of new music are urged to subscribe to the TCF Composer News and to make additional tax-deductible contributions to help sustain TCF services and programs. In a newsletter appeal for contributions, Rodriguez declares: "We believe Texas Composers Forum provides an essential service in bringing composers, audiences, and performers together, and we invite all of our readers to work together with us to enrich and preserve the music for which our generation will be remembered."

TCF began as part of a country-wide network of Meet-the-Composer affiliated organizations. Based in New York, the largest MTC organization and the "parent" of the affiliates was established in 1974 and brilliantly led since then by composer John Duffy. Composers around the country can now benefit from MTC grants through one of the eight regional affiliated programs, including MTC/Arizona in Phoenix, MTC/California in Los Angeles, MTC/Mid–America in Kansas City, MTC/Midwest in Minneapolis, MTC/New York, MTC/Texas in Dallas, MTC/Southeast in Atlanta, MTC/West in Santa Fe, and, independently serving New England states, the Visiting Composers Program in Cambridge.

A National Organization. Founded in New York in 1937 by composers Aaron Copland, Wallingford Riegger, and Virgil Thomson as a cooperative venture to promote the interests of American composers, the American Composers Alliance (ACA) continues to prosper today as the oldest national membership organization for professional composers of concert music in the United

States. Through its half century of service to composers, it has been dedicated to promoting, reproducing, and distributing members' compositions through American Composers Edition, its sales and rental division, and composers Facsimile Edition, an economical reproduction service for nonmembers. ACA reproduction and distribution services are modeled after commercial music publishers, except that composer members retain copyrights to their music. Royalty and rental payments to composers from ACA are about 50 percent higher than standard publisher rates.

Complementing its publishing and distribution services, ACA has been effective through the years in its ongoing promotion of members' works through the ACA Catalogue, the ACA Recording Award, concert sponsorships, and the ACA Radio Series. These activities have brought forth two very successful and influential ACA ventures, which have become independent entities. Composer Recordings, Inc. (CRI) began in 1954, producing recordings under the auspices of ACA until 1976, when it became an independent, nonprofit record company. Through CRI, ACA has subsidized more than 140 recordings of its members' works on the CRI label. CRI has independently produced hundreds more recordings of significant American concert music. The American Composers Orchestra (ACO), organized by ACA in 1977, independently continues its concert seasons today in New York as the only professional orchestra in the United States completely dedicated to the performance of new American orchestral music. In its ten seasons since 1977, the ACO has presented the works of more than 140 American composers, including nearly 60 world premieres and an even larger number of first New York performances. The orchestra has commissioned thirty-seven works, two of which have won the Pulitzer Prize. Both CRI and the ACO continue to nurture closer relations with their "parent," the ACA.

Over three hundred composer members of ACA govern their cooperative ventures through an elected Board. Past Presidents comprise an impressive list of American professional composers: Aaron Copland, Henry Cowell, Robert Ward, Ben Weber, Richard Donovan, Quincy Porter, Hall Overton, Vladimir Ussachevsky, Charles Dodge, Nicolas Roussakis, Frank Wigglesworth, and Eleanor Cory. The professional staff not only fills orders for music scores, parts, and electronic tape materials, but also provides assistance to composers with licenses, contracts, fees, and copyrights. They also have useful, up-to-date information about copyists, lawyers, accountants, and many other business aspects of professional composing.

Since 1972, ACA has been affiliated with the performing rights society, Broadcast Music, Inc. (BMI), which subsidizes ACA's staff salaries and office rental in New York. Admission to membership in ACA, then, requires composers to be affiliated with BMI, which collects performance royalties for members. An admission committee of peer composers reviews all applications. ACA's address is 170 West 74th Street, New York, NY 10023.

ACA serves a national constituency of professional composers, who cooperate to publish, distribute, and promote their own music. Other established national composer organizations serve their members and participants primarily by promoting and presenting composers' music in annual concert series and national conference/festivals. These organizations include American Women Composers, Composers Forum, Computer Music Association, Independent Composers Association, League of Composers ISCM, League of Women Composers, National Association of Composers USA, New Music Alliance, Society of Composers/ASUC, and Society of Electro-Acoustic Music in the United States.

State, regional and metropolitan areas of the United States abound with thriving composer organizations; here are only a few: the previously profiled TCF; Minnesota Composers Forum; in New York, the Experimental Intermedia Foundation, The Kitchen, P.A.S.S., Roulette, the Group for Contemporary Music, Alternative Museum, Dance Theater Workshop, Franklin Furnace, Clocktower, and P.S. 122; Arizona Composers Forum; Cincinnati Composers Guild; New Music Chicago; Boston chapter, ISCM; New Music Circle of St. Louis; and many, many more. Add to these composers' groups the many series of new music throughout the United States and university sponsored festivals and performing ensembles. Altogether, a composer in the United States has a wide diversity of performance venues, distribution and promotional opportunities from which to choose and in which to participate.

Participation in cooperative professional composers' organizations can be fruitful and very important for composers at the beginning of their career. As their music becomes better known and appreciated among their peers through such participation, real benefits accrue. Recognition for the excellence of one's work among peers can lead to important commissions and performance opportunities beyond the organization. Many composers feel a responsibility that, as their careers mature and performances and commissions increase, they should continue to participate in the leadership of these organizations, insuring that younger composers will continue to enjoy the same benefits that helped their own careers "take off."

The Independent Composer. Of course, belonging to a composers' organization does not guarantee advancement and success in the profession. As a matter of fact, many very successful composers choose an independent course, preferring to advance their music through personal enterprise alone. If their music gains national prominence through such efforts, they engage personal managers and enter into contractual agreements with commercial music publishers. Like composer Donald Martino, they may even start their own publishing concern (Dantalian, Inc.), or, like composer Pauline Oliveros, their own foundation (the Pauline Oliveros Foundation). A small but notable sampling of other independently successful composers include Steve Reich, Philip Glass, Laurie Anderson, David Amram, John Cage, Earle Brown, Suzanne Ciani, John Corigliano, David Del Tredici, Paul Dresher, Jacob Druckman, Lukas Foss, William Hellerman, Leonard Bernstein, Barton and Priscilla McLean, Laurie Spiegel, Morton Subotnick, David Tudor and many, many more. Each has modeled their personal career largely outside of composers' organizations. Instead, they perform, promote, publish, and record their own music, or they have managers and publishers contracted to promote its performance and distribution.

Other equally independent composers choose not to participate in composers' organizations for practical and/or philosophical reasons. Noted composer Martin Mailman, a valued colleague of the authors at the University of North Texas, has not chosen to participate in or join composers' groups throughout his very successful career. He states, "Back in the sixties, when I was a Ford Foundation Composer-in-Residence in Jacksonville, Florida, I felt it was important in that position for me to join my fellow composers in that region as a member of the Southeastern League of Composers. But since then, the only group I have been associated with is the Texas Composers Forum." When asked why he hadn't seen fit to join composers' groups, he was careful to point out that he was only speaking for himself and not at all recommending these views, necessarily, for any other composer. "I have not joined composers' groups for three reasons: one, I feel that new music should be performed in concerts just like any other kind of traditional concert music. Performing my music strictly for other composers doesn't hold a great amount of interest for me. Two, the political reason: I don't know now, but at one time, it seemed to me that composers' organizations served a few composers well and a great many composers not at all. I haven't felt it was necessary to participate in something that seemed to me was not always on the up-and-up. Three, there's the time and money. When I get involved in things, I get involved heavily, and that ends up being very time consuming, time I could be devoting to composing. And there is a limit to the amount of money one can spend on dues, etc." Asked how he felt about national organizations like the American Music Center, which distributes information and promotes the performance of music by American composers while maintaining an extensive library of scores for consideration by performers and conductors, Mailman replied, "My own distribution and promotional needs are met by my publisher (Boosey-Hawkes) and by my own efforts. As for AMC, I personally feel that they have a very idealistic view of how music gets discovered and performed." Finally, Mailman was asked what advice he gives student composers about advancing their careers and finding performance opportunities for their pieces. He responded, "Early in their careers, certainly, they need to develop associations with more experienced composers, and that can come from membership in such groups. But another way to go is to enter pieces in competitions and apply for composition fellowships."

No matter how independent, there is one type of organization to which Mailman himself and thousands of other professional composers in the United States belong. Membership in composers' performing rights societies has become a basic imperative. Martin Mailman is *very much* a member of ASCAP, the American Society of Composers, Authors, and Publishers. The authors of this book happen both to be affiliates of a similar organization, BMI, Broadcast Music, Inc.

COMPOSERS' RIGHTS

Composers have rights? When composers or their publishers in the USA own the copyright for a piece, they have all the exclusive economic rights guaranteed by the legal provisions of Public Law 94–553 (94th Congress, Oct. 19, 1976, Title 17, US Code, Copyrights), which took effect on January 1, 1978.

The question is often asked, especially by those who have just succeeded in their first modest efforts at composition, "How can I copyright my song?" First of all, a copyright is yours in principle from the moment you produce the first copy of your piece, showing that it is your creative work. However, your rights can be protected much more dependably in any eventual legal dispute by registering your copyright of the work with the Library of Congress. The composition is not likely to be misused or your rights to it abused, though, until it has proven its commercial value by important performances or the interest of a film or recording producer or a publisher. When a publisher accepts a piece for publication, it usually buys the copyright from the composer and registers the copyright for itself. It is only at this point of some mass distribution scheme for the piece that a copyright registered by its publisher or, if not, by its composer, becomes crucial.

The provisions of the law describe three kinds of exclusive rights enjoyed by the copyright owner: 1) "performing rights," covering the important right of public performance; 2) "mechanical rights," covering the right to reproduce a piece on a recording; and 3) "synchronization rights," covering soundtracks for films and television. These rights are economically powerful for composers, because royalty fees can be levied each time a copyrighted piece is performed publically, a recording of it is sold, or a film or video frame containing a moment of its music is made part of a film or television production. With recordings and film or television soundtracks, the process for receiving payment is almost always part of a negotiated agreement between the composer and the recording company or production company. Payment of royalty fees for a concert performance or for the broadcast of a copyrighted piece are much more difficult for the composer to collect.

It is also nearly impossible for individual composers or publishers to monitor and account for every single public performance or broadcast of every single piece they have composed and copyrighted. Even if they are able to keep track of all performances nationwide and around the world, composers alone lack the expertise and negotiating skills to deal directly with performers, conductors, radio/televison stations and musical entrepreneurs about how much the royalty fee should be or how a renewable license to play the piece can be agreed upon.

Performing rights societies were organized to do all these things, but most importantly to collect royalties for performances of copyrighted music and to distribute the funds collected to the composers and publishers whose pieces have been performed. The practice of centralizing in a large agency the monitoring, accounting, licensing, collection, and payment of copyright royalties to composers and publishers is well established. The first such agency in the world was founded in the United States in 1914 as the American Society of Composers, Authors, and Publishers, known universally as ASCAP. Today, there are three such organizations in the United States, two international agencies, and at least one such organization in virtually every country in the world. All are linked by international agreements. For instance, when a piece by a United States composer affiliated with a performing rights society in the United States is presented in a concert broadcast in, say, Vancouver, British Columbia, that licensed performance is reported to the Performing Rights Organization of Canada (PROC). In turn, the royalty fee is eventually remitted to the appropriate United States society, which pays the composers and publishers their shares.

How can such societies monitor *all* public performances of *all* copyrighted "concert" and "popular" music by *all* the composers affiliated with *all* the societies in almost *all* of the countries of the world? Phew! They can't. By a combination of actual concert reporting and scientific sampling methods, however, the societies have developed sophisticated techniques for monitoring performances. They can, with credible accuracy, keep tabs on the relative number and kind, if not an actual record, of performances a composer's pieces log in all licensed performance venues for a given period of time.

Why and how would a performing organization be obliged to pay a copyright collecting society? Naturally, music presenters would rather not pay royalty fees of any kind, but the performing rights societies have demonstrated their determination to collect the fees, early in this century establishing the composer's rights in a succession of successful court actions. These court decisions also established the validity of the "blanket license" concept, where a music presenter is issued a license by the society and charged an annual, negotiated fee for all copyrighted music presented in public concerts or broadcasts. Today, in the United States, all major professional music presenters—orchestras, chamber music series, radio and television stations, and, more recently, almost every university and college—pay annual fees for blanket performance licenses from each of the three performing rights societies in the United States.

ASCAP, representing over 35,000 composers, lyricists, and publishers, is the largest performing rights society in the United States in terms of the number of works assigned to its protection and the amount of revenue it annually collects—almost $200 million! **BMI,** founded in 1940, on the other hand, is the world's largest performing rights organization in the number of affiliated "writers" (composers and lyricists), numbering almost 50,000, and publishers, numbering 28,000. BMI is no slouch either in collecting royalties of almost $150 million annually. **SESAC Inc.** was founded in 1931 as the Society of European Stage Authors and Composers. It is a relatively small, private licensing firm representing almost 2,000 authors and composers and about 500 music publishers, collecting about $5 million per year in royalty fees.

How and when can a composer become a member of ASCAP or an affiliate of BMI or SESAC, and which society should the composer join? First, a composer cannot concurrently belong to more than one society. Nor can a publisher, except that publishers can form separate companies for each society; for example, Peters Corporation of New York as the publisher for all composers affiliated with BMI, and its Henmar Press division for all ASCAP composers. Second, deciding which society to join is usually based on personal research by the composer into the effectiveness and reputation of each. Usually, composers join a society to which many of their composer friends or former teachers belong. All three societies are good at what they do, and strong cases can be made for joining each.

The "how and when" of joining are linked. Certain minimal standards have been established through the years by the societies and have served as criteria for composers to gain membership or affiliation. For instance, the composer has just had a new piece recorded for commercial distribution. The societies recognize that as a major professional accomplishment and, more importantly, a prime candidate for broadcast royalties. Or, the composer has had several recent performances in significant professional concert venues—a performance in New York at Weill Recital Hall (formerly Carnegie Recital Hall) on the League of Composers ISCM series or inclusion of a piece on a concert during an annual New Music America festival. The main criterion for acceptance is, in short, demonstrated evidence that potential royalty revenue can be expected from performance of the composer's works. "How and when" are linked, then, by the fact that the composer must work to accomplish minimal monetary aspects of the profession and will then know "when the time is ripe."

However large and powerful ASCAP, BMI, and SESAC might seem to an individual composer, they are also dynamic, composer-oriented, intent on encouraging the composition and performance of all types of new and older copyrighted music. Each, for instance, has established generous and enlightened composition competitions annually held for young composers: the ASCAP Foundation Grants to Young Composers; the BMI Awards to Student Composers; and the SESAC/Society for Composers, Inc. Student Composers Contest. ASCAP and BMI both have been especially active in granting substantial funds to nonprofit composers' organizations devoted to presenting new works, such as the American Composers Orchestra described earlier. Generous annual "awards" from ASCAP and "guarantees" from BMI are made to active composers of concert music, whose performance records rarely approach the thousands or even millions of concert and broadcast performances an affiliate like popular music composer Michael Jackson logs. It is, in fact, thanks to composers like Jackson that such awards can be made to the composers of less lucrative concert music.

Finally, it is up to the individual composer to understand and exercise all the rights entailed in creating a new composition. In a very real sense, a composer's professional career is officially launched when the first royalty check for a licensed public performance is received. This small occasion is a personal triumph, encouraging more freely composed works to emerge from the studio of a now thriving professional composer.

CONCEPTS AND TERMS

Composing is largely a solitary endeavor; up until the preparations for a performance, it takes place in the realm of a single mind. We work alone with ideas and relationships, imagining our music in our mind's ear as it takes shape. As composers, we communicate through our music, and we quite naturally want to let it speak for itself. Those who describe and analyze our compositions, then, are often the critics, the performers, the musicologists. The terms they use describe musical results but not the thought processes that went into creating the music's design. The composer needs a unique language to describe composing.

To articulate the actual processes of invention in this book has meant avoiding categories and definitions that might limit thought. Instead, metaphors rich with stimulating possibilities of connection are invoked. Explaining concepts of composing through these metaphors, we have sought to open doors in the imagination. Indeed, language itself refines and deepens thought processes. It may be, in fact, that only language makes thought possible. We believe this is as true for creative as for analytic processes. Concepts are verbalized here to help a composer speak about composition, if only to write more illuminating program notes for a new piece. Beyond that and much more important, it is hoped that a collection of statements and explanations taken from the chapters of this book will help crystalize concepts vital to composers' thought and work, enhancing their intuitive craft and creative art.

acceleration Acceleration and deceleration are gradual changes in the rate of what is perceived to be the relative regularity of a pulse.

action symbol A notation is a communication or a record of musical ideas, expressing one or both of two things: instructions for certain performer actions, or some quality of a sound or pattern or complex of events. Invented action symbols represent (through a self-defining and often pictorial meaning) a performer's action rather than representing the resulting sound's qualities.

agogic stress One of the most persuasive factors differentiating elements is called agogic stress, the prominence of a rhythmic element due to being a longer duration than recent previous elements. As with all other stress factors, there can be an infinity of shadings of relative agogic or length stress. The placement of agogically stressed elements in a rhythmic stream is important insofar as they are understood as interruptions in rhythmic flow or as goals of motion, the moments when motion in an event stream temporarily ceases.

algorithm A process that can be precisely explained step-by-step is called an algorithm. If the kinds of patterns it takes as models and is meant to produce can be architecturally analyzed and described, then the process can be programmed.

alignment The patterns of durations in each strand of a counterpoint interact, sometimes coinciding, at other times independent. There may be alignment of their points of change in time or divergence of timing or, commonly, a mixture of these configurations. Rhythmic alignment is the extent to which the beginnings of time intervals in two or more streams of events are simultaneous, synchronous in time.

analog An analog is, at every point in time and space, generated directly by the thing it is tracking. A map, for instance, is an analog of the features of the land area it represents, and this relationship between the land and the analog map is itself a metaphor.

angularity The quality of angularity is what the composer thinks of and wishes to control when planning and building the shape of a line's architecture. Angularity is just a way to think about how changeably the elements of a line behave.

antiphonal placement Score designs can be specifically tailored to represent antiphonal placement of performers in space.

arch The arch is a classic shape, its opening expressed as an ascending growth and development curve, reaching its peak usually past midway; then descending to its resolution and closure.

architecture Architecture connotes the deep structure, the large organizing elements of entire sections of a piece, their proportions, relations, and functions in the overall coherence of structure. We define musical architecture as the interrelationship of elements of musical structure—rhythmic, pitch space, sound color and loudness patterns—as they form musical materials. An idiom is a particular architectural pattern, described by the specific ways these domains relate. How all the musical elements and the patterns made with them go together, fit and support and cross and connect with each other, is what we call the architecture of a musical composition.

art Composition is an art, not just a craft. Art is the ultimate end, striving to create works that are elegant in conception and thorough in realization, original to the best of the composer's ability.

art object The musical art object is beautiful, complete, having no corporeal model but itself, transcendent from the "real" world. A piece of music is an object of sounding art, a thing created for itself, for the artist's conscious expression of beauty. The entire tradition of music in the West has been devoted to defining further the beauty of the musical object, to refining our understanding of musical processes so that the processes can yield desired results.

ASCAP American Society of Composers, Authors and Publishers Representing over 35,000 composers, lyricists, and publishers, ASCAP is the largest performing rights society in the United States in terms of the number of works assigned to its protection and the amount of revenue it annually collects.

assimilation Assimilation, the intuitive phenomenon in the modeling process, is the combustion of the fuel in the engine, the all-important melding force. It is learning about our composition in progress. Assimilation smooths rough edges, corrects imbalances, puts things in order and relation.

basic interval stack Although a single interval has a definite sound quality, the smallest and most basic interval stacks of significance as transforming sources are those of relatively compact three-pitch constellations.

BMI Broadcast Music, Inc. Founded in 1940, BMI is the world's largest performing rights organization in the number of affiliated "writers" (composers and lyricists), numbering almost 50,000, and publishers, numbering 28,000.

box music Collections of pitches and/or rhythmic values or fragments placed in boxes provide source material for controlled improvisation within limits specified by an otherwise conventional notation.

calligraphy The technique of drawing or printing musical notation, calligraphy is only the final step in a process.

canon In the traditionally accepted sense, a canon involves contrapuntal imitation of a line by other lines removed by a time delay and possibly some pitch interval from the original.

carrier In traditional scoring, where musical color represented in the instrumental timbres is principally the carrier of pitch, sensitivity is critical.

chain of constellations A basic stack could generate a long chain of related but diverse constellations transformed one to another.

choosing a medium The medium chosen directly affects the form the piece takes; the composer should make such an important compositional decision a part of the modeling process.

clock time Clock time is a uniform system for measuring the passage of time, but it is meaningless without changing events to measure.

cluster Cluster symbols show a range of possible pitches to be included in a very dense sonority.

cognition Cognition is the result of the process of knowing in the broadest sense, including consciousness, memory, perception, conception, and judgement. Cognitive process at work is both deductive and inductive—deductive, where the composer proceeds from a known assumption to an unknown, from the general to the specific, from a premise to a logical conclusion; and inductive, where the composer proceeds by method, logically reasoning from particular facts to general conclusions.

collaboration Successful collaboration with another artist involves learning to trust shared experiences and insights and their ability to transcend individual limits.

color The nature of a sound is its timbre, its color. A sound is identified by its color, as it unfolds in time. A colorless instrument or voice is a physical contradiction. Color changes not only as pitch changes but also as time evolves. Color is the spectral envelope of a sound, for example, not only its timbre but the evolution of its pitch, loudness and timbral characteristics in time. Color, by its informed and thoughtful use, is form-giving.

coloration Coloration is the modeling of sound color from the smallest to largest detail of form to create a sound color image for the piece, a complex, dynamic phenomenon where the composer models specific colors in succession and combination. As in modeling rhythmic qualities, the composer can model the coloration in a piece by creating a coloration curve through the course of the piece.

color chain A single line of a texture that is recolored, one instrument taking over for another in relay fashion, was a technique extensively developed in the music of early twentieth century composer Anton Webern, and is often referred to in German as *Klangfarbenmelodie.* It is essentially a color chain elaborately building a single architectural line.

color highlighting Percussion instruments are often used for color highlighting, reinforcing certain notes of an important line and its basic color with other isolated colors.

color refraction Assigning different instruments to different "voices," clearly differentiating them as separate although simultaneous, is the simplest and most common kind of color refraction.

color span The simplest distinction of color "intervals" is to think of any significant color difference as a large span and no overt color difference as a very small color span (allowing for the minute color differences in an instrument's various pitch registers, for example).

combined mediums Unchanging vocal and instrumental combinations that constitute our established, traditional combined mediums include opera; music theater, bringing together elements from music and drama that are distinct from operatic traditions; music for film and television; music for the dance; and concertos, combining a soloist or small group of soloists with orchestra. To these well-known traditional combinations we add the now widely accepted combination of taped electroacoustic music with instrumental and vocal mediums. Many kinds of interaction can arise between an instrument or instruments and taped electronically produced sounds, two unique mediums combined. Nontraditional combinations of mediums—open and determined by the nature of the piece—are variously referred to as mixed media, multi-media, theater pieces, performance art, and intermedia, as well as happenings, environments, and installations.

commission The most direct and beneficial form of sponsorship of a composer's work comes in the form of commisssions and performances. At the heart of a professional composer's career are the quality, frequency, and significance of the commissions for and performances of compositions.

common tone A specific pitch shared by two constellations makes a strong connection.

composition Etymologically, the term "composition" is rooted in the concept of "a putting together." Today, it connotes putting music together, integrating the materials with skill, planning, and artful originality to satisfy the requirements of a particular musical genre.

compression Compression occurs when initiating time points get closer and closer together.

computer-assisted composition Computer-assisted composition is a very young field, but already the computer programmed use of compositional algorithms has developed into a rigorous and well documented endeavor.

concentration Exclusive use of only one color in paintings or pieces is unusual: concentration of color in extreme.

conclusion Conclusion requires the certainty of two kinds of information: that an event is readily recognizable as an idea important enough to be the last; and that it is marked by some "last-minute" alteration to warn that it is, indeed, the last event. Entropy is a good concept for understanding conclusions. To achieve what would normally be called a cadence, a convincing completion and satisfying closure of a musical form, information must build up to a certainty of outcome that outweighs remaining entropy.

consciousness The history of music as art and of musical composition is a history of the development of growing consciousness—the consciousness of change, consciousness of the beauty of change, and the resulting consciousness of creating processes of change as beauty.

conciseness Conciseness and consistency promote efficency in notational representations.

conjunction Conjunction, the simplest and most common linkage of event streams, follows a stream immediately as it ends with the start of a new stream.

constant condition A constant condition is an unchanging constraint or limit the composer invokes uniformly in the modeling process.

constellation A constellation is a real and specific pattern segmenting a particular chunk of pitch space. Pitch constellations have both a registral order and a time order. The pitches in a constellation may be simultaneous or successive in time.

contests One measure of the quality of a composer's work exists in the number, competitive quality, prize amount, and historical distinction of the composition contests that composer has won. Winning one composition contest does not, of course, "a composer make," but it does establish the probability that future works by this composer will be equal to or better than that composition.

continuity Continuity in the unfolding of events in time requires memory to appreciate, referring back and comparing new events with previous ones. Continuity, with its metaphorical aspects, is an all-important cohesive force in musical change through time. Continuity need not mean large doses of sameness; recurring use of bold contrast could as easily operate as a continuity, with great momentum of change.

contour In linear patterns, changing the direction or the rate of upward or downward registral motion makes contours. The simplest contour stress occurs with a sound or event at the turning point of a line, a change in registral direction, thus becoming the highest or lowest sound or event in its vicinity. Sounds or events suddenly much higher or lower than those preceding may possess contour stress even if not ultimate turning points in a registral curve.

contrapuntal accent In a rich stream of pitch intervals between lines, those whose pitches do fall into alignment, beginning at the same moment, are marked by contrapuntal accent. They tend to stand out and form in the ear a set of principal intervals dominating the contrapuntal quality.

control Compositional thinking is a dynamic interplay of intuitive and cognitive reasoning, of heart and brain, of *yin* and *yang,* of fluency and control. The degree of control the composer exerts over the materials of a composition is, in our time, a central issue.

copyright When composers or their publishers in the USA own the copyright for a piece, they have all the exclusive economic rights guaranteed by the legal provisions of Public Law 94–553 (94th Congress, Oct. 19, 1976, Title 17, US Code, Copyrights), which took effect on January 1, 1978. The provisions of the law describe three kinds of exclusive rights enjoyed by the copyright owner: 1) "performing rights," covering the important right of public performance; 2) "mechanical rights," covering the right to reproduce a piece on a recording; and 3) "synchronization rights," covering soundtracks for films and television.

counterpoint Combining lines within the same time frame forms counterpoint, the most essential kind of texture, a weaving together of distinct lines. Independent successions of events may coexist in time, forming a counterpoint of event streams with overlapping and coincident durations. Counterpoint is a complex phenomenon, embodying so many of the important features of musical structure: rhythmic conformity/elasticity of individual lines; rhythmic alignment; complexity of composite rhythm; variety of pitch intervals in individual lines; quality and prevalence of principal contrapuntal intervals. Works for combined mediums intensify interactions in time, establishing a contrapuntal dialogue between the mediums.

craft Much has been written exploring the craft of composition, particular ideas and methods for constructing various aspects of musical structure. Craft is an essential discipline of execution and absolutely necessary for the composer to become a masterful artist.

cut-out score Scores, with staff lines "cut out" when an instrument is not active, visually highlight changes in texture.

delete An interval can be removed, shortening a stack's height.

density Transformations of texture can be brought about by increasing or decreasing only the density of time, pitch, and/or color factors without reconfiguring their distinctions of basic textural parts.

diatonic All the church modes and major and minor scales are seven-note scales classed as diatonic because there are two basic building intervals in their collections, the wholetone and semitone.

diffusion Just as artists do not normally choose to paint all possible colors everywhere on their canvas, composers do not normally use all possible sound colors at all times in an orchestral work: diffusion of color in extreme. The modern symphony orchestra has, by any measurement, a vast potential of diffusion of different sound colors, as well as large and various concentrations of the same sound colors. The impressive potential for both color diffusion and concentration in the orchestra is, naturally, conditioned not only by tradition but by acoustical and perceptual considerations.

distributed color A distributed color configuration combines different but generally similar colors, often making a good supporting or "middle-ground" part.

duration Elements of rhythm can be measured in time, creating a stream of durations. Inevitably, all rhythmic phenomena end up being understood in terms of durations, articulated divisions of time.

elaboration A phase of form, elaboration is an infinity of possibilities for transforming and developing ideas, spinning a maze-like network of doors and corridors connecting events.

elasticity of change From the smallest, most detailed level of rhythm to the broadest levels of time and large segmentation, streams of durations form relationships of magnitude and proportion giving rise to trends or processes of change, the elasticity of which is the most profound quality of the unfolding of events in time. Processes of change can be enacted by very gradual, subtle degrees, by lurching, rapid increases or decreases, even by abrupt reversals of the processes themselves. We can think of a vague notion of rates of change created by temporal or rhythmic trends. Perhaps most significant is the rate at which trends are reversed, terminated, interrupted, replaced—the elasticity of change.

electroacoustic The rise and the now ubiquitous development of electroacoustic music systems has offered composers the potential of creating not just one musical microcosm in a particular system but a whole new world every time a new piece is conceived. The term, electroacoustic, connotes the extraordinarily broad reach of these contemporary mediums into every kind of music there is today: any means to make music that involves electronic and/or digital technology with or without the involvement of acoustic sound sources.

elision Elision involves one actually shared element, event, or time point that can be understood as the final element of one stream and simultaneously the initiating element of another.

energy curve We can think of the unfolding of time as an energy curve, waves of rhythmic momentum with ebb and flow and possibly splashes or glassy calms.

entropy Information science calls uncertainty entropy, stemming from a lack of complete predictive information.

entry point At the very beginning of a piece's modeling, we normally choose a particular, usually familiar strategy as an entry point into one sphere. Only if our entry point is the temporal sphere must we create an immediate, assimilated image in time of spatial and narrative metaphors in our modeling process.

equal-tempered Equal-tempered twelve-tone tuning is the basis not only for chromatic tonality and so-called "twelve-tone" music and "atonal" music but also for other current modes of pitch organization with familiar or synthetic scales.

ergodic Ergodic is the term for a process of moment-to-moment change in trajectory, a complex curve "whose statistical properties as a whole are the same as the statistical properties of each part at the next lower hierarchical level." [Tenney 1985]

event-complex Whole events are successions of single sounds and silences, and event-complexes, in turn, consist of successive whole events, making even longer segments of a time stream.

event rate As distinguished from tempo (the rate of implicit, regular divisions of time), event rate is the irregular, fluctuating speed of actual events.

expand/compress intervals All the intervals in a stack can be uniformly altered by adding, subtracting, multiplying or dividing by some constant number, preserving only the possible symmetry of the original stack.

exploring a medium Exploring a medium's nature involves thorough research, experimentation in a kind of performance laboratory context, and analysis of the effectiveness of the particular use of a medium.

extended resources Explorations with acoustic instruments began to be formalized in the sixties and seventies with the publication of several books devoted to the detailed explication of special techniques involved in producing and controlling, for instance, a variety of multiple sounds—multiphonics—and microtonal pitch control on conventional wind and brass instruments. These special performance techniques, extended resources, have been employed by composers in designing the coloration of their compositions, especially for soloists and small ensembles. The development of "extended instrumental resources" and "extended vocal techniques" has come about, for one thing, because composers and performers specializing in contemporary music have found themselves increasingly sensitive to the need for modeling the integration of acoustical and electroacoustical sound colors.

fellowship "Fellowship" and "grant" normally refer to a sum of money allocated from funds dedicated to advanced work by an individual in some particular field of study. "Residency" refers to the formal period of time devoted to such study while in residence at an institution specializing in that field.

Fibonacci Mathematical pattern models are of great interest to composers, such as the Fibonacci series, in which each term is the sum of the previous two terms (1 2 3 5 8 13 21 34 55 and so on).

field A field is a set of lines or other delineators with significant spacings or dimensions. Ideally, a field represents a density and distribution of possibilities suitable to the range of some important musical feature.

form In music, form is the shaping of musical time through change. Form is the wholeness in time of a piece. Form is all the attributes the composer gives a piece, its whole sonic and temporal effect, its essence.

formal process Combinations of rhythmic data, pitch selection, loudness behavior, and color assignment for streams of sound events can be determined by formal processes.

framework A stack's framework is revealed by adding adjacent interval sizes, bringing to the surface its larger underlying intervals. Hidden intervals are important in selecting source interval stacks and guiding their coherent transformation.

freeform Freeform composition is free of restrictions, defined only by constraints the composer invokes. Freely composed music is, by nature, speculative, even experimental. To what degree is up to the artist. Each piece or series of pieces should be a new adventure for the composer, new imagery, a new land of free composing to explore.

frequency Frequency and amplitude—pitch and loudness—are both functions of time.

fuse Two adjacent intervals can be joined to make a larger interval, the sum of their sizes.

gesture Timbre and gesture explorations involve discovering new ways of producing sound events.

graphic notation The simplest form of graphic notation replaces the traditional pitchfield of staves with bands of space vertically representing registral realms of pitch.

heightened color When, in the progress of a piece, the composer models the pitch space to be essentially undifferentiated, the composer correspondingly heightens the importance of color in the texture, causing us to focus on the richness of color and mass of sonority in the sound color image of a sonic atmosphere. In modeling the coloration of a piece, the composer can enhance the effect of the composition by heightening—or lessening—our sense of color's relative importance at any one moment in the piece.

idea Ideas are the fuel for the engine driving a piece; ideas are nothing without the engine. "Idea" has to do with the spontaneous, innocent, improvisatory thinking on the periphery of serious conception in the act of composition.

idiom The performance, communication and transmission of music through its many mediums involves an ever-changing, always expanding range of characteristic musical expressions, gestures and meanings—its idioms. As composers, we use idioms and sometimes even cause musical idioms to come into existence: the way we express these idioms in our music constitutes what we often refer to as our compositional style.

image Master composers focus on achieving a coalescence of ideas around a particular musical image, a focus likely to result in a compelling piece of music.

improvisation Improvisation is the incorporation of performer action and choice in the design of events. Improvisation is both impelled and controlled by the expression of a partial architecture which it works to complete.

independence The most basic relationship is a simple independence of inherently different mediums, coexisting in time and sounding space, mixing to form a composite texture but not pointedly interacting.

information Information about a musical architecture is a clear impression of how patterns in the domains of structure relate to each other.

initiating time point All the moments at which some sound begins, initiating time points mark off durational units of rhythm on a surface level.

innovation The notational innovations of contemporary music can be described in broad categories: extensions of traditional notation; space-proportional time notation; graphic (nonsymbolic) representations of texture and action; and musical "mobiles."

instrumentation Instrumentation is the musical medium(s) chosen to create particular kinds of sound color and color combinations, including all mediums of musical expression: vocal, instrumental, electroacoustic, intermedia, and/or any combination of musical means designated by the composer.

integration Integration shares a segment of time in which final elements of one stream overlap and coexist with initial elements of another stream. The integration may be brief and make a casual link or so extensive that it can be thought of as complete contrapuntal merging of the streams.

interpretation We know that a performer playing all the proper pitches in tune and in proper rhythm never impresses beyond nominal skill until control over the color nuances of his/her instrument and the music performed yield the beauty of what we term interpretation in performance.

interval Creative thinking about pitch primarily involves proportioning segments of space, intervals.

interval quality group Interval quality groups are just initial aural assessments to help start becoming familiar with the vast variety of constellations possible in pitch space. Basic three-note constellations whose interval stacks contain the most acoustically complex intervals only one semitone different in size from an octave or unison—1, 11, and 13 semitones—are marked by the acoustically complex quality of dissonance or tension of interval quality **GROUP 1.** Interval stacks with none of these intervals: 1, 11, or 13 semitones, but containing an interval two semitones different in size from an octave or unison—2, 10, or 14—comprise interval quality **GROUP 2.** Those intervals possess some of the tension of 11's, and 1's, but their brightness is warmer or more rounded. Those basic interval stacks without intervals close to an octave or unison are in a final interval quality **GROUP 3** with familiar qualities associated with their identities as triads of various sorts. A group of constellations, all of which are relatively simple transformations of one basic stack, will have a related, similar interval sound quality.

interval stack Measured simply in semitones, a registral succession of intervals might be thought of as an ascending arpeggio of a chord, an interval stack. Constellations and their interval stacks are not really categories but actual descriptions of interval patterns in pitch space. They provide a way of thinking about a pitch combination that suggests how to move on to other pitch combinations in a coherent fashion.

intuition Intuition is the direct knowing or learning of something without conscious use of reason, immediate apprehension or understanding. If intuition is something known or learned in this subconscious way, and if intuition is the ability to know or perceive things without conscious reasoning, it certainly doesn't seem to fit the profile of the master composer—they consciously reason; they plan their pieces; they know what they're doing.

invention In a venerable tradition of composition, our "inventions" are creative projects with guidelines designed to suggest many outcomes, permitting and requiring the exercise of real creative choice and evaluation. They are road maps for individual exploration of possibilities.

inversion Having the same scale pattern in reverse direction indicates an inverse relationship, an interval set configuration turned upside-down. Making an inversion of a row is simple, turning each successive interval in the opposite direction. The sizes of the original ascending serial interval and the ascending equivalent of the inverted interval always add up to twelve.

invert Reversing the entire registral order of intervals in a stack only mildly transforms it.

isolated color A stream of sounds would be an isolated color if unlike the colors of surrounding sounds.

license Court decisions established the validity of the "blanket license" concept, where a music presenter is issued a license by the performing rights society and charged an annual, negotiated fee for all copyrighted music presented in public concerts or broadcasts. Today, in the United States, all major professional music presenters—orchestras, chamber music series, radio and television stations, and, more recently, almost every university and college—pay annual fees for blanket performance licenses from each of the three performing rights societies in the United States.

line It is in a single line that we can most easily illustrate and explore the concept of shape. Since a line exists not only in pitch space but in time and in sound color, its shape is a composite of many characteristics, including but much more than the direction and size of pitch intervals. Successive lines of various character and angularity make much of the contrast and variety needed for the continuity of a well-modeled form.

link Kinds of intervals can be matched or otherwise linked to give rhythms to a pitch pattern, to color a rhythm, to select constellations for fitting together instrumental colors.

linkage Event streams normally follow one another in time. The different ways they may do this or otherwise relate can be understood in four categories, or kinds of linkage: separation, conjunction, integration, and elision.

loudness An obvious stress is created by loudness—notes marked with an accent or events occurring at specified dynamic levels greater than preceding events. The louder a sound is, the more complex the relation of its partials, the more transformed with modulating distortion. These changes in sound not only affect amplitude but cause complex changes in sound color. We get our cues for loudness not only from the strength of the sound (its loudness measured in decibels, its impact measured by the membrane of the eardrum) but from the relative distortion of its composite partials—its color—and the amount of resonance or reverberation it possesses. Heightened loudness in the coloration of a piece can immediately focus our attention to the color of the sound. Sustained, excessive loudness, however, can have a dulling effect on our ability to perceive and appreciate sound color. With heightened, sustained softness, our acuities for color, pitch, and texture are highly sensitized. Loudness of sound, like a splash of red or yellow in a painting, can brighten and articulate. Composers sense this intuitively, using loudness to energize their music with vivid contrast.

luminosity Synaesthetic processes having to do with sound nominally involve only the degree of luminosity in colors, ranging from, say, brilliant to dark or from transparent to opaque.

mapping Mapping involves some way of converting information from spatial or numerical patterns onto the elements of a rhythmic stream or the constellations of a pitch space design.

medium Medium in music connotes modes of invention, the means of communicating musical ideas and the methods of transmitting musical sounds.

metaphor A piece of music, out of time, is imagined as an object with qualities and measurable quantities—a spatial metaphor; or as chains of events happening in consequence to one another—a narrative metaphor; and a piece of music as an elaborately articulated piece of time's flow—a temporal metaphor.

meter Rhythmic patterns can relate to a meter in a counterpoint between the explicit and the implicit. Meter is an underlying implied hierarchy of conforming time divisions.

metric stress Metric stress is the rhythmic prominence a sound or event exhibits when its point of inception coincides with the beginning of a metric time unit. On the many hierarchical levels that a regulated time sense may operate, the beginnings of its equal units of time become points of focus for potential stress.

micro/macro-composition Micro- and macro-composition extend the extremes of compositional specification and control to both minute details and to the broadest perspectives of conceptualization. The sketching process is most effective when it proceeds from the broadest, most general conception of image, intent, and form—the macro-composition—gradually toward the more and more detailed aspects of material and structure—the micro-composition. This process of filling in form with detail should be well organized if the work is to achieve coherence in all its dimensions.

microtones Microtonal specifications include quarter-tone inflections of basic chromatic pitches.

mobile The sculptural mobiles of artists such as Alexander Calder suggest an exciting possibility of form: a set of material components "hung" in a floating system of suspension so that the parts can freely take on many possible relationships to each other in metamorphic flux. Musical materials can be thus "suspended" by breaking the customary assumption of left-to-right sequence in score reading.

model A model represents some real thing. Music's models are its own vast array of musical compositions.

modeling What we often fail to understand is that the modeling process is aesthetically creative, not analytically derivative. The modeling process is not analytical method turned around to generate the form a piece will take. It is, instead, a staging process for the form of a piece, evolving from its first blurred image, in turn becoming a series of trial realizations, exploring ways its materials can be made and combined. Modeling a piece calls for the composer to imagine, then assimilate the image of the form it will take. An effective modeling process must balance all three spheres of image, bringing from each its unique contribution to architecture, trajectory, and continuity.

momentum All qualities of rhythm influence the trajectory of an energy curve, weighing toward one side or the other of a basic polarity, momentum and inertia. Musical recurrence and contrast are like physical inertia and momentum. Momentum, the extent of contrast or alteration of patterns—the flow of the stream—is manifested in qualities of mobility and stability. A succession of constellations, each on some pitch level, is like a stream; its flow or sense of progression is a kind of momentum.

morphology The morphology of a piece means tracing its course, what events occur, when and how they relate.

narrative modeling Narrative modeling involves the plot or the eventfulness of a piece.

nonpitched Nonpitched refers to those instruments and sounds that have complex sound spectra not centered on one fundamental frequency, especially including kinds of percussion instruments. Sustained, centered pitches being absent, we focus our perception on sound colors, their spectra, in turn, yielding hierarchical ranges of color registrations, broader than pitch constellations but modeled nonetheless.

notation Notation is the process of expressing and recording ideas, of conveying a work's substance and the means of its realization. The notational medium chosen to convey musical ideas strongly influences the nature of the ideas to be expressed.

notational systems In an interactive way, the nature of ideas can suggest suitable notations, but a notational system can in turn spawn ideas through a ready potential for certain patterns or configurations. With an appreciation for the great diversity of notational systems and styles that can be adopted, and with a theoretical understanding of the basic representational and perceptual processes universal to them all, the composer can design notations best suited to the musical ideas being explored.

octave The octave is indeed rather universal, recognized in most cultures and most historical periods of music as the most primary interval or division of pitch space to make a smaller segment. Octaves are really circular in nature like the face of a clock; finishing one octave, a pattern starts over in the next. Any basic three-pitch constellation containing an octave, twelve semitones, or a multiple of octaves, has a special quality. The pure and simple but hollow interval of the octave and the focus it places on its two pitches affects a constellation's consonance and balance.

open An interval can be opened, expanded by an octave, by adding twelve semitones.

orchestration Orchestration refers, as it has traditionally, to both the instrumentation and coloration of the medium of the modern symphony orchestra, chamber orchestra, or other comparable grouping of primarily traditional orchestral instruments, sometimes including voices.

organizations Established national composer organizations serve their members and participants primarily by promoting and presenting composers' music in annual concert series and national conference/festivals. Some, such as the American Composers Alliance, serve composers who cooperatively publish, distribute, and promote their own music.

palindrome A process of matching a pattern with its retrograde to make a form symmetrical around its middle or, in other words, the same overall sequence forward or backward, is called a palindrome.

performing rights Performing rights societies were organized to collect royalties for performances and broadcasts of copyrighted music and to distribute the funds collected to the composers and publishers whose pieces have been performed.

personal medium Composing is normally a highly personalized endeavor, ideally in the quiet and solitude of the composer's own studio. The composer's personal medium of in-studio music making is, then, all-important.

phases of form Although the essence of form is continuous and connected change, some notion of separate, defineable maneuvers is useful. A form of any scope could be said to consist of three phases: a presentation, an elaboration, and a conclusion of material.

pitch When we hear a tone's pitch, we perceive it as being metaphorically high or low in a kind of sounding space. Acoustically and physiologically, we are perceiving the rate of periodic cycles of sound producing that tone's pitch: the greater or lesser the cycles' frequency, the higher or lower the tone's placement in our imagined pitch space. Rather than being identified apart from musical color—timbre—pitch is identifiable because it is integral to timbre. Pitch is an attribute of and ascribed by its timbre.

pitch approximation Note-stems with rhythmic information but no note-heads allow for improvised pitch within a generally depicted contour.

pitch center Some scales have a focal point in the interval structure, a place for a pitch we are accustomed to understand as the center for the entire configuration of all intervals in the scale. Such a pitch center or tonic, as it is traditionally called, may exist in a scale.

pitch class Octave related pitches (or, for that matter, enharmonically related pitches like D-sharp and E-flat) are considered members of the same pitch class, so that a collection's pitch classes can be represented within one octave of pitch space, usually in ascending order.

pitch fabric The mixture or variety of intervals used in individual lines establishes the basic character of a counterpoint's pitch fabric.

pitch language An important part of the sound character of a composition is its pitch language, in a general sense any coherent quality of patterns in pitch space.

pitch momentum Pitch momentum in a stream of constellations, the degree of interval and pitch change, can be assessed by identifying the extent of interval transformation (which contributes momentum) and the degree of pitch connection (which retards momentum) in each succession from one constellation to the next.

pitch pattern The universe of possible pitch patterns to explore is virtually infinite, and so are the variations one can devise in a personal technique. Rows and constellations, for instance, are modes of thinking about arrangements in pitch space, ways to explore that vast universe of possibilities.

pointillism Generally, the proportion of a time span not filled with sound is thus a degree of isolation, a disconnectedness of sounds. When pervasive, such separateness of sounds in time is often called pointillism, after the century-old technique in oil painting of dots of color separated on a canvas.

presentation The presentation phase of a musical form needs these features of architecture: a fixed relationship of rhythm, pitch, color, and loudness patterns; a texture with vivid distinction of parts, whether by register, loudness, color, or rhythm, probably with more than one factor at work linked to strengthen each other in distinguishing parts; single streams of events without significant transformation of their architecture, clearly delineated from other event streams that may present a different architecture.

professional A professional composer is a person who receives fees and other forms of compensation through commissions for compositions. These might include royalty payments for professional performances of his or her compositions; royalties from published and recorded works; and fees for consultation services, as well as lecturing, writing about and participating in performances of his or her work.

propagate Appending or inserting in the right place an interval of a size already present in a stack can make another basic stack identical to one in the original.

proportion A quantitative comparison of any two successive durations in a stream forms a proportion. Proportional complexity and simplicity might, then, be understood in either of two ways, the magnitude of arithmetic ratios or the intricacy of common perceptible subunits. By comparing and assessing proportions and subpulses, temporal trends such as complication, simplification, and continuation can be understood, especially over broad musical time spans such as the various sections of an entire piece.

proportional time Representing time without pulse, meter, or note-value symbols can be accomplished using a simple, basic metaphor: durations of time are represented proportionally by horizontal spatial extensity. Absence of bar lines allows patterns of accent to flow freely without interaction against a regular scheme of potential metric accents.

pulse Durations may relate to an implied regularity of time division, a sense of pulse.

ramp Pitches of a constellation can be represented in a straight ascending or descending order.

recurrence Presented more than once in the ordering of a constellation's pitches, tones begin to take on a role as focal points within the space.

redistribute Two intervals are fused and then the resulting interval is subdivided into two smaller intervals different than those originally fused.

register Orchestration textbooks and treatises discuss registers, divisions of the full range of instruments or voices into two, three, or four areas of different sound production quality.

registral order Registral order is identified by arranging the pitches of a constellation from lowest to highest (even though they may appear in some other time order) without changing any octaves—in other words, representing the constellation as a chord.

relating forces Relating forces assimilate and fuse distinctly modeled but incomplete images, synthesizing the ultimate form of a composition. These relating forces are fluid, channels of flow where images of time, space, and plot intermingle simultaneously and gravitate toward a common pool.

repeated pitch Actually more a function of rhythm, immediately repeated pitches affect the pitch shape of a line even more emphatically than just sustaining it longer than others.

retrograde A transformation can be applied to any original, transposed, or inverted form in which the time order of pitches is reversed, making what is called a retrograde. Any sequence exactly reversed in time order can be called a retrograde.

rhythmic complexity Ratios of two durational values range from the simplest, a one-to-one equality, to such irreducible ratios of primes as 7 : 5 or 1 : 13. A ratio's complexity, how big its numbers are, is one way to appreciate the complexity of a rhythmic proportion. The magnitude of the largest possible whole subunit common to two durations therefore represents the complexity of their proportion; the shorter the perceived subdivision of time needed to grasp the proportion, the more intricate or complex it seems.

rhythmic density A simple mathematical expression for rhythmic density is the number of events divided by the total duration of the stream (in beats or seconds).

rhythmic range Expressing rhythmic range as a comparison of the longest duration to the shortest duration in a stream is a simple way to appraise the variety of durations in succession.

rotation Choosing to place a different pitch at the start (the bottom) of a representative collection will simply rotate the scale pattern which expresses it.

row The most common kind of row is a series of intervals which will present in some order all twelve possible pitch classes. In the generating constellations of a twelve-tone row, there are no common tones from one to the next or between any two of the constellations. In a twelve-tone row, each of the twelve semitone divisions of octaves is represented, and since there are only twelve notes, no pitch class (as these semitone divisions of every octave are called) is represented more than once. One row, transformed and segmented many possible ways, is a highly fertile source for making patterns in pitch space.

rules As a piece is formed, the composer is at the same time modeling the piece on its own "rules." As temporal modeling tests new materials for the piece, applying earlier rules may not work. Then the composer either invents new material, invents a new rule, or alters the now unapplicable rule. There is a conciliation of rule and material or object and event. This part of the modeling process is the synthesis of form.

scale Scales are the basis of most harmonic languages, an embodiment of all the interval potentials of a pitch organizing system. A scale is an abstract collection of pitches constituting the resources for building lines and chords.

scale pattern When pitches are collected—arranged close together within an octave in ascending order—the successive intervals from one pitch to the next form a scale pattern. A scale pattern expresses only one arbitrary octave of a scale or set collection.

score The score is not the musical entity but only a necessary conveyor of its identity, in most cases simply a catalog of performers' parts.

scoring At the scoring stage, if it has been preceded by an orderly and effective sketching process, the composer is not bound by the restrictions of working only "note-to-note" in a chronological tunnel but, by being able to glimpse the broad picture, can move freely from one part of a score to another, filling in details directly while following the various confluences of coherence.

segmentation A row can be used to make chords as well as lines simply by collecting up a few successive pitches to sound together. Collecting adjacent pitches of the row into a chord can form many different successive constellations, depending on how the collecting process is segmented.

semitone Dividing pitch space into octaves, each octave can be further divided into six equal "tones" or twelve semitones. The ratio of the basic semitone interval is roughly 1.06 to 1.

semitone displacement A pitch in a constellation only one semitone away from a pitch in the previous constellation makes a connection with a significant quality of motion.

separation Separation involves a pause, a rest, or another not closely related event interrupting the connection between the end of one stream and the beginning of another.

series The selection of intervals to construct constellations and the pitch connections between them as well as the ordering of their pitches in time, makes what is called a pitch series.

serial interval If all the intervals are the smallest possible ascending interval to get to some pitch of the next class, we can do the simplest transformation, transposition, quite easily. Start on any pitch and just move up by the same serial intervals through all the other pitch classes.

serial process Serial processes with rows are a traditional means of organizing pitch space by establishing and continually reusing a particular way of ordering pitches.

SESAC Founded in 1931 as the Society of European Stage Authors and Composers, SESAC Inc. is a relatively small, private licensing firm representing almost 2,000 authors and composers and about 500 music publishers.

set A set is the abstract representation of fundamental interval structure in a pitch collection of any size.

set type Two sets with scale patterns inverted in relation to each other are considered the same set type. In this way, any set of three pitch classes can be placed in one of twelve possible types.

silence Silence or pause is an effective delineator if the architectures of two event-complexes are similar and might be confused if joined or overlapped.

sketching A process of sketching a piece records the stages of creative design of a composition. Sketching should utilize the means best suited to the particular image that is being formed. Sketches should be custom designed so they convey to the composer the character and potential of his/her thoughts as they are reconsidered and refined. Sketching effectively addresses the broad initial concerns of image and form—texture, character of events, the flow and elasticity of time, the shaping of basic energy curves. The nature or means of the sketching process and the most crucial conceptions of a musical work influence and even determine each other.

sonority Color-and-pitch, color-through-time, color-and-texture are mutually interacting qualities of sonorities.

sound color image The creation of a sound color image for a composition is a dynamic concept: it is temporal in the flow and confluence of sonorities in the event streams; it is spatial in its expression of textural dimensions in the work. The sound color image reflects the quality, combination, mutuality, and merging of the confluent sonorities in a composition.

sound object The name of a particular genre of tape music celebrated the compositional approach of musique concrete or objectified music, referring to the materials of such compositions as *objets sonore,* sound objects.

source stack Transforming interval stacks to create a stream of constellations starts from some chosen source stack. It likely would be one of the basic interval stacks of three-pitch constellations, but a very large source interval stack is also possible, thinking of a process of filtering or carving out instead of amplifying and filling out.

span We normally think of an interval as a distance in pitch space, the difference in location of two "points" in that pitch space. A time span is the duration of time from one event or time point to another. Applied to sound color and to loudness, the concept of a span can be thought of similarly as the degree of difference between two sounds. Each domain of structure, time, pitch, color, works on a concept of differences, intervals—spans.

spatial modeling Spatial modeling is the conscious visualization in "mind-space" of the piece of music as an object with measurable dimensions in a network of spatial characteristics: how long, how many, how few, how high, how low, how thick or thin, what color, what texture, where placed, where heard, what structure—all metaphors for spatial images, thinking of the piece as an object.

spiral Just as in the general unfolding of pitch spaces, ramps and waves can spiral and take detours, compounding themselves while maintaining the progress of their general shapes.

stress The perceived prominence of individual elements due to various kinds of stress differentiates their roles. Goals of motion may be perceived, rhythmic focal points created by means of these stress factors. A stress rhythm can be decisive in forming rhythmic character, more so than the surface stream of sounds and silences, especially when the surface is realtively conformed and undifferentiated.

stress point The stress points in distinct domains each make their own strata of time divisions. The pattern of durations from one focal pitch to the next, the pattern of time intervals of agogic stress, of color changes—all these patterns interact. When they correspond in time, there is a special sense of focus, of resolution. When the stress points of rhythm, pitch, and color change do not correspond, tension is built up. The pattern of stress points in one domain can take over from another domain or compete with it as the principal shaping of a stream of events.

stretch/shrink One interval in a stack can be altered in size, leaving others unchanged.

subdivide By inserting a pitch, an interval can be divided into two smaller intervals whose sum will equal the original interval.

subdivision Complex subdivisions of metric time values make groups of notes that interact in complex ways with each other and with metric divisions.

suggestiveness A notation is enhanced if it is suggestive in looks or form to its musical meaning.

symbol A symbol is a mark with visual autonomy and distinguishable identity.

symmetry The acoustical complexity, simplicity, and/or possible symmetry of intervals are some considerations in designing constellations.

synaesthetic The faculty to "hear color" is sometimes referred to as synaesthetic: a sensory impression from an impression of another sense. Our perceptive sense of color in music is synaesthetic: the experience of music is "seen" as more than strictly an acoustical phenomenon.

synthesis of form Through fluency and control of creative thought, through testing and revising, by seeking balanced but vivid images of time, shape, and plot, synthesis of form becomes fully realized.

temporal modeling The most readily understood modeling process is temporal modeling, where the sonic materials of the piece are invented and shaped in real or imagined performance time.

textural contrast Thinking of the various factors that distinguish textural parts—event rate, elasticity, and alignment; registral isolation, size of prominent intervals; color distribution; loudness differential—we can make textural contrast by rearranging several distinguishing differences to create new parts.

textural parts Factors that distinguish musical events, making distinct parts of a texture, can come from any domain of musical structure—time, pitch, space, color, or loudness. Each can also contribute to a sense of depth in a texture, foreground/background distinction of parts. In the time domain, parts of a texture can be distinguished by event rate. Rhythmic elasticity can play a role, with more varied or elastic parts of a texture standing out as prominent foreground events. With streams of events relatively similar in rate and elasticity, a lack of rhythmic alignment can keep separate the parts without making foreground/background distinctions. Separation of sounds in pitch space can isolate a stream of events as a foreground part; distributing aligned or matching sounds over a wide register of pitch space can create a diffuse textural background. Color usually plays an important role in creating and clarifying texture; color can define texture, while the texture can, in turn, articulate its colors.

textural stress Contrapuntal parts may reinforce each other by their simultaneous attacks. This textural stress is closely related to loudness, the greater strength or mass a sound may have by containing a larger aggregate of pitches or an event by containing more instrumental colors or more activity.

texture Musical texture is a broad concept that includes counterpoint; it is the combination of distinct events within a time frame.

texture piece A new array of instrumental colors have been explored, evoked rarely in instrumental scores before the last half of the twentieth century. Such explorations and use of these "extra-instrumental," nonidiomatic colors have given rise to an era of textural pieces where change in textural color detail is paramount in the continuity of the piece.

theory A theory is the relationship or similarity the model has to the thing it models. It is a metaphor between a model and data.

timbre Timbre modifications, symbols applied to conventional notes, designate alterations in the basic methods of tone production. As they are subliminally perceived, partial vibrations play an important role in our perception of tone quality or musical color, sometimes called timbre.

timbral object Robert Erickson refers to sounds as "timbral objects," made distinct not only because they are "recognizable" but because they are "multidimensional wholes, individual and various: it is that they exist in time, exhibit changes during their time course," still retaining their particular identity [Erickson 1975].

time Music exists in time, and its substance is the articulation of time. Time exists as we sense it articulated on many levels by changing and cyclically recurring events.

time span A significant kind of duration is the time span from the beginning of one event or pattern to the beginning of the next—whatever is perceived as the next in succession, a comparable event.

time stream In a hierarchical model of time, each level of time, from surface to deep structure, contains elements which form into streams; on the next broader or deeper level these streams in turn become the elements of yet longer streams.

tone Each musical tone an instrument or voice produces is, in itself, a stream of constantly changing relationships of pitch, loudness, timbre, and expressive nuance—or, as acousticians prefer, frequency, amplitude, harmonic spectrum and format. The attack, prolongation, and release of a musical tone are termed the onset, steady-state and decay of the spectral envelope.

traditional notation Traditional notation works through the chronologically ordered placement of notes signifying metrically proportionate time values in the field of a five-line staff.

trajectory A trajectory can be a complex wave form, increasing gradually in activity, backing off, surging to a peak of continuous activity, gradually relaxing to a low point of energy, interrupting with surges of rapid events. A piece of music is "a moving object," so to speak, and before we can determine its mass of material content, we must design and understand its intended trajectory through time.

transformation Transformations are operations demonstrating similarities between two constellations by showing how the interval stack of one could be derived from the other, the basic means of variation in a coherent compositional process.

transformed row A row can be transformed in any of three simple ways: transposed, inverted, retrogressed. Each kind of transformation preserves the general pattern of intervals in the original row but supplies a new succession of pitch classes to express those intervals.

transforming operation While generating many closely related interval stacks, transforming operations bring out interval differences in a rich diversity of qualities. Composers instinctively think this way, starting with some choice of pattern, then varying it, exploring its transformational potential.

truncation Often, compression or expansion of time is brought about simply by truncating or extending a rhythmic pattern.

variable condition A variable condition is a changeable constraint or limit invoked when deemed appropriate. The variables of coloration, for instance, can range both over the surface of the event streams of a piece and through the depths of the texture, from whole portions of the piece to the millisecond by millisecond transformation of one sound.

variation A basic procedure for variation techniques is to change textural factors one by one while keeping other factors and parts consistent.

wave An alternation of ascending and descending ramps makes a line with wave-like shape. A wave can travel through a constellation then turn to go back through it again in the other direction to make recurring pitches, or it can move through one constellation then turn to go through the next constellation in the opposite direction.

wedge "Wedge" rhythms gradually expand or contract the number of beams within a group of notes to represent quick accelerations and decelerations.

INDEX